SAINT PATRICK

His Origins and Career

SAINT PATRICK

His Origins and Career

BY

R. P. C. HANSON

OXFORD
AT THE CLARENDON PRESS

Oxford University Press, Great Clarendon Street, Oxford OX2 6DP

Oxford New York

Athens Auckland Bangkok Bogota Bombay
Buenos Aires Calcutta Cape Town Dar es Salaam
Delhi Florence Hong Kong Istanbul Karachi
Kuala Lumpur Madras Madrid Melbourne
Mexico City Nairobi Paris Singapore
Taipei Tokyo Toronto Warsaw
and associated companies in
Berlin Ibadan

Oxford is a trade mark of Oxford University Press

Published in the United States by
Oxford University Press Inc., New York

© Oxford University Press 1968

Special edition for Sandpiper Books Ltd., 1997

British Library Cataloguing in Publication Data
Data available

ISBN 0-19-826616-2

1 3 5 7 9 10 8 6 4 2

Printed in Great Britain
on acid-free paper by
Bookcraft (Bath) Ltd.,
Midsomer Norton

This book is dedicated to the memory of the late

GEORGE VIVILIERS JOURDAN
D.D., D.Litt.

*formerly Beresford Professor of Ecclesiastical History
in the University of Dublin*

FLAMMAM ACCENDENTI

ACKNOWLEDGEMENTS

THIS book owes much of any merit that it may possess to the kind interest shown and scholarly advice supplied by Professor D. A. Binchy, D.Litt. to its author while it was being composed. Warm thanks are also due to Mr. R. P. Wright, the eminent authority on Roman British Archaeology in the University of Durham, and to Professor E. A. Thompson, F.B.A. and Mr. G. R. Watson, M.Litt., of the Department of Classics in the University of Nottingham, for answering the author's queries on various important points. The author also thanks his wife and daughters for their help in compiling the Indexes.

R. P. C. H.

CONTENTS

ABBREVIATIONS

I. BRITAIN IN THE FIFTH CENTURY   I

II. THE BRITISH CHURCH IN THE FIFTH CENTURY   29

III. ASSESSMENT OF THE SOURCES   72
    1. *Writings of St. Patrick himself*
    2. *Later Traditions about St. Patrick*
    3. *Entries about St. Patrick in the Irish Annals*

IV. ST. PATRICK'S CAREER   106

V. ST. PATRICK'S BACKGROUND   141

VI. ST. PATRICK'S DATE   171

VII. ST. PATRICK   189

APPENDIXES
    1. *Mention of St. Patrick in the Irish Annals*   213
    2. *The 'High-King' of Ireland*   225

BIBLIOGRAPHY   230

INDEXES   236

ABBREVIATIONS

ACW	Bieler's translation of the works of St. Patrick in the series 'Ancient Christian Writers'.
ASCC	Norah Chadwick, *Age of the Saints in the Early Celtic Church.*
CB	Norah Chadwick, *Celtic Britain.*
CEB	H. Williams, *Christianity in Early Britain.*
Councils, etc.	Haddan and Stubbs, *Councils and Ecclesiastical Documents relating to Great Britain and Ireland,* vol. i.
CS	*Celt and Saxon,* ed. Norah Chadwick.
Latin	Christine Mohrmann, *The Latin of St. Patrick.*
LE	Bieler's commentary on the Latin text of St. Patrick's works, called *Libri Epistolarum.*
LHB	K. Jackson, *Language and History in Early Britain.*
LP	Bury, *Life of St. Patrick.*
MGH or *Mon. Germ. Hist.*	*Monumenta Germaniae Historica.*
Ninian and Origins	W. D. Simpson, *St. Ninian and the Origins of the Christian Church in Scotland.*
Patrick, Apostle	J. H. Todd, *St. Patrick, Apostle of Ireland.*
PB	Binchy's article 'Patrick and his Biographers'.
PG	Migne, *Patrologia Graeca.*
PL	Migne, *Patrologia Latina.*
PLG	Norah Chadwick, *Poetry and Letters in Early Christian Gaul.*
RBES	Collingwood and Myres, *Roman Britain and the English Settlements.*
SBC	*Studies in the Early British Church,* ed. Norah Chadwick.
SBH	*Studies in Early British History,* ed. Norah Chadwick.
Sources	J. F. Kenney, *Sources for the Early History of Ireland.*
TL	Stokes, *The Tripartite Life of Patrick, with other documents.*

I

BRITAIN IN THE FIFTH CENTURY

IT is certain that Patrick was born in Britain. It is virtually certain that he was born at some time late in the fourth century and that most of his career falls in the first half of the fifth.[1] It is fitting therefore to begin our consideration of the historical background to Patrick's life with Britain in the middle of the fourth century. There is some evidence that Britain was enjoying a measure of prosperity at that time. The historian Zosimus tells us that at the beginning of his campaigns against the barbarians on the Rhine frontier (356–61) Julian, then Caesar and later to be sole Emperor, sent across from the mouth of the Rhine to Britain in order to secure food and other supplies for a vast number of prisoners returned by the barbarians whom he had heavily defeated.[2] This suggests that the island must at that time have been well under Roman control, and in a reasonably good state economically. But this prosperity and security were soon to be roughly shattered. In the year 367 there took place what the historian Ammianus Marcellinus called the *barbarica conspiratio*. In a concerted movement, the Picts and Scots and Attacotti attacked Hadrian's wall, some of the local troops posted there to defend it joined hands with the invaders, and at the same time Saxons and Franks attacked the south and east of Britain. In the resulting fighting a *comes litoris Saxonici* was killed and a *dux Brittanniarum* was cut off (*circumventus*, which could mean killed. Amm. Marc. 27. 8. 1). According to a recent authority[3] one of the results of this series of disasters was that the Romanized civil population disappeared from most parts of Britain between York and the Antonine Wall, except for a few towns, such as Corbridge and Brougham, where civilians could live near a Roman garrison. But the disaster in most of the rest of Britain was retrieved when

[1] For the evidence for these conclusions, see below, Chapter VI.
[2] Zosimus, *Historia* iii. 5 (117–18).
[3] P. Salway, *The Frontier People of Roman Britain*, p. 18.

B

Valentinian I in 368 sent Theodosius the Elder (father of the Emperor of the same name) to Britain.¹ After some campaigning, during which he had to relieve a siege of London by barbarian forces, Theodosius restored the situation, though hardly to the *status quo ante*. One of the results of his reorganization was that a fifth province, called Valentia, was created in Britain,² and that for a brief period London enjoyed the title of *Augusta*. It may be that Theodosius entrusted the defence of the new province to *foederati*, that is to say barbarian troops under a chief or leader who was bound by treaty to Rome, and perhaps was a Roman citizen, but who administered the territory entrusted to him independently of the Roman military and taxation system.³ This is to assume that Valentia covered the modern principality of Wales, or some part of it, an assumption for which we have no proof. But we shall see reason to believe that this system of employing *foederati* was used later in the history of Britain, and it is not fantastic to conjecture that Theodosius made use of it.

The next important event in the history of Britain is the successful rebellion of Magnus Maximus. Britain, which Jerome in his *Letter to Ctesiphon* called *fertilis provincia tyrannorum*,⁴ had produced usurpers before. Zosimus tells us that a certain Valentinianus or Valentinus at some point between 364 and

---

¹ It is easy, but undesirable, to confuse the Emperor Theodosius I with his father. J. L. Gough Meissner does so (*History of the Church of Ireland*, vol. i, p. 53, and all through cap. ii).

² The other four were Britannia Prima, Britannia Secunda, Flavia Caesariensis, and Maxima Caesariensis. The location and limits of these provinces are unknown. *The Atlas of the Early Christian World* and Map II attached to A. H. M. Jones's *Later Roman Empire* give quite different positions to them. London had hitherto been neither a *colonia* nor a *municipium*, and, in spite of its new title, retained the same status as it had held before the *barbarica conspiratio*. Colchester, Gloucester, Lincoln, and York were the only *coloniae*, and Verulamium the only *municipium*. Such distinctions were no longer relevant by the middle of the fourth century. J. L. Gough Meissner has failed to appreciate that ever since the time of Diocletian Britain had not been 'the province', but several, and he unjustifiably locates Valentia between the walls (*History of the Church of Ireland*, vol. i, cap. ii). As far as the references to it in Ammianus Marcellinus go, Valentia could have been merely an existing province (Amm. Marc. 28. 3. 7).

³ The evidence for this is the fact that the *Notitia Dignitatum*, a document drawn up between 420 and 430, but perhaps relating to conditions at a rather earlier period, purports to give the military strength of the Roman army in all parts of the Empire, but has no entries at all detailing forts or the stationing of soldiers in the west of Britain.

⁴ *Epistles* 133. 9 (*PL* 22. 1157–8). See below, p. 7.

375, on being banished to Britain, had started an attempt at usurpation which cost him his life.[1] Earlier still, in the reign of Diocletian, Carausius had successfully maintained an independent Kingdom of Britain for six years (287–93) before being murdered by one of his staff, Allectus, who had survived in independence for three more years. Orosius tells us that Carausius was originally appointed to suppress Frankish and Saxon raiders.[2] A Gallic chronicle written about the year 452 relates, after recording Maximus's elevation by his soldiers, *incursantes Pictos et Scottos Maximus strenue superavit.*[3] Later usurpers originating from Britain spent their entire short and trouble-filled careers contending against barbarians, as we shall see. It may be that it was Britain's search for security that led her so frequently to attempt to produce her own emperors, who might deal more effectively with the enemy at the gates than the distant Augustus, beset by other cares in Milan or Constantinople. Orosius has some surprisingly favourable words to say about Maximus. He calls him 'a man of vigour and integrity, worthy to be an Augustus', and says that he was made Emperor by the army in Britain against his will.[4] This praise may be due to the fact that Maximus was on his elevation a newly baptized Christian, and on reaching the Continent he posed as a champion of orthodoxy. In a letter to Pope Siricius written in 385 he says *imperium ab ipso statim salutari fonte conscenderim*, and declares that he consequently regards himself as having a special obligation to protect the Catholic faith, and later (in 386 or 387) he wrote a sententious piece of propaganda to Valentinian II urging him to abandon his support of the Arians.[5] Zosimus says that Maximus had fought in Britain under Theodosius the Elder, and that he obtained his elevation by playing on the feelings of the soldiers in Britain, who regarded themselves as slighted by the Emperor Gratian's preference for foreign mercenaries.[6] Norah Chadwick, on the strength of Old Welsh

---

[1] Zosimus, *Historia* iv. 29 (168). See also Amm. Marc. 28. 3. 3–6.

[2] Orosius, *Historia adversus Paganos* vii. 25 (1125–6).

[3] *Two Gallic Chronicles*, ed. T. Mommsen (*Mon. Germ. Hist. Auct. Ant.* ix: *Chron. Min.* i), p. 646.

[4] Orosius, *Hist. adv. Pag.* vii. 3, 4 (1149)—*vir quidem strenuus et probus et Augusto dignus.*

[5] *Epistulae Imperatorum, Pontificum, Aliorum*, 40. 1 (90); 39. 4 (89).

[6] Zosimus, *Hist.* iv. 35 (190, 191).

genealogies and the silence of the *Notitia Dignitatum* about Roman military forces in the west of Britain, has advanced a theory that Magnus Maximus was a Welsh chieftain entrusted as a *foederatus* with the defence of Wales, or its south-western frontier, against further Irish encroachments.[1] It does, indeed, appear to be true that by this period the south-west of Wales was much open to Irish influence, was perhaps bilingual, and numbered many people of Irish stock among its inhabitants, and this fact will have to be taken into consideration when we come to discuss the place of Patrick's birth.[2] But it is wholly unlikely that Magnus Maximus was the Romanized chief of barbarian *foederati*. Zosimus describes him as Spanish.[3] The idea that a barbarian, even a Romanized one, whose power lay in his being the leader of barbarians, should aspire to the purple was a quite unacceptable one to the average Roman citizen of that day. Zosimus and Orosius would certainly have pointed this out as a scandal, had it occurred in Maximus's case, Zosimus all the more readily because as a pagan he had a prejudice against Christian emperors. Orosius in his history gives very short shrift to barbarians who aspire to power, such as Gildo, Firmus, and Stilicho, using language about them which he does not use of Magnus Maximus.[4] And, anyway, one of the most remarkable features about the Roman Empire in the fifth century is the refusal of powerful barbarian war-lords to aim directly at the imperial throne. We may instance Alaric, Gainas, Atalphus, Aetius, Ricimer, Odoacer, and finally Theodoric, who apparently preferred to abolish the title of Emperor rather than usurp it himself.[5]

Magnus Maximus is said to have pursued a ruthless financial

---

[1] Norah K. Chadwick, *CS*, pp. 41–42. Part of her evidence rests upon the discovery in the *Notitia Dignitatum* of a detachment of troops called *Seguntienses* in Illyricum, who probably derive their name from Segontium (Caernarvon); it is thought that they accompanied Maximus on his continental adventure; archaeological evidence from the Roman fort at Caernarvon suggests that Roman occupation of it ended in 380. But interesting though this evidence is, it does not make Maximus into a British chieftain.

[2] See below, pp. 12, 114.

[3] *Hist.* iv. 35 (190) Ἴβηρ τῷ γένει.

[4] *Hist. adv. Pag.* vii. 36 (1155–7), Gildo and Firmus, 38 (1162) Stilicho.

[5] Magnus Maximus was not Welsh, but he left a lasting impression upon the Welsh folk-memory; he figures in the *Mabinogion* as the great Emperor Machsen. Perhaps it was his successful campaign against the Picts and Scots that originally produced this impression.

policy, and probably those writers are correct who assume that
when he crossed to the Continent in a successful bid to exter-
minate Gratian and make himself Emperor of the West he
denuded Britain of troops.[1] Archaeological evidence suggests
that after his reign Hadrian's wall was not regularly repaired
nor regularly garrisoned. The *Notitia Dignitatum*, consistently
with this conclusion, assigns to the *Dux Britanniarum*, whose
command would lie in the Highland Zone of Britain, almost
no troops at all. The north of Britain may have been exposed
again to attacks from the Picts, and the western coasts must
have been vulnerable to raids from the Scots (i.e. the Irish).
Collingwood and Myres describe the years after Magnus Maximus's death in 388 as 'the classical period of Irish piracy', and,
with several other authorities, they associate this period with
the *floruit* of the famous Irish war-lord and raider, Niall of the
Nine Hostages.[2] This is the period to which the signal-towers
found in prominent places along the Yorkshire coast are to be
attributed. Hunter Blair attributes them to Theodosius the
Elder,[3] and L. E. Stevens places them between 369 and 395.[4]
The inscription on the signal-tower on Ravenscar, above Robin
Hood Bay in Yorkshire, was put up by a *praepositus*, the commander of a detachment of a legion under the ultimate control
of a *dux Britanniarum*, and a *praefectus*, the commander of a body
of auxiliaries, perhaps from the *numerus supervenientium Petueren-
sium* known to have been stationed at Malton, not far away.[5]
These signal-towers would imply the likelihood of Saxon raids
on the eastern coasts of Britain.[6]

But the erection of signal-towers suggests the existence of
a government able to build and man them. We must not

[1] So Bury, *LP*, pp. 21–22 and 383–8; W. D. Simpson, *St. Ninian and the Origins*,
pp. 9–10; Collingwood and Myres, *RBES*, p. 287.

[2] Ibid., p. 312; so also Bury, *LP*, pp. 25–26 and 334, and Norah Chadwick,
SBC, p. 34. But it is not certain that we can assign the career of Niall to this period.
See below, pp. 171–2, 223–5.

[3] P. Hunter Blair, *Roman Britain and Early England*, p. 153.

[4] C. E. Stevens, 'The British Sections of the *Notitia Dignitatum*', pp. 151–4.

[5] This is the reconstruction of Stevens op. cit.

[6] The large 'Saxon forts', which still survive in considerable ruins in several
places (e.g. Pevensey, Portchester, and Burgh Castle in Suffolk), were probably
built either by Carausius to resist invasion from the forces of the central Roman
government coming from the Continent, or by Constantius I or his successors, as
a defence against Saxon raids early in the fourth century (Norah Chadwick, *CB*,
p. 25; Hunter Blair, *Roman Britain and Early England*, p. 85).

exaggerate the tribulations of this period in British history. Theodosius the Great, after being compelled for a short period to recognize Magnus Maximus as Western Emperor, was able to defeat him and put him to death in 388. It is likely that the central Roman government was too much distracted by other pressing necessities to regain effective control in Britain for some years after that. It was probably not till the arrival of Stilicho some time between 395 and 399 that this was achieved. Meanwhile Britons, in the Lowland Zone at any rate, may have enjoyed a modest prosperity. It is not till about 395 that series of coins found on excavated sites peter out. There is evidence for rebuilding and a revival of civilized living in some Roman villas at the end of the fifth century.[1] It is from this period that the very impressive temple to the Celtic god Nodens at Lydney in Gloucestershire dates, and there are signs of the rebuilding of pagan shrines elsewhere.[2] It is known that a State woollen mill was still operating at Winchester early in the fifth century. When Stilicho did arrive he inflicted defeats on Irish raiders, as far as can be made out from the confused and scanty evidence, and may have left some more troops in Britain, though it is likely that he withdrew many soldiers during the panic caused by the invasion of Italy by Radagaesus in 405. It is likely that the fort at Pevensey was repaired in the reign of Honorius, probably under Stilicho.[3] C. E. Stevens calculates that about the year 400 the commander of military forces in the Lowland Zone, the *comes Saxonici litoris*, must have had a fair number of troops at his disposal.[4]

The next phase in the history of Britain of which we can have any knowledge includes the circumstances under which Roman rule there ended. This obscure and much debated series of events can for purposes of discussion be divided into three heads: the immediate cause of the break with the Roman government; the actual achievement of independence itself; and the question of whether there was a brief and partial Roman reoccupation of Britain after the formal break. There can be no doubt that what caused the break with the Roman government was the fear of

---

[1] Hunter Blair, *Roman Britain and Early England*, p. 130.

[2] Ibid., pp. 141–3.

[3] See F. Haverfield in *Ephemeris Epigraphica* ix, p. 649, no. 1281, who derives this conclusion from an inscription which runs HONAUG ANDRIA.

[4] C. E. Stevens, op. cit., pp. 145–6.

barbarian invasion and the failure to remove this threat of the usurper elevated in Britain in order to deal with it. On the last day of the year 406 a vast horde of barbarians of different races, Vandals, Suevi, and Alans, crossed the frozen Rhine and burst into the Gallic provinces, brushing away by force of numbers any opposition they met. They streamed westward across Gaul as they went, pillaging and destroying, until they reached the barrier of the Pyrenees, when they spread out over the neighbouring provinces to the east of this mountain barrier. This was the worst invasion of barbarians that the Gallic provinces (perhaps that the Western Roman Empire) had ever experienced, and it might even be described as the moment when the Western Roman Empire expired, for most of these barbarians never returned home, and the central Roman government never recovered control of its northern Gallic provinces for any long period after this irruption. Enough of the invading masses turned northwards towards the coast of Gaul to alarm thoroughly the British provincials. It must have looked as if the barbarians had only to seize enough ships to be able to continue their apparently irresistible drive in the direction of Britain. The Britons' sense of insecurity expressed itself, as it had before, in the elevation of usurping Emperors. During the year 407 the army in Britain elevated in quick succession three men, the first two of whom were speedily murdered, a man called Marcus, a man called Gratian, and finally a man from the lower ranks of the army called Constantine. This Constantine (who is often distinguished as Constantine III by historians, though the later Byzantine Emperors called Constantine did not recognize him as the third in their succession) was able quickly to gather a large force, to cross the Channel with it to Gaul, and to begin a career as claimant to the imperial throne full of vicissitudes and struggles. This career included one short period in the year 409 when Honorius (son of Theodosius the Great), the nominal Western Roman Emperor, with his headquarters at Ravenna, found it expedient to recognize Constantine as co-Emperor. But though Honorius was quite incapable himself of preventing the Western Roman Empire dissolving before the assaults of the barbarians, he had an amazing capacity for ensuring that he, and only he, should preside over its dissolution. He was able in the year 411 to get rid of this usurper as he eventually got rid of all usurpers. Constantine was decisively defeated in battle in north Italy, captured, and executed. Constantine had been attempting, not very successfully, to deal with the barbarians who were spreading havoc in Gaul, finding his lieutenants insubordinate, and his son, whom he had made Caesar and later Augustus, incapable of securing the allegiance of the rebels. He also witnessed the incursion into Spain of both the Vandals and the Suevi, and of some of the troops that Constantine himself had introduced into Gaul from Britain. Meanwhile, his native land, Britain, suffered a severe raid from Saxons, which Constantine was quite unable to prevent or avenge. At this point the patience of the British provincials broke. They threw off allegiance to Roman rule as represented by Constantine III. They were unable to restore the rule of Honorius, who was at the time suffering under the shock of Alaric's sack of Rome. They declared themselves independent of the Roman government. Never again was Britain destined to return to Roman rule.[1] The form which this British movement for independence took is uncertain. Zosimus, who is at this point thought to be dependent upon an earlier and more reliable historian, Olympiodorus, describes the affair thus:

> As they advanced the barbarians gained control of everything and brought the inhabitants of the British island and some of the peoples who lived among the Celts to the necessity of revolting from the Roman government and managing their own affairs without observing the laws of the Romans.

> Consequently the people of Britain armed themselves and took their lives in their hands in order to rid their cities of the barbarians who were menacing them, and all Armorica and other provinces of the Gauls followed the example of the Britons and in a similar way made themselves independent, throwing out the Romans' officials and setting up their own independent government.[2]

---

[1] This account of the events leading up to the withdrawal of Britain from Roman rule is based on the following sources: Zosimus, *Hist.* v; Orosius, *Hist. adv. Pag.* vii. 40–42; *Gallic Chronicle, MGH Auct. Ant.* ix, p. 654 (which confirms Zosimus's information about the Saxon raid on Britain); Collingwood and Myres, *RBES*, pp. 10–11; E. A. Thompson, 'Zosimus on the End of Roman Britain', pp. 163–6; C. E. Stevens, 'Marcus, Gratian, Constantine', pp. 317–27, 328–38; A. H. M. Jones, *The Later Roman Empire*, vol. i, pp. 185–91; P. Hunter Blair, *Roman Britain and Early England*, pp. 155–6.

[2] *Hist.* vi. 5 (286–7): πάντα κατ' ἐξουσίαν ἐπιόντες οἱ ὑπὲρ τὸν Ῥῆνον βάρβαροι κατέστησαν εἰς ἀνάγκην τούς τε τὴν Βρεττανικὴν νῆσον οἰκοῦντας καὶ τῶν ἐν Κέλτοις ἐθνῶν ἔνια τῆς Ῥωμαίων ἀρχῆς ἀποστῆναι καὶ καθ' ἑαυτὰ βιοτεύειν οὐκέτι τοῖς τούτων

Writing about a hundred years later than Zosimus, Procopius says, 'The Romans in fact were never able to recover Britain but it remained from that time under tyrants.'[1] Zosimus also later tells us that 'Honorius wrote a letter to the cities in Britain telling them to look to their own defence.'[2] J. Morris interprets this as implying that the *Concilium Britanniarum*, the body composed of the leading men in each of the *civitates* of Britain (a council which he assumes to have existed, by analogy with the *concilium Galliarum*), wrote to Honorius in 410, and that this letter was Honorius's reply.[3] J. N. L. Myres suggests that Honorius's letter repeated for the benefit of the Britons the repeal of the *Lex Julia de Vi Publica*, which had been enacted in 406 during the panic at Radagaesus's invasion of Italy, an enactment which the Britons, owing to the troubled times, might never have heard of.[4] As Honorius's letter was apparently addressed directly to the *civitates*, we may assume that the normal recipients of an Imperial missive in Britain had departed, the *vicarius* of Britain, the *dux Britanniarum*, and the *comes litoris Saxonici*. It also means that all units of the field army of the Roman Empire, the *comitatenses*, would have left (no doubt having accompanied Constantine III in his military enterprise on the continent). This does not, however, mean that no soldiers were left in Britain. The *limitanei*, the locally recruited forces who had not through the emergencies and vicissitudes of the last few years been drafted into the field army as *comitatenses* or *pseudo-comitatenses*, would have remained, not as a peasant militia,[5] but simply as locally recruited full-time soldiers who were expected to give all their service in much the same place.[6]

ὑπακούοντα νόμοις. οἵ τε ἐκ τῆς Βρεττανίας ὅπλα ἐνδύντες καὶ σφῶν αὐτῶν προκινδυνεύσαντες ἠλευθέρωσαν τῶν ἐπικειμένων βαρβάρων τάς πόλεις, καὶ ὁ Ἀρμόριχος ἅπας καὶ ἕτεραι Γαλάτων ἐπαρχίαι, Βρεττάνους μιμησάμεναι, κατὰ τὸν ἴσον σφᾶς ἠλευθέρωσαν τρόπον, ἐκβάλλουσαι μὲν τοὺς Ῥωμαίων ἄρχοντας, οἰκεῖον δὲ κατ' ἐξουσίαν πολίτευμα καθιστᾶσαι.

[1] Procopius, *Bellum Vandalicum* i. 2, 38, quoted by C. E. Stevens, 'Marcus, Gratian and Constantine', p. 341 (the translation is that of Stevens); the Greek of Procopius runs Βρεττανίαν μέντοι Ῥωμαῖοι ἀνασώσασθαι οὐκέτι ἔσχον, ἀλλ' οὖσα ὑπὸ τυράννοις ἀπ' αὐτοῦ ἔμεινε.

[2] *Hist.* vi. 10 (291): Ὀνωρίου δὲ γράμμασι πρὸς τὰς ἐν Βρεττανίᾳ χρησαμένου πόλεις φυλάττεσθαι παραγγέλλουσι. [3] J. Morris, 'Dark Age Dates', p. 147.

[4] J. N. L. Myres, 'Pelagius and the End of Roman Rule in Britain', p. 33.

[5] See below, p. 115–16.

[6] For this interpretation of events, see C. E. Stevens, 'Marcus, Gratian, Constantine', pp. 317–25, 328–38; J. N. L. Myres, 'Pelagius and the End of Roman Rule

Did the Roman government ever re-establish its control over Britain? Some eminent authorities have thought that it did. Collingwood, arguing from the disposition of troops given in one list in the *Notitia Dignitatum* and assigned to the *comes Britanniarum*, from the discovery of coins in Richborough, where finds show an intensive occupation lasting well into the fifth century, and from other sites in East Anglia, in Wiltshire, and in Weymouth where the same situation appears to have occurred on a smaller scale, conjured up a picture of a brief Roman reoccupation of Britain. A Roman army, he suggested, reoccupied south-eastern England, perhaps by means of a *vicarius* in London, largely in walled towns, but without garrisoning the forts of the Saxon shore. He conjectured that the reoccupation was the work of the Patrician Constantius, who re-established Roman control in Brittany about 417, and that this re-established régime had withdrawn by 429.[1] H. M. Chadwick was convinced by these arguments,[2] and A. H. M. Jones, in his recent magisterial *The Later Roman Empire*,[3] has endorsed them too. But the evidence upon which this reconstruction is based is very flimsy, and it has met some criticisms from other scholars. C. E. Stevens has analysed the evidence in the *Notitia Dignitatum* to show how frail are the arguments based upon the assumption that it gives us reliable evidence of the disposition of the Roman army in Britain as late as 420,[4] and he and E. A. Thompson have pointed to the significance of the fact that Zosimus is relying upon an earlier and trustworthy historian, Olympiodorus, in recording that the departure of the Roman administration in 410 was not followed by any reoccupation.[5] Thompson, indeed, advanced in the same article a theory, which is not without support in Zosimus, that after the departure of Constantine III a peasant and slave revolt, called by contemporaries a 'Bacauda', broke out in Britain, similar to that which certainly occurred in

in Britain', pp. 21–23, 32–33; J. Morris, 'Dark Age Dates', pp. 147–8; E. A. Thompson, 'Zosimus on the End of the Roman Empire', pp. 164–7.

[1] Collingwood and Myres, *RBES*, pp. 295–301.

[2] In 'The End of Roman Britain', printed in *SEBH* (ed. Norah Chadwick), pp. 11–13.

[3] p. 191.

[4] C. E. Stevens, 'The British Sections of the *Notitia Dignitatum*', pp. 124–40.

[5] C. E. Stevens, 'Marcus, Gratian, Constantine', pp. 317, 340–1; E. A. Thompson, 'Zosimus on the End of the Roman Empire', pp. 163–7.

Armorica in 417, and in northern Gaul under Tibatto in 435–7, and that Honorius's letter was sent in response to an appeal from the upper and middle classes of Britain to save them from the British working classes in revolt. However we may estimate this suggestion, it is difficult not to agree with these last two scholars that the evidence for a Roman reoccupation of Britain at this time is quite insufficient, especially as there is no evidence of the Saxon forts being garrisoned at this period. Britain, once a diocese of the Roman Empire, did early in the fifth century 'eject Roman administrators, receive no Roman legislation and pay no taxes',[1] even though it remained what Prosper later called it, and what Patrick so clearly thought it to be, *Romana insula*.[2]

It is not difficult to discern, at least in dim outline, the type of policy which succeeded the régime of the central Roman government in Britain. The original *civitates*, which had been Celtic and then were Romanized, territories of varying size associated with a chief town, formed themselves into independent kingdoms, ruled first by people whom we should call dictators and later by hereditary royal dynasties. The ruler of each was called in British speech a *ti(g)ern* (Welsh *teyrn*), a word which originally meant 'lord of the land'. It may be conjectured that the Latin word *tyrannus* (Gildas, Patrick) was adopted as an equivalent because it sounded like *ti(g)ern*. *Reges habet Britannia, sed tyrannos*, says Gildas, writing of Britain in the first half of the sixth century,[3] as if the word *tyrannus* was a reproach, and Patrick's statement that the devil was using *tyrannidem Corotici*[4] suggests the same sense. But Zosimus translates the Latin sentence *misero regi servantur* by ἀθλίῳ τυράννῳ φυλάττονται.[5] Patrick speaks of Irish *reges* and *reguli*, though never of a single *rex*.[6] Some of these successor-kingdoms to the Roman Empire in Britain can be roughly located. One of them comprised the

---

[1] C. E. Stevens, 'Marcus, Gratian, Constantine', pp. 340–1.

[2] Prosper, *Contra Collatorem* 21. 2. Cf. the judgement of Salway: 'There is in fact absolutely no evidence for anything but the most wholehearted desire on the part of the heterogeneous population of the *vici* to be considered Roman, at least in public' (*The Frontier People*, p. 18).

[3] Gildas, *De Excidio Britanniae* 27 (66).

[4] Epistle 6.

[5] *Hist.* v. 38 (267).

[6] *Confession* 41. 52. The bearing of this upon the theory that there was a 'High-King' of Ireland in Patrick's day is discussed below Appendix 2, pp. 223–7.

basin of the Severn in central Wales and Shropshire, with its capital at Wroxeter (Viroconium), originally the territory of the Cornovii. Another, originally the territory of the Silures, included parts of Monmouthshire and Herefordshire, perhaps extending eastward to Gloucestershire (the Forest of Dean) and westward to Glamorgan; its capital was Caerwent (*Venta*). Early in the fifth century this state became a monarchy. Another derived from the *civitas* of the Dummonii, with its capital at Exeter (Isca Dumnoniorum), and included Cornwall and Devon. Another was the Kingdom called Demetia, covering south-west Wales, a survival of the numerous Irish colonies which had been established on the west coasts of Britain during the fourth century, but which were mostly reduced during the fifth, where it is probable that the population was bilingual and well mixed with Irish stock. Two more were the British Kingdom of Strathclyde in the north, with its capital at Dumbarton in the Firth of Clyde, and the Kingdom of Manau Gododdin (originally the territory of the Votadini), stretching southward from the shores of the Firth of Forth. Another was the Kingdom of Rheged, including both the shores of the Solway estuary and some extent of hinterland on both sides;[1] and still another was the Kingdom of Elmet, which corresponded roughly to the modern West Riding of Yorkshire. In the far north, beyond the Kingdom of Strathclyde, after the year 495 the purely Irish Kingdom of the Scots (i.e. Irish) of Dalriada was established, in what is now Argyll and the islands to the west and north of it, by invading Irish settlers.[2] As will shortly be seen, we can identify at least two of these *tyranni* in charge of successor-states in fifth-century Britain by name. Some of them issued coinage modelled on the coins of the Constantinian dynasty still current in

[1] J. MacQueen (*St. Nynia*, caps. vii and viii) does his best to show that the Kingdom of Rheged did not lie in this position but included territory on the *east* coast of Scotland. But his arguments upon a question which can only be decided by slender evidence rest upon proofs so tenuous as to leave the matter quite indecisive.

[2] The reconstruction of this list of kingdoms is based on H. M. Chadwick, 'The Foundation of the Early British Kingdoms' (pp. 47–60 in Norah Chadwick's *SBH*); Norah Chadwick, *CS*, pp. 11 ff.; P. Hunter Blair, *Roman Britain and Early England*, pp. 153–4; and J. Morris, 'The Dates of the Celtic Saints', p. 351. The reason why almost all the successor states that can be recognized are in the west of Britain is that those in the east were obliterated so early by the Anglo-Saxon intruders that all trace of them has disappeared.

Britain.[1] On the whole, we may conjecture that these successor-states enjoyed comparative peace and prosperity, broken only by occasional incursions of Picts and Scots, until at least the middle of the fifth century. This may correspond to the period of unprecedented prosperity placed by Gildas's very much muddled narrative at about this time.[2]

The conventional history of early Britain would next relate that this relatively untroubled period was ended by the Saxon, or Anglo-Saxon, invasion. The evidence for this is usually thought to be found in two sources. First, the *Gallic Chronicle*, of about 452, has against the year 441/2 the entry: *Brittaniae usque ad hoc tempus variis cladibus eventibusque latae in dicionem Saxonum rediguntur.*[3] Second, Gildas relates that the 'remnants' (*reliquiae*) of the Britons sent a letter *ad Agitium Romanae potestatis virum* asking for aid against invading barbarians, and he quotes some sentences from it: *Agitio ter consuli gemitus Britannorum . . . repellunt barbari ad mare, repellit mare ad barbaros; inter haec duo genera funerum aut iugulamur aut mergimur.*[4] Agitius is generally identified as Aetius, and the third consulship of Aetius can be dated to 446. This letter is usually reckoned as an historical fact and dated to this year.[5] And it is difficult to explain away the evidence of the *Gallic Chronicle*, which must have been composed not long after the event chronicled.[6] But we should hesitate before accepting the *Gallic Chronicle*'s account quite literally. Gildas himself does not encourage such a course, because he goes on to relate that, unable to secure Roman aid, the Britons pulled themselves together and gained a victory over the barbarians, that this victory was followed by a long period of prosperity, and that this period was only ended when, in the face of a threatened raid on a large scale (apparently by Picts and Scots), *omnes consilarii cum superbo tyranno* agreed to call in the aid of the Saxons against

---

[1] Collingwood and Myres, *RBES*, p. 308. See also C. H. V. Sutherland, 'Coinage in Britain in the Fifth and Sixth Centuries', in *Dark Age Britain* (ed. D. B. Harden), especially pp. 9–10.

[2] *De Excidio* 21 (48).

[3] *Two Gallic Chronicles*, MGH *Auct. Ant.* ix. 660.

[4] Gildas, *De Excidio* 20 (46).

[5] e.g. by C. E. Stevens, 'Marcus, Gratian, Constantine', p. 342.

[6] E. A. Thompson, for instance, thinks that the Saxons 'inflicted a severe blow on Britain in 441/2' ('Zosimus on the End of Roman Britain', p. 166). H. Williams (*CEB*, p. 334) for reasons of his own wished to place this event twenty years earlier, but he has not been followed by many scholars in this.

these impending enemies.[1] As far as Gildas is concerned, the merciless enemies of the Letter to Aetius of 446 are the Picts and Scots, not the Saxons, and there was no sudden, single, and overwhelming invasion of Saxons, such as the *Gallic Chronicle* suggests. As far as it goes, archaeological evidence appears to support Gildas. Recent work at Verulamium has shown that the town must have been inhabited well into the middle of the fifth century.[2] Earlier, Collingwood had noted that the fate that overtook Verulamium, Silchester, Wroxeter, and Caistor-next-to-Norwich in the fifth century was not destruction by fire and sword but simply desertion.[3] With this is consistent the fact that the great majority of the Roman villas which have been excavated were not burnt or violently destroyed, but apparently just left to decay, and that it is likely that very few of them were inhabited by the middle of the fifth century. In view of this and similar evidence,[4] C. H. V. Sutherland has suggested that 'the main vanguard of the Anglo-Saxon invasion consisted of sizeable armies which entered Britain in the mid fifth century by East Anglia and the Wash at the invitation of Romano-British communities, to act as mercenaries against the growing Pictish threat',[5] and several other scholars have taken a similar view.

In fact the history of Britain in the second half of the fifth century, which begins with this question of the exact nature of the Saxon intervention, is so obscure and uncertain that it will be necessary to give at this point a brief account of our two main

[1] Gildas, *De Excidio* 22 (52) and 23 (52–54).

[2] See S. S. Frere, 'Excavations at Verulamium 1959' and 'Excavations at Verulamium 1960', and especially in the former the words on p. 20, 'Thus at a date well into the fifth century, and probably at least as late as 450, we find that the technical skill necessary to maintain the city's aqueduct and to install a piped supply from the *castellum divisorium* was still available and that the civilized needs implicit in such a demand were still continuing.'

[3] Collingwood and Myres, *RBES*, pp. 317–18.

[4] Cf. the statement of C. H. V. Sutherland ('Coinage in Britain in the Fifth and Sixth Centuries', p. 6) 'walled cities in south and south-east Britain could stand without interruption substantially down the fifth century' (cf. pp. 9, 10), and the archaeological evidence discovered by W. D. Simpson that Brougham (*Brocavum*) was occupied in the fifth and later centuries (see P. Salway, *The Frontier People*, p. 136, referring to Simpson, *Transactions of the Cumberland and Westmorland Archaeological Society* (2) lviii, 68 ff.). Perhaps it is significant for our estimate of the continuity of life in Britain at this time that the names of several of the places examined by Salway appear to derive from or incorporate the Romano-Celtic names, e.g. Brougham, Carlisle (*Luguvalium*), and Binchester (*Vinovia*).

[5] C. H. V. Sutherland, 'Coinage in Britain in the Fifth and Sixth Centuries', p. 7.

sources, Gildas's *De Excidio* and Nennius's *Historia Brittonum*. It is generally agreed among scholars that Gildas must have been born about 500 and must have written between 540 and 550.[1] His description of the history of Britain before the middle of the fifth century does not inspire confidence, though some scholars have attempted to make sense of it.[2] He ascribes the building of the Hadrianic and Antonine walls and the *vallum* of the former to the successors of Magnus Maximus in Britain up to the period when the Romans left Britain.[3] He schematizes the history of that period into three attacks of barbarians and three repulses of them by the Romans,[4] and he gives a fanciful picture of Britons as helpless, unarmed civilians in contrast to the foreign Roman soldiers, which does not in the least correspond to reality.[5] But there is no valid reason for disbelieving Gildas when he is writing about events which may be said to have fallen within living memory in Gildas's day. The difficulty is to determine the limits of living memory. He gives us no dates at all, except the reference to Aetius's third consulship, which we have already noted.[6] According to his account, the unsuccessful appeal of the Britons to Aetius was followed by a successful counter-attack on their part against the Picts and Scots (not the Saxons), a period of great prosperity, another threat by Picts and Scots, the introduction of forces of Saxons to assist them against this threat by a 'proud king and all the counsellors' (*omnes consilarii cum superbo tyranno*), and the rebellion of the Saxons, which caused immense destruction and loss of life. He then[7] goes on to relate that after the first shock of the rebellion many of the Saxons returned home, and the Britons rallied under a man called Ambrosius Aurelianus and won a victory.[8] There followed a war of varying

---

[1] So H. Williams, *CEB*, pp. 366 ff.; K. Jackson, *LHB*, p. 12; J. Morris, 'Dark Age Dates', pp. 150–1.

[2] H. Williams, in his edition of Gildas, and P. Hunter Blair, *Roman Britain and Early England*, pp. 159–66.

[3] Gildas, *De Excidio* 15 (32–34), 17 (34–36), 18 (36–38).

[4] Ibid. 17 (34–36).

[5] Ibid. 18 (36–38). H. M. Chadwick (*Early Scotland*, p. 141) and J. Morris ('Dark Age Dates', p. 151) agree in rejecting these narratives as worthless.

[6] See above, p. 13.

[7] Gildas, *De Excidio* 20 (46), 22 (52), 23 (52–54).

[8] Ibid. 25 (60). Gildas describes Ambrosius Aurelianus in these words: *viro modesto qui solus forte Romanae gentis tantae tempestatis collisione occisis in eadem parentibus purpura nimirum indutis superfuerat, cuius nunc temporibus nostris suboles magnopere avita bonitate degeneravit.*

fortunes, which ended with a siege (called *obsessio Badonici montis*) that resulted in an overwhelming defeat for the Saxons. Since that time to the point at which Gildas is writing there has been quiet. Clearly the Saxons are in possession of part of Britain, but clearly their penetration has been halted.[1] The dating of these events presents a problem, for if we accept the *Gallic Chronicle*'s year of 441/2 as that of the outbreak of the Saxon rebellion, we shall have to place the introduction of the Saxons as mercenaries well before that date, the period of prosperity before that, and the appeal of the Britons to Aetius in the face of attacks by Picts and Scots before that. And yet Gildas dates this appeal to 446!

The analysis of the evidence provided by Nennius's *Historia Brittonum* is a much more complicated matter. It is clear that this work was edited rather than written *de novo* by Nennius. It survives in several different forms. Nennius must have made additions between 796 and 801 to an already existing work, and additions to Nennius's own edition may have been made as late as 830. The work, which is in Latin, can be divided into eight parts, as follows:

1. The Six Ages of the World (caps. 1–6).
2. The History of Britain (caps. 7–49).
3. The Life of St. Patrick (caps. 50–55).
4. The Account of Arthur (cap. 56).
5. The Anglo-Saxon Genealogies and Northern Material (caps. 57–66).
6. The Computus of Easter (cap. 66).

To this most manuscripts add

7. The List of the Cities of Britain (cap. 66a).
8. The List of the Marvels of Britain (caps. 67–76).

The best and most complete version of this work is to be found in the manuscript called H, i.e. Harleian 3859, assigned to the period shortly before or after 1100. It makes no reference to any author, but it is generally reckoned to be a version of the *Historia* as it was edited about 800 by Nennius (with perhaps an appendix added 828/9). The name Nennius does not occur in any extant version before the twelfth century. The whole work

---

[1] Gildas, *De Excidio* 26 (60–62).

is more like a gradually growing organism than a composition, or even an edition, done at one time. It probably began with a small British nucleus of the late seventh century, and in some of the recensions of this other matter has been included (such as the *Liber Sancti Germani* and the *Vita Patricii*). Nennius's recension of this organism may have been made, as has been said, about 800, in Bangor in Wales. In the MS. Harleian 3859 there is also included a Latin text called the *Annales Cambriae*, and also the genealogies of several Welsh and north British princes. The *Annales Cambriae* was very probably drawn up in its latest form not later than 956, though it contains much earlier material. The genealogies appear to have been copied in the second half of the tenth century. Much of the material in the *Annales Cambriae* was originally compiled in the seventh century, and this compilation was motivated by a desire to support the pro-Roman side in the controversy about the calculation of Easter that troubled the Irish and the British Churches in that century and was settled at the end of it. The union of the *Annales Cambriae* and the *Historia Brittonum* took place in Gwynnedd (north Wales) in the late tenth century, under the patronage of the ruling family of that country, who were anxious to remind their people of the original connexion of Wales with north Britain in order to encourage resistance to the encroaching power of the Anglo-Saxons.[1]

The parts of the text of the *Historia Brittonum*[2] relevant to this study are Sections 2 ('The History of Britain', caps. 7–49), 4 ('The account of Arthur', cap. 56), and 5 ('The Anglo-Saxon

[1] This account of the *Historia Brittonum* relies on three books edited by Norah Chadwick: *SBH* ('The End of Roman Britain' and 'Vortigern' by H. M. Chadwick, pp. 9–20 and 21–33); *SBC* (Norah Chadwick herself, 'Early Culture and Learning in North Wales' (pp. 37–92)); *CS* ('On the Northern British Section in Nennius', by K. Jackson (pp. 48–54)). This last essay gives a fascinating reconstruction of how one part of Nennius's work was gradually compiled, though space forbids an account of it here.

[2] The text of Nennius followed here is that of T. Mommsen, *Historia Brittonum, cum additamentis Nennii* (*MGH Auct. Antiquiss.* xiii, pp. 113–222). Throughout his edition Mommsen relies mainly on the MS. Harleian 3859, but for the parts contributed by Nennius he gives in a parallel column another version, headed 'Nennius Interpretatus', which is a Latin translation made by Zimmer of an Irish version of Nennius made *c.* 1040 by a certain Gilla Coemgin, of which several manuscripts are extant (the oldest dated *c.* 1100), and which has been edited by Todd, Zimmer, and others. Mommsen's edition of Nennius has here been deliberately preferred to Loth's later edition.

Genealogies and Northern Material', caps. 57–66). With Chapter 31 in Section 2 (170 ff.) begins the story of Vortigern (*Guorthigirnus*). Up to this point the history has been a jumbled and unconvincing mixture of Gildas, Prosper, and Jerome. It cannot be said that at this point the narrative becomes less jumbled or more convincing. In the next chapter (32 (172 ff.)) the account of the romantic adventures of Germanus begins. Vortigern is represented as a ruler controlling most of Britain, and as pursued by the avenging and righteous wrath of Germanus for a sin he has committed. Vortigern's son Guorthemir and the Saxon leader Henghist are introduced into the story. The narrative on the whole suggests an historical kernel, based originally on oral tradition, surrounded by a luxurious growth of legend and folk-lore. The part assigned to Germanus appears to be wholly legendary, and devoid of any basis in history except the single fact that Germanus did at least once visit Britain. It could easily be detached from the rest. The section devoted to Arthur (Section 4, cap. 56 (199–201)) seems extremely vague and unreliable. It connects Arthur with nobody else except Ochta, son of Henghist. Section 5 conveys to the discerning reader a much more promising impression; it has a clearer ring of truth than any of the preceding narrative. In particular Chapter 66 (209) impresses one as providing securer ground for historical reconstruction. As well as describing the reign of Vortigern it mentions someone called Guitolinus, the discord between him and Ambrosius, and a battle at Wallop in Shropshire. It has naturally formed the chief source for those who have tried to trace the history of Britain in the second half of the fifth century from the work of Nennius.

There have been several reconstructions of this sort, all envisaging roughly the same pattern of events.[1] They all agree that Vortigern was an historical character, one who was born at the end of the fourth century, probably of an aristocratic British family, and who, on the withdrawal of the Romans, built up for himself a large though temporary empire, ranging,

---

[1] See J. N. L. Myres, 'Pelagius and the End of Roman Rule in Britain', pp. 34–36; H. M. Chadwick, 'The End of Roman Rule in Britain' (in Norah Chadwick, *SBH*, pp. 26–33); Rachel Bromwich in the same volume ('The Character of the Early Welsh Tradition', pp. 108–18); P. Hunter Blair, *Roman Britain and Early England*, pp. 159–66; J. Morris, 'Dark Age Dates', pp. 150–70. Cf. also Norah Chadwick, *CB*, pp. 41–48.

perhaps, from the Roman wall to Wales and even Cornwall. He introduced Saxon troops into the country to act as *foederati*, and settled them on the east coast in order to deal with raids from the Picts on that coast.[1] The Saxons at one point revolted, gained control of the whole of south-east Britain, and began to extend their conquests as far as the Solent, but were driven back and contained by the action of Ambrosius, and perhaps of Arthur. The final victory of Mons Badonis, which is usually said to have been situated in the Iron-Age hill fort called Badbury Rings, near Wimborne in Dorset, is assigned by all the authorities to about the year 500. Different scholars add different details to this reconstruction. Norah Chadwick, followed by Rachel Bromwich, rather romantically makes Vortigern son-in-law of Magnus Maximus, and Morris (more romantically still) makes him the father-in-law of a high-king of Ireland. Several of the authorities (Myres, Norah Chadwick, Hunter Blair) accept the picture of Germanus relentlessly pursuing Vortigern because of his sin as a reflection of Germanus's attack on Pelagianism in Ireland, and envisage Vortigern as an arch-Pelagian, with what appears to me to be excessive credulity. The reconstruction offered by Morris is the most detailed of all. He manages to fit in almost all the evidence, though he does not resolve the difficulty created by Gildas's attribution to the year 446 of an attack by Picts and Scots which, on Morris's account, must have taken place long before that. He places the appearance of the Saxons, invited by Vortigern, about 430, and thinks that he can detect in caps. 36–38 and 43–46 of Nennius a 'Kentish Chronicle' of the fifth century, written between 430 and 460, a document whose existence is far from obvious to the ordinary reader of Nennius's work. All these writers accept Ambrosius Aurelianus as an historical character, a leader of the Britons in a successful movement against the Saxons a generation after Vortigern. The extent to which it is thought that we can reconstruct his campaigns varies from writer to writer. For instance, Rachel Bromwich can describe the battle of Longborth, mentioned in a very old Welsh poem, a contest in which a figure called Gereint ap Erbin was slain and at which Arthur was present, as 'a further example of the attraction of the hero

[1] Hunter Blair produces several earlier historical precedents for this from British history, *Roman Britain and Early England*, p. 160.

of an originally independent saga into the Arthurian vortex',[1] whereas Morris can see it as a victory of Arthur at Portchester, at the head of Portsmouth harbour, over a Saxon leader, perhaps the ruler of the *civitas* of the Belgae at Winchester, commanding a partly Saxon and partly British army.[2] Norah Chadwick displays a scepticism about Arthur not unlike that of Rachel Bromwich; if he did exist (and she is not sure of this) it was in north Britain, whence his legend has been transferred to Wales and Cornwall.[3] It would perhaps be wise for the historian who is attempting to reconstruct the history of Britain in the fifth century as a preliminary to exploring the date and background of St. Patrick to accept the main outlines of the story as agreed upon by all these scholars, but to suspend his judgement about the details, and in particular to recognize that, though the people of southern Britain must have experienced a period of intense assault, danger, and confusion from at least the year 460 onwards, there is a direct contradiction concerning the exact date when this period began, and the circumstances that began it, in the two sources which are nearest to being contemporary, Gildas and the *Gallic Chronicle*.

There are several other pieces of evidence which must be taken into account before we finish our sketch of the history of Britain in the fifth century. One of these is the immigration to Armorica, later to be called Brittany, of large numbers of Britons, which took place at some point during this century. An even larger immigration to Armorica took place in the sixth century, as a result of the forward movement of the Anglo-Saxons during the second half of that century, but here we are only concerned with the first immigration. Gildas mentions it,[4] placing it between the introduction of the Saxons by Vortigern on the one hand and on the other the return home of several of the Saxons and the *revanche* of the Britons under Ambrosius. This immigration cannot be dated exactly. One of the best indications is that in the year 461 a small council of bishops was

[1] *SBH*, p. 118.
[2] 'Dark Age Dates', pp. 166–70.
[3] *CB*, pp. 47–48. On the other hand, H. M. Chadwick in *SBH* (pp. 50–55) takes Arthur to be an historical character associated with the rulers of the *civitas* of the Dumnonii, including Devon and Cornwall; he was born, according to this view, 450–70, and took part in the battle of *Mons Badonis*, 490–500.
[4] *De Excidio* 25 (58).

held at Tours, and this was attended by a British bishop called Mansuetus. It is unlikely that so unimportant a council would have summoned a bishop from the island of Britain to Tours; probably this one attended because there were already by that date large numbers of Britons in Armorica and Mansuetus represented them.[1] There are references to Britons settled on the north bank of the Loire in Sidonius Apollinaris[2] and in Jordanes.[3] E. A. Thompson suggests that it was shortly after the failure of the Roman government to respond to the Britons' appeal to Aetius in 446 that this immigration took place, that the intruding Britons subjugated the dangerous peasantry in Armorica and settled the country, and that this accounts for the cessation of 'Bacaudae' in Gaul after 445.[4] K. Jackson is not disinclined to accept the evidence of the Council of Tours, but prefers to leave the date of the British immigration into Armorica undetermined between 450 and 470. He does not think that it is possible, on linguistic or on any other evidence, to determine from what parts of Britain the first move of immigration to Armorica was made, because most of its traces in Brittany were obliterated by the much larger immigration which took place, from Devon and Cornwall, in the second half of the sixth century.[5]

Next we must consider two British leaders who figure, albeit mistily and ephemerally, in the history of fifth-century Britain, one of whom entered dramatically into Patrick's career. The first is a man called Cunedag (modern Welsh Cunedda) by Nennius, who mentions him as the great-grandfather (*atavus*) of a well-known figure of the second half of the sixth century, a king in or of north Wales (Gwynnedd) called Maileunus or Mailuin (Old Welsh Maelgwynn). Cunedag came from the left part (*sinistrali*, i.e. the north), which is called Manau Guotodin (i.e. the original territory of the Votadini extending southwards from the Firth of Forth), with eight of his sons to north

---

[1] This point is dealt with more fully below, pp. 65–66.

[2] *Epistles* 1. 7.

[3] *History of Gothic War*, ed. Mommsen, pp. 118, 119. See H. Williams, *CEB*, pp. 281–2. Morris accepts this Council as a valid indication of the date of the immigration, 'Dark Age Dates', p. 156.

[4] 'Zosimus on the End of Roman Britain', p. 167. Thompson thinks that Germanus had shortly before this become involved in a 'Bacauda' in Armorica. See below, p. 50.

[5] K. Jackson, *LHB*, pp. 13, 14, 25–27.

Wales and expelled the Irish (Scotti) from that region so that they never returned, and this took place 146 years before Mael-gwyn reigned.[1] Most scholars accept this as a genuine piece of historical information, but there is considerable variation about the date of this move by a northern British chieftain to a not very fertile or attractive region, Cardiganshire, which still bears the name of his fifth son Ceretic.[2] Cunedag can be placed early, as he is by Simpson, who thinks that he and his people were *foederati* moved by Stilicho to guard against Irish raids such as that of Niall of the Nine Hostages,[3] and by most scholars writing before his day. Or Cunedag can be placed later, as by H. M. Chadwick, who dates his move from the Firth of Forth to north Wales about 460 and sees this as part of a movement whereby barbarian war-lords on the frontiers of Britain were being encouraged to settle with their followers in places where they could protect the British Kingdom, after the removal of Roman rule.[4]

The other figure, resembling Cunedag, is Coroticus, the ruler to whom Patrick addressed his *Epistle to Coroticus*. We face here a question of identification and a question of date. One Coroti-cus we have just met already, Ceretic, fifth son of Cunedag. The other is mentioned in at least two, and possibly three, documents whose information may go back to the fifth century. In the work of Muirchu, the Irish cleric who wrote a life of Patrick in the second half of the seventh century, the table of contents (which is displaced, and also contains some headings to which nothing in the narrative corresponds) includes the heading *De Conflictu*

---

[1] Nennius, *Historia Brittonum* 62 (205–6), from Section 5.
[2] See D. A. Binchy, *PB*, pp. 106–11.
[3] W. D. Simpson, *Ninian and Origins*, pp. 17–18.
[4] H. M. Chadwick, *Early Scotland*, pp. 147–9; so, apparently, Rachel Bromwich, *SBH*, p. 84; and so Morris, 'Dark Age Dates', p. 240. Norah Chadwick's attitude to Cunedag is uncertain, not to say contradictory. In *SBC*, pp. 32–34, she assigns the date of Cunedag's move to 460, but dismisses the whole story as worthless because 'belonging to the same class of eponymous stories as those related of the Picts and the rulers of Scottish Dalriada' (p. 34); but almost immediately after-wards (pp. 34–35) she speaks of 'the date 450 favoured by the most recent scholar-ship for the invasion of Cunedag and his sons into Wales', and alleges that 'it receives confirmation from the Genealogies of the founders of those Welsh King-doms claiming descent from his eponymous sons'; but in *CB* (pp. 66–68) she declares that though there is nothing incredible about the migration from the north into Wales, yet the genealogy of Cunedag's sons may be late and unreliable, and the Irish certainly were not driven out so early.

sancti Patricii adversum Coirtech regem Aloo;[1] this clearly means Ceretic, king of Ail, i.e. Ail-Cluaide, Rock of Clyde, that is Dumbarton. Old Welsh genealogies also mention a Ceretic Guletic (i.e. Ceretic Imperator or Generalissimo) who ruled over what was later called Strathclyde.[2] He can be roughly dated by the fact that Adomnan's *Vita Columbae* places a contemporary of Columba, *Rodercus filius Tothail* (Riderch Hen, son of Tutwal), as fifth in descent from this Ceretic. This would place Ceretic (580, less $30 \times 5 = 150$) about 430, say between 420 and 470. Nennius also mentions a Ceretic in a characteristically obscure manner. At one point in the romance of Vortigern, Henghist the Saxon chief makes a feast for *Guorthigirno et comitibus eius in domo regis cui est nomen Ceretic*.[3] This might be a confused memory of a fifth-century Ceretic. But Nennius the editor has at this point added the word *Elmet* as a gloss on Ceretic, assuming that *cui* refers to the place and not the king. This is explained later, in Chapter 63, where reference is made to another, much later, Ceretic, who lived at the beginning of the seventh century and was driven out of the Kingdom of Elmet by the Anglian king of Northumbria. We have to decide, therefore, whether the Ceretic of Dumbarton was Patrick's Coroticus or whether the son of Cunedag, Ceretic, was Patrick's foe. And we have to choose whether we are to attempt to date Coroticus by Patrick or to date Patrick by Coroticus, for scholars have freely taken both courses.

O'Rahilly, with very few supporters, argues that Patrick's Coroticus is the son of Cunedag, presumably by the time Patrick encountered him a Welsh prince. He disagrees that the career of Ceretic of Dumbarton should be placed in the first half of the fifth century rather than the second, *c.* 410–40, as he is convinced that Patrick's career fell mainly in the second half of the fifth century. This is an argument which, it is hoped, will be disposed of altogether in later pages of this work.[4] He maintains that Latin would not have been used at the court of Dumbarton, yet Patrick addresses a letter to Coroticus in Latin. But this too is an assumption which can readily be challenged. We have

---

[1] Stokes, *TL* ii. 271, 20 b 1 (Gwynn 40).
[2] Binchy, *PB*, p. 106; the genealogy is Pedigree V in MS. Harl. 3859.
[3] Nennius, *Historia Brittonum* 37 (177).
[4] See below, Chapter VI.

the evidence of K. Jackson to the contrary. He maintains that as the Roman culture in the Lowland Zone of Britain broke up, there was a brief resurgence of Latin, because the princes of the Highland Zone tried to succeed the Romans as representatives of Roman government and civilization: 'Some fair knowledge of Latin can be traced there, and signs of a self-conscious Romanisation, no doubt partly owing to the influence of refugees from the Lowland Zone, as well as to the widening influence of the Church.'[1] Finally, O'Rahilly objects that Patrick would not have regarded the subjects of the king of Dumbarton as Roman citizens.[2] But this too is a questionable argument. After the year 410 there were, formally speaking, no Roman citizens in Britain, but it is clear that for Patrick all Christians were *ipso facto* Roman citizens; in *Epistle* 14 he has the famous expression: *consuetudo Romanorum Gallorum Christianorum*.[3] What O'Rahilly should have proved is that the people of Strathclyde could not have been Christians. In short, the arguments against the identification of Patrick's Coroticus with Ceretic of Dumbarton are weak. It is better to accept the verdict of the majority of scholars and assume that the two were the same man.[4] If we do this, we can draw upon some information about Ceretic which Patrick gives us in his *Epistle*. There is no doubt at all that Ceretic and his soldiers were nominal Christians,[5] and as it is clear that they were not Irish,[6] and not Picts, because Patrick accuses Coroticus of selling his captives to the Picts,[7] they must have been British. The date of Coroticus must at the moment be kept open, within the limits, already imposed, 440–70. On the problem of whether to date Coroticus by Patrick or date Patrick by Coroti-

---

[1] K. Jackson, 'The British Language during the Period of the English Settlements' (in Norah Chadwick's *SBH*), p. 62.

[2] All these arguments are to be found in T. F. O'Rahilly, *The Two Patricks*, p. 39.

[3] I accept, of course, the reading of Bieler's text here. See below, p. 108.

[4] So Bury, *LP*, pp. 313–14; P. Grosjean ('Les Pictes Apostats dans l'Épitre de S. Patrice', pp. 363–4); H. M. Chadwick (*Early Christian Scotland*, pp. 149–51); W. D. Simpson (*Ninian and Origins*, pp. 19–20); and Norah Chadwick (*SBH*, p. 217, and *CS*, p. 326). Bieler (*Life and Legend of St. Patrick*, p. 37) inclines to O'Rahilly's view.

[5] *Epistle* 5, 6, 7, 12, 14, 16, 19. The question of whether they were formally, and not just practically, apostates, is dealt with below, pp. 107–8.

[6] *Epistle* 16: *Indignum est illis Hiberionaci sumus.*

[7] *Epistle* 12.

cus, the solution of which has been attempted quite differently by different scholars, we prefer to take the former alternative, and therefore to reserve our verdict. Suffice it to say that what we can discover of Coroticus is consistent with the picture already built up of a number of British successor-states to the Roman Empire preserving some tincture of Roman culture, and perhaps some faint claim to imperial authority, for a period keeping at bay the most serious enemies of Britain, the Picts and the Scots (during the first half and the middle of the fifth century). Clearly Coroticus was on good terms with the Picts and held himself free to conduct raids on the Scots.[1]

Finally, it should perhaps be noted that the attempt to correlate Irish history in the fifth century with British history, or to fix the dates of Patrick's career in Britain or Ireland by reference to known dates in Irish history, is apparently doomed to failure, because while there are very few known dates in British history there are absolutely no known dates in Irish secular history during the fifth century. Bury was confident that he could date the death of Niall of the Nine Hostages to 405, relying on the Irish Annals.[2] But O'Rahilly and Carney (who certainly know more about Irish annals than Bury would have claimed to know) both reject this date and propose others.[3] H. M. Chadwick was anxious to place the career of Niall more than thirty years after the period allotted to it by the annalists, because he detected a serious chronological dislocation whereby at least a generation was lost between the traditional date assigned to Niall and the dates ascribed to his sons; so he suggested c. 435 as the date of Niall's death.[4] The same uncertainty attends the date of Loeghaire, the high-king of Ireland with whom, according to

---

[1] We may dismiss Grosjean's theory put forward in his article last referred to (pp. 363-4) that the Roman fleet stationed at Ravenglas was ordered by Coroticus to go to the Clyde and on the way massacred Patrick's converts. Once we have disposed of his view that Ravenglas was Patrick's home town, this theory becomes absurd. The Roman government would no doubt have been delighted had there been a fleet during the period of Patrick's missionary work in Ireland at its disposal, or anybody's. But there can have been no such thing. For the reasons for abandoning Grosjean's theory about Ravenglas, see below, pp. 115-16.

[2] LP, pp. 25-26, 334.

[3] O'Rahilly (The Two Patricks, pp. 142-3) maintains that Niall died in 427 and Loeghaire in 463 (Early Irish History and Mythology, p. 165 and cap. xii, pp. 209-34); Carney believes that Niall must have been killed in the second half of the fifth century (The Problem of Patrick, pp. 8-9).

[4] Early Scotland, pp. 123, 133-6.

the narratives of Muirchu and Tirechan,[1] Patrick came in
contact. Bury had accepted the traditional account of Loeghaire,
based on the Irish annals. He regarded Loeghaire as the son of
Niall, and believed that he succeeded Dathi or Nath I (presumably his uncle or his brother) as high-king of Ireland about 428.
He thought that Dathi or Nath I died while assisting Aetius to
drive back the Franks from eastern Gaul about that year. He
suggested that the traditional view that Loeghaire produced a
law code was correct, and that he did so in imitation of the
Theodosian Code of 435.[2] He accepted, at least in outline,
the account of Patrick's encounter with Loeghaire given in
the narratives of Muirchu and Tirechan. But O'Rahilly had no
difficulty in showing that the evidence upon which Bury had
relied for his account of Dathi or Nath I and of Loeghaire was
worthless.[3] It should be remembered that while Bury was a very
eminent scholar indeed on all matters relating to the late Roman
Empire, he was not, and did not pretend to be, an authority on
ancient Irish history and language, and that O'Rahilly could
claim considerable knowledge in these subjects. O'Rahilly himself believed that Loeghaire directly succeeded Niall and that
he was dead by the year 463. Further, he held that to speak of
a 'High-King' at all in fifth-century Ireland is an anachronism,
because no such institution then existed. He regarded both this
concept and the association of Loeghaire, or anybody else in the
fifth century, with a spring festival at Tara, such as Muirchu
and Tirechan describe, as utterly inappropriate to Patrick's
day.[4] Carney allows a single festival at Tara to Loeghaire, but
wishes to place him between 454 and 461.[5] But if anyone will
take the trouble to read the very thorough refutation of Carney
carried out by Binchy in his famous essay on 'St. Patrick and
his Biographers'[6] he will find it difficult to avoid the conclusion
that not only is the evidence of Muirchu and Tirechan for
Loeghaire's (or anybody else's) celebrating a spring festival at

---

[1] See Chapter III.
[2] *LP*, pp. 95, 113–14. J. Ryan (*St. Patrick*, p. 16) and E. McNeill (*St. Patrick*,
p. 72) were among the many that followed him.
[3] *The Two Patricks*, p. 8 and n. 5 (p. 48).
[4] Ibid., p. 31. See also D. A. Binchy, 'The Fair of Tailtu and the Feast of Tara'.
[5] J. Carney, 'A New Chronology of the Saint's Life', in *St. Patrick* (ed. J. Ryan),
p. 27.
[6] pp. 99–103.

Tara entirely worthless, but that in effect we have in the Irish annals, in spite of their apparently careful attention to detail, no means whatever of dating Loeghaire's succession, career, or death. Binchy endorses emphatically the view that there was no high-king of Ireland in Patrick's day, and that the statements of Muirchu and Tirechan to the effect that there was are no more than the reflection of the situation as it existed in their own day —the seventh century.[1] Lastly, it must be observed that Patrick in his own works at no point ever refers to Loeghaire or to a high-king, though there were places in his *Confession* at least where he could have done so had he wanted to. The reader may well conclude that the maxim that in the multitude of counsellors there is safety does not apply to the history of Ireland in the fifth century, and that to attempt to secure a firm chronological footing here to assist in reconstructing the history of fifth-century Britain is a hopeless task.[2]

This survey of the history of Britain in the fifth century will at least have given the reader some idea of what is not known about this subject, and that in itself is no bad thing. But the survey has not been altogether barren. There is a great dearth of known events, but there is a surprising amount of material to give us information about conditions. If anybody has had the idea, such as an uncritical reading of Gildas might give him, that the departure of the Romans left Britain defenceless, unarmed, and naked to her enemies, a prey to ceaseless attacks of Picts and Scots until the coming of the Saxons in a final and decisive invasion, this survey should have dispelled that idea. If we are to apply this survey to the case of Patrick, we can say with some confidence that there is plenty of room between about 410 and about 440, and perhaps a little later, for the British Church to send a mission to Ireland in the person of Patrick, and to keep him supplied with funds and personnel, if other circumstances can permit of our placing Patrick's mission to Ireland in this period. But it should be clear that the further we

---

[1] *PB*, p. 12. Morris ('The Dates of the Celtic Saints', pp. 387, n. 4; cf. pp. 355, 361), after passing stringent criticism upon Binchy for his treatment of the annals and the later tradition concerning Patrick, attempts to reinstate a fifth-century high-king. For a fuller treatment of this subject, see Appendix II.

[2] For a useful short summary of what is known of the political and social condition of Ireland at the time of St. Patrick see Françoise Henry, *Irish Art in the Early Christian Period to A.D. 800*, pp. 17–21.

are anxious to place Patrick's career into the second half of the fifth century the more difficult it becomes to envisage his being sent to Ireland by the British Church. Those scholars who have entertained theories of Patrick's being dispatched to Ireland in the 460s, or even the 470s, have formidable difficulties to face in the history of Britain in the fifth century.

II

THE BRITISH CHURCH IN THE FIFTH CENTURY

BY the time that Nennius compiled his *Historia Brittonum* a legendary origin in the second century had been ascribed to the British Church. Nennius relates the story of the British King Leucius, who accepted baptism with the sub-kings of the whole of Britain at the hands of the representatives of the Pope in the year 167.[1] But in the fourth century Chrysostom had believed in the apostolic origin of British Christianity. Speaking of the original apostles, he says, 'They did not stop there, but went even further, and not satisfied with the world known to us they went out as far as the Ocean itself and enclosed in their own nets the countries of the barbarians and the British Isles.'[2] It is possible that Chrysostom picked up this legend from some British Christian, but, of course, we must discount this and the later and more detailed story from Nennius. It is unknown how Christianity reached Britain. We may conjecture that it did so through traders or soldiers. There are a number of vague references to the existence of Christianity in Britain to be found in Christian writings in the first half of the third century, in Tertullian, in Origen, and in Hippolytus,[3] all of them designed to

---

[1] *Hist. Brit.* 22 (164).

[2] Chrysostom, *Homiliae* viii (*PG* 63. 501) : οὐ μέχρι δὲ τούτων, ἀλλὰ καὶ περαιτέρω προῆλθον, καὶ τῇ καθ᾽ ἡμᾶς οὐκ ἀρκεσθέντες οἰκουμένῃ πρὸς αὐτὸν ἐξέβησαν τὸν Ὠκεανὸν, καὶ τὰς βαρβαρικὰς χώρας καὶ τὰς Βρεττανικὰς νήσους εἴσω τῶν οἰκείων δικτύων ἔλαβον. This passage is also printed in J. Zwicker, *Fontes Historicae Religionis Celticae, Pars Altera*, p. 125 ; cf. Haddan and Stubbs, *Councils, etc.*, col. i, pp. 5, 12–13, where passages from Hilary of Poictiers, Augustine, and Theodoret are quoted voicing similar sentiments.

[3] Tertullian, *Adversus Judaeos*, 7. 4; Origen, *Hom. in Ezekiel* 4 (*PL* 25. 723), *Hom. in Luke* 6 or 14.1.24 (*PG* 13. 1816); Hippolytus, *Elenchos*, 10. 34. It is not generally noticed by those who cite these references that Tertullian's authorship of *Adv. Jud.* is not certain. Cf. H. Williams (*CEB*, pp. 74, 96–100) and J. A. Duke (*The Columban Church*, p. 3, where Duke quite unjustifiably accuses Origen of 'highly-coloured rhetoric'; he cannot have read Origen if he thinks that this is a true account of his style).

show the great extent to which the Christian Church had grown. We know almost nothing of the Christian Church in Britain in the third century. Archaeology has been able to detect a few faint clues, such as a cryptogram scratched on the plaster of a Roman house in Cirencester (Corinium), which should be interpreted as meaning A PATER NOSTER O, written horizontally and vertically with N as the common letter, dating from before the peace of the Church, and perhaps a basin bearing a Christian monogram, which was dug up at Corbridge in 1867 and melted down shortly afterwards.[1] The only other indication of the existence of a Church in Britain in the third century is the story of the martyrdom of Alban, of Aaron, and of Julius. These martyrdoms are only mentioned in late sources, the first of which is the monk Constantius's *Vita Germani*, who tells us that Germanus and his companion Lupus, on reaching Britain, seek *beatum Albanum martyrem*, though we are not told where he was to be found.[2] Germanus and Lupus were in Britain in 429, and Constantius was writing about 480. The other source is Gildas, writing about 540, who gives an account, in the traditional style of early medieval saints' lives embroidered with miracles, of the martyrdoms of Alban in Verulamium and Aaron and Julius at Caerleon.[3] It is uncertain to which persecution we are supposed to assign these events, whether to that of Diocletian or to the earlier persecution of Decius. On the whole it would be unreasonable to doubt that these martyrdoms did take place, and it is more satisfactory to place them in the Decian than in the Diocletian persecutions.

In the fourth century our information about Christianity in Britain becomes rather fuller, though still far from ample. Archaeology has been able to unearth some villas with Christian mosaics, such as those at Frampton, at Cirencester, and at Hinton St. Mary. A fountain with crosses inscribed on it has been found at Chedworth. Brading has a pavement representing Abraxas, the Gnostic deity. At Lullingstone a whole room has

---

[1] The archaeological evidence is admirably dealt with in Jocelyn Toynbee, 'Christianity in Roman Britain' and W. H. C. Frend, 'Religion in Roman Britain in the Fourth Century A.D.'. The basin is mentioned in P. Salway, *The Frontier People*, p. 45. See also I. Richmond, *Roman Britain*, pp. 180, 186–202 and Kathleen Hughes, *The Church in Early Irish Society*, pp. 25–29.

[2] *Vita Germani* 16.

[3] *De Excidio* 10 (24, 26) and 11 (28).

been discovered, devoted, as the paintings on its walls make clear, to Christian worship. The traces of buildings which probably were Christian churches have been found at Silchester and at Caerwent. The fact that at Verulamium in the fourth century the theatre seems to have been abandoned and allowed to decay, at a time when in other respects the town was flourishing economically, may represent Christian influence, and the same influence may be seen in the deliberate desecration at Carrawburgh of a Mithraic temple and of a well dedicated to the Celtic goddess Coventina.[1] There survive also some Christian inscriptions on rings and some on tombstones.[2]

In the fourth century also we encounter for the first time clear contemporary references to the British Church in literature. The Acts of the Council of Arles held in 314 list five persons as attending from Britain.[3] They were *Eborius episcopus de civitate Eboracensi provincia Britannia Restitutus episcopus de civitate Londinensi provincia suprascripta Adelfius episcopus de civitate Colonia Londinensium Exinde Sacerdos presbyter, Arminius diaconus.* It is curious that the Bishop of York should bear a name so reminiscent of his own see. But *Eboracum* may originally mean 'estate of Eburus', Eburos being the original landowner,[4] which makes the likelihood rather stronger that this is a personal name and not the result of a confusion on the part of a scribe between the bishop and the name of his see. *Colonia Londinensium* must be a corruption of some other original name. There have been suggested as alternatives *Colonia Legionensium*, i.e. Caerleon-on-Usk, which was sometimes known as *Castra Legionum*, or *Camulodunensium*, i.e. Colchester, and it has

---

[1] I. Richmond, *Roman Britain*, pp. 196, 210; the first desecration took place in the fourth century, the second early in the fifth. For most of the other evidence see the articles of Jocelyn Toynbee and of W. H. C. Frend just cited. See also Collingwood and Myres, *RBES*, pp. 270–3; P. Hunter Blair, *Roman Britain and Early England*, pp. 104, 144; and Norah Chadwick's final chapter on the Church in *CB*.

[2] e.g. the fourth-century ring found at Silchester, with the inscription *Seniciane Vivas in De[o]*; a small leaden seal found in the Forum there, with the design A?⳨Ω scratched on each side; a silver ring found in the Roman villa at Fifehead Neville in Dorset, with a *Chi-Rho* monogram inscribed on it; and also another, with a dove between olive branches and the device ⳨. See F. Haverfield, *Victoria History of Hampshire*, pp. 283, 284, and *Ephemeris Epigraphica* vii, p. 350, no. 1174. See also the list in J. Wall, *Christian Evidences in the Roman Period*, part i, pp. 216–24. For several examples of Christian tombstones see J. Wall, op. cit., pp. 202–14.

[3] The text is given in H. Williams, *CEB*, pp. 141–2, and Jocelyn Toynbee, 'Christianity in Roman Britain', p. 4.

[4] K. Jackson, *LHB*, p. 39.

even been suggested that Adelfius was Metropolitan of Britain, on the grounds that Colchester was the oldest British town there. But the proper Roman name of Caerleon was *Isca* or *Urbs Legionum*, and it was not a *colonia*. The conjecture *Camulodunensium* is unnecessarily complicated, and it is anachronistic to see a metropolitan system in a remote part of the Empire early in the fourth century, when the system was hardly developed in parts where Christians were more populous and traditions older.[1] The best conjecture to emend this corruption is *Colonia Lindunensium*, i.e. Lincoln, which certainly was a Roman *colonia*. According to Athanasius, the British Church accepted the decrees of the Council of Nicaea in 325, was represented at the Council of Sardica of 343, and supported Athanasius there.[2] In the year 358 Hilary of Poictiers in the opening sentence of his *De Synodis* addressed his reading public thus: *Dilectissimis et beatissimis fratribus et coepiscopis provinciae Germanicae Primae . . . et ex Narbonensi plebibus et clericis Tolosanis, et provinciarum Britanniarum episcopis, Hilarius servus Christi in Deo et Domino nostro aeternam salutem.*[3] This suggests that the Church in Britain numbered enough bishops to make it worth Hilary's while to enrol them on his side in the Arian controversy.

The same impression is given by an interesting piece of information which we possess about the British delegation at the Council of Ariminum held in 359. Sulpicius Severus in his *Historia Sacra*[4] tells us of what a certain Bishop Gavidius, whom he knew personally and who had been present at this Council, had told him. The imperial treasury provided the travelling expenses of all the bishops attending this Council, or was ready to do so. Sulpicius then continues:

But this did not seem right to our bishops [that is, those from Aquitania], to the bishops from Gaul and from Britain: they refused the treasury's funds and preferred to live at their own expense.

---

[1] So, quite rightly, H. Williams, *CEB*, p. 87.
[2] For references see Haddan and Stubbs, *Councils, etc.*, vol. i, pp. 7–9.
[3] Text in ibid., p. 9, and H. Williams, *CEB*, p. 99.
[4] xli. 152; *sed id nostris (id est Aquitanis), Gallis et Britannis indecus visum; repudiatis fiscalibus, propriis sumptibus vivere maluerunt. Tres tantum ex Britannia inopia proprii publico usi sunt, cum oblatam a ceteris collationem respuissent, sanctius putantes fiscum gravare quam singulos. Hoc ego Gavidium episcopum nostrum quasi obtrectantem referre solitum audivi. Sed longe aliter senserim: laudique attribuo episcopis tam pauperes fuisse ut nihil proprium haberent, neque ab aliis potius quam fisco sumerent, ubi neminem gravabant.*

Only three bishops from Britain used the public funds because of the poverty of their own resources, even though they had scorned a contribution offered by other people, and thought it a holier action to burden the treasury than private individuals. I have heard our Bishop Gavidius referring to this often and inclined to blame them. But I would take quite a different view; and I think that it is to the credit of the bishops that they were so poor that they had no private property and that they would not accept help from others rather than from the treasury, so that they were a burden to nobody.

Several interesting pieces of information can be gleaned from this passage. In the first place, a careful reading of the passage must convince the reader that there must have been many more than three British bishops, even though a number of people have unreflectingly assumed that the three poor British bishops represented the total British delegation at Ariminum. In fact it must be obvious that the majority of the British bishops were wealthy enough, or had wealthy enough flocks, to be able to pay their own not inconsiderable expenses, and that the three poverty-stricken bishops were the exception, not the rule. Another point is that we might detect here a consultation or collusion between the British and the Gallic bishops; it would not be surprising to discover that there was a special relationship between the bishops of two parts of the Roman Empire so near to each other and so much involved in each other's destinies, and we shall see plenty of examples of close relations between the two Churches later. Finally, Norah Chadwick has made the suggestion that the reason why the three British bishops were poor is that they were following a monastic or semi-monastic discipline, and that this is the reason why Sulpicius Severus, himself a great admirer and exponent of monasticism on the plan of St. Martin, championed them.[1] Certainly it seems unlikely that really poor men, and not merely those who were poor for the sake of ascetic discipline, should have achieved no less than three sees in Britain. There are very few precedents for poor men being made bishops in the fourth century. Patrick uses the phrase *sacerdotibus nostris*[2] of the bishops of his

[1] Norah Chadwick, *PLG*, pp. 166–7; *SBH*, pp. 202–3; *CB*, p. 142. Haddan and Stubbs, *Councils, etc.*, vol. i, pp. 9 and 10.

[2] *Confession* 1. Patrick, following contemporary usage, always means 'bishop' by *sacerdos*. In his deplorably tendentious essay in *The History of the Church of Ireland*

boyhood in Britain about the same time as Sulpicius Severus was writing, conveying the same impression that there were plenty of them.

In the year 383 Magnus Maximus was a newly baptized Christian when he became Emperor; he had conducted a correspondence about Arianism with Pope Siricius. Baptism was probably part of his preparation for imperial rule.[1] This is yet another indication that by this time the Church in Britain had gained considerable importance and that its numbers must have grown greatly since the beginning of the century. We must therefore modify the statement of Simpson that 'all our evidence goes to show that Britain was predominantly pagan down to the end of the Roman period'.[2] No doubt the British Church was mainly confined to the towns, as Norah Chadwick and J. Morris declare,[3] but it is hard to accept as strictly accurate the opinion of Frend that 'fourth Century Christianity remained an official and somewhat extraneous worship which had still to make its impact on those who lived beyond the walls of town, fort, or villa'.[4] By the time that Patrick is writing it seems pretty clear that most Britons were Christian, so much so that he can identify Christians with Roman citizens, and Christianity has reached far enough to convert many of the people of the remote Kingdom of Strathclyde. By the end of the fourth century it must have been in a stronger position than Frend's words suggest in order to have achieved this state by the middle of the fifth.[5]

Evidence for the general condition of the British Church in the fifth century, apart from that which is involved in the careers of a number of prominent individuals, to whom most of the rest of this chapter is devoted, is very scanty. Early Celtic inscriptions

(vol. i, cap. iv), Newport White made the mistake of thinking that *sacerdos* meant 'priest' in Patrick (p. 110).

[1] H. Williams, *CEB*, p. 170. See above, p. 3.

[2] *Ninian and Origins*, p. 29.

[3] Norah Chadwick, *ASCC*, p. 9; J. Morris, 'Celtic Saints', pp. 351–2.

[4] 'Religion in Roman Britain', pp. 7–8.

[5] See also the surprisingly extensive evidence for Christianity in the north of England in the fourth and fifth centuries accumulated by J. Wall in *Christian Evidences in the Roman Period*, Part I, which is scarcely compatible with Frend's verdict. In an unpublished dissertation submitted to the University of Bristol the same author shows that nearly as many stones and other objects bearing the *Chi-Rho* sign have been discovered in the north of Britain as in the south.

in Latin do not come from the Lowland Zone of Britain, the more Romanized part, even during the period when there was no Saxon occupation.[1] Some linguistic evidence enables us to identify the existence of a British centre of population with organized Christian worship, such as the place-names Eccles and Eccleston, derived from the British word for 'church'.[2] The British Church can have left no very strongly entrenched ecclesiastical tradition attached to any place in the east of Britain, for the title of early Anglo-Saxon bishoprics are all taken from the residences of English kings, and, with very few exceptions, not even based on Roman towns.[3] But there can be no doubt that the Church in Britain was gaining in numbers and influence during at least the first half of the fifth century.[4] Constantius in his *Vita Germani* says that a large number of the British army, which was about to fight the battle that ended in the 'Alleluia Victory', were baptized,[5] suggesting that the country was still largely pagan, but we cannot take this as serious history, any more than we can accept as reliable information the same author's statement that since Germanus's second visit to Britain *in illis locis etiam nunc fides intemerata perduret.*[6] We know that at some point in the second half of the century there was a British bishop who was also a monk.[7] Grosjean envisages the British bishops about the year 445 as 'prélats relativement riches et bien dotés, peu enclins à pratiquer l'ascèse'.[8] Morris reminds us of the references in Patrick's *Confession* to people, probably bishops, who were learned lawyers and skilled speakers,[9] evidence which suggests a prosperous and successful Church.

We must now turn from attempting to sketch the general conditions and development of the British Church during the fifth century to considering a number of eminent figures in the Church, who were or may have been, connected with Britain. The first of these are the famous heresiarch Pelagius and the shadowy and enigmatic figure Fastidius, whose existence cannot be discussed separately from discussion of Pelagius. Pelagius

---

[1] K. Jackson, *LHB*, p. 165.
[2] Ibid., p. 227; also the same author in *SBH*, p. 65.
[3] *LHB*, p. 230.　　[4] Ibid., *SBH*, p. 62.　　[5] *Vita Germani* 17.　　　[6] Ibid. 27.
[7] The case of Riochatus is discussed fully below, pp. 64–66.
[8] P. Grosjean, 'Notes d'Hagiographie Celtique' (1957), p. 173.
[9] 'Dark Age Dates', p. 150; cf. *Confession* 9, 13.

certainly was a Briton and probably not an Irishman. There is no evidence at all that Caelestius, Pelagius's fellow-Pelagian, was an Irishman. Had all the scholars who have been anxious to derive Caelestius from Ireland read an important early article of J. B. Bury on the subject in the periodical *Hermathena*,[1] they would have found it unnecessary to indulge in these speculations. Bury begins by pointing out the impressive number of authors contemporary with Pelagius who described him as a Briton: Alypius, Augustine,[2] Orosius,[3] Prosper,[4] and Marius Mercator.[5] He then quotes in full two passages in Jerome's *Commentary on Jeremiah*[6] which refer to somebody who has been calumniating Jerome. In the first extract Jerome says that *Grunnius* (by whom he always means Rufinus) was the *praecursor* of the calumniator. Jerome describes the calumniator as *Scottorum pultibus praegravatus*.[7] In the second extract there occurs a long passage in which, as Bury insists with entire justice, the subject is, and can only be, the Devil: *ipse mutus latrat per Alpinum*[8] *canem grandem et corpulentum et qui calcibus magis possit saevire quam dentibus. Habet enim progeniem Scotticae gentis de Britannorum vicinia qui iuxta fabulas poetarum instar Cerberi spirituali percutiendus est clava ut aeterno cum suo magistro Plutone silentio conticescat.* 'The Devil is dumb but barks by the agency of a large and fat Alpine dog, one who is able to do damage rather with his feet than his teeth. For the Devil has an offspring of the Scottic race, neighbours of the Britons, who, in accordance with the poets' fairy-stories, should, like Cerberus, be struck with a spiritual club to make him voiceless in eternal silence along with his master Pluto.'[9] Jerome does indeed refer in two other passages of his work to an enemy of his in Sicily, but this enemy is clearly dead, and can be no other than Rufinus, who died in

---

[1] *Hermathena* xiii (1905), pp. 26–35, 'The Origins of Pelagius'.

[2] Augustine, *Epistles* 186 (*PL* 33. 816).

[3] Orosius, *Liber Apologeticus* 12 (*PL* 31. 1182).

[4] Prosper, *Chronicle*, s.a. 413; *De Ingratis* 1 (*PL* 51. 94).

[5] Marius Mercator, *Liber Subnotationum in Verba Iuliani*, Praef. 2. 1 (*PL* 48. 777). Rufinus, says Marius, first began the Pelagian heresy, then *Pelagium gente Britannum monachum decepit*. The texts of these authors are given, with inadequate references, in Haddan and Stubbs, *Councils, etc.*, vol. i, p. 15.

[6] *PL* 24. 680–2, 757–8.

[7] 'The Origins of Pelagius', pp. 27–28.

[8] Bury reads *Alpinum*, but wonders whether there might not be support for the reading *Albinum*; see below, p. 38.

[9] 'The Origins of Pelagius', pp. 29–30, but the translation is mine.

Sicily.[1] It is, therefore, quite clear that in the extracts from Jerome's *Commentary on Jeremiah* the calumniator and the person fed on Irish porridge and of Irish ancestry are one and the same. This person can only be Pelagius, not Caelestius, for while Jerome was writing the *Commentary on Jeremiah* he was much agitated about the controversy concerning Pelagius's views which was taking place at the time in Palestine. Pelagius certainly was in Palestine at the time and Caelestius certainly was not; or rather, if Caelestius was there, no word of his is recorded, and this is incompatible with Jerome's statement that while the Devil was dumb his dog was barking for him. Anyway, the description of the calumniator as large and fat fits descriptions of Pelagius given in Orosius and elsewhere in Jerome.[2] The only evidence that connects Caelestius with Ireland or with Britain thus disappears.[3]

But does not this evidence connect Pelagius with Ireland? Bury thinks that it is not necessary to draw this conclusion. Jerome, he thinks, maliciously preferred to call Pelagius Irish, but he may have come from a family which belonged to the Irish settlements in south-western Britain.[4] 'Irish' (or rather *Scotticus*) was a term of opprobrium in Jerome's day. Bury quotes another passage of Jerome, written well before the Pelagian controversy, where Jerome links Britain and Ireland—*Britanni fertilis provincia tyrannorum et Scotticae gentes omnesque usque ad Oceanum per circuitum barbarae nationes*,[5] and Souter points to passages where Jerome had used the insulting attribution of Irish nationality against other opponents before Pelagius.[6]

---

[1] *Scorpiusque inter Enceladum et Porphyrionem Trinacriae humo premitur*, *Comm.* on *Ezekiel*, Pref. to Book i (*PL* 25. 15), and *putabam quod medio serpente confosso non reviviscerunt hydrae novellae plantaria et iuxta fabulas poetarum scylla mortua nequaquam in me Scyllaei saevirent canes qui latrare non cessant*, ibid., Pref. to Book vi (*PL* 25. 165 sq.). This was composed after 410, but before the *Commentary on Jeremiah*.

[2] 'Origins of Pelagius', pp. 30–32.

[3] Ibid., p. 35. This final refutation, perhaps because the periodical in which it appeared has not had a wide circulation, has been ignored by several scholars, e.g. H. Williams, *CEB*, p. 203; Norah Chadwick, *PLG*, pp. 173–4, *SBH*, p. 208; J. Morris, 'Pelagian Literature', pp. 40–43. But Plinval rejected an Irish ancestry for Caelestius (*Pélage, ses Écrits, sa Vie et sa Réforme*, p. 212).

[4] 'Origins of Pelagius', pp. 33–35.

[5] Ibid., p. 34. The quotation is from Jerome's *Letter to Ctesiphon*, *PL* 22. 1157–8 (*Ep.* 133. 9). See above, p. 2.

[6] *Scottorum et Aticottorum ritu . . . promiscuas uxores, communes liberos habeant* (*Ep.* 69, 3, 6 (*C.S.E.L.* liv. 684) written *c.* 397); and *Scottorum natio uxores proprias non habet*

Grosjean has shown, further, that when Jerome attaches the word *Scotticus* to Pelagius or his followers, he does not mean it in a racial sense, especially when he describes Pelagius as a dog. Grosjean adopts the reading in the second extract from Jerome's *Commentary on Jeremiah* just quoted, *Albinum canem* rather than *Alpinum*, meaning a British dog. When the statement that the Devil is barking through his British dog is followed by the sentence '*habet enim progeniem Scotticae gentis de vicinia Brittanorum*', all he means is that the Devil has an Irish terrier, not that the terrier came from Ireland.[1] Jerome may have distinguished the British from the Irish race, but he can hardly have regarded the distinction as important. To him the two nations were alike in remoteness and in vicinity to barbarism. Even in Jerome's day it was customary to use the expression 'the British isles'.[2] It is unlikely that Jerome had such detailed information about Pelagius's ancestry as to know (and record) that he came from an Irish family settled in Britain. It is much more likely that Jerome knew Pelagius to be British, but found it useful for purposes of insulting him to call him an Irish dog.[3]

We must briefly outline what can be discovered of Pelagius's career and movements before we approach the subject of Pelagian literature and its connexion with Britain. He was, we can confidently assume, born in Britain and of parents who were wealthy enough to give him a good education, for the two books which can be unhesitatingly attributed to him, *Expositions on the Letters of St. Paul* and the *Letter to Demetrias*, sufficiently assure us that he was well educated. There can be little doubt that the educational resources of Britain were equal to this. He was born

(*Adv. Iovinianum*, ii. 7 (*PL* 23. 296)), written *c.* 392. See A. Souter, *Pelagius' Expositions of Thirteen Epistles of St. Paul*, vol. i, pp. 1–4, quoting Zimmer, *Pelagius in Ireland* (1901), p. 20, n. 4.

[1] P. Grosjean, 'Notes d'Hagiographie Celtique' (1957), pp. 206–11.

[2] e.g. Zosimus, *Hist.*, i. 64 (46), iv. 35 (190, 191). Several other examples occur in contemporary texts quoted in Haddan and Stubbs, *Councils, etc.*, vol. i, p. 5 (one example), p. 10 (three examples), and pp. 11 and 12 (one example each).

[3] After all, he either called him an Alpine dog without wishing to imply that he was Swiss, or he did in fact call him a British (*Albinus*) dog. Plinval adopts the view put forward here (*Pélage*, pp. 55–58). Kenney gives a good summary of the whole question (*Sources*, pp. 161–3). We may dismiss the curious theory of Esposito that Pelagius not only came from Ireland but may have converted Patrick there ('The Patrician Problem and a Possible Solution', pp. 134–5). The theory that Pelagius's name is Celtic in origin seems now to be abandoned by all (see H. Williams, *CEB*, p. 203; A. Souter, *Pelagius' Expositions*, vol. i, pp. 1–4).

and brought up a Christian, but, following the widespread custom of the day, may not have been baptized until adolescence. He left Britain for Rome about 375 or 380.[1] He may have been educated as a lawyer, either in Britain or in Rome, but the evidence for this is slight.[2] About the year 394 he wrote a work, which has not survived, in protest against the violence and exaggeration of Jerome's *Contra Iovinianum*.[3] He wrote his *Expositions on the Letters of St. Paul* at some point between 404 and 409.[4] The sack of Rome by Alaric in 410 drove him and Caelestius out of Rome to Africa, and later Pelagius travelled to Palestine, where in 415 he attended an informal hearing of charges raised against him in Jerusalem before the bishop of that place, and later a formal synod at Diospolis convened to discuss his doctrine. Both gatherings acquitted him of the charge of heresy. It is probable that he later returned to Rome, because in 417, though Pope Innocent I had recently declared an opinion unfavourable to Pelagius's views, Innocent's successor Zosimus pronounced him guiltless of holding dangerous opinions. But when the Emperor Honorius early in 418 issued a particularly fierce decree banishing Pelagius, Caelestius, and their adherents from Rome and, indeed, from Italy, Zosimus yielded to this *fait accompli* and to the pressure which the African Church had for some time been exerting on the papal see against Pelagius, and condemned and excommunicated Pelagius and Caelestius. Pelagius left Italy, but it is not known where he went. It is calculated that he died at some point between 423 and 429. It is not impossible, especially in view of the later history of Pelagianism, that the place he went to on being banished from Italy was Britain. Not only are there several instances of exiled victims of imperial displeasure going to Britain,[5] but he would in Britain at that time have been beyond the reach of Honorius's arm.

[1] Plinval, *Pélage*, pp. 60–63; cf. K. Jackson, *LHB*, p. 114. Plinval (*Pélage*, pp. 69–71) conjectures that Pelagius was baptized in Rome, *c*. 382.

[2] It depends upon our identification of Pelagius with the person mentioned by Jerome (though not by name) in *Epistles* 50. 2 (*PL* 22. 513), and otherwise only on arguments drawn by Plinval from Pelagius's style and his cast of mind. The question of whether Pelagius was a monk is discussed below in Chapter VI.

[3] Plinval, *Pélage*, p. 50.

[4] See the evidence in Souter, *Pelagius' Expositions*, vol. i, pp. 4–5, 189.

[5] e.g. The Priscillianists banished by Magnus Maximus to the Scilly Isles, and the case of Valentinus, referred to above, pp. 2–3.

It is necessary to approach the complicated and much debated subject of Pelagian literature, because several scholars have believed that quite a large proportion of the works attributed in antiquity to others (Jerome or Pelagius or Augustine) were in fact written by authors who were either at the time they wrote living in Britain or had recently lived there. We need not here detail all the works which have been ascribed by scholars to Pelagius (Plinval lists no less than twenty-two). But the following must be mentioned:[1]

De Vita Christiana (*PL* 40. 1031 ff., henceforth known as *De VC*). Six tracts edited together by Caspari in 1890 and ascribed by him to the same author, a Pelagian, viz.

> *Letter I* (*Honorificentiae tuae*, *PL* Supp. i. 1687 ff.).
> *Letter II* (*Humanae referunt litterae*, *PL* Supp. i. 1375 ff.).
> *De Divitiis* (*PL* Supp. i. 1380 ff., henceforth known as *De Div*).
> *De Operibus* (*PL* Supp. i. 1418 ff., henceforth known as *De Op*).
> *De Possibilitate non Peccandi* (*PL* Supp. i. 1457 ff.).
> *De Castitate* (*PL* Supp. i. 1464 ff., henceforth known as *De Cast*).

Two other tracts which in antiquity had been attributed to Jerome, but which Caspari claimed to belong to his group:

> *De Virginitate* (Jerome, *Ep.* 13, *PL* 30. 162, henceforth known as *De Virg*).
> *De Divina Lege* (Jerome, *Ep.* 7, *PL* 30. 104, henceforth known as *De Div Leg*).

These six tracts and the other two tracts Caspari attributed to the same author, a Pelagian. Plinval believed that Pelagius had written all the nine works just mentioned.

We must first deal with *De VC* because it can be isolated from the others. This little work has often been attributed to a person called Fastidius. Fastidius is known from a heading of the Monte

---

[1] The three fullest recent discussions are those of Plinval (*Pélage*, pp. 27–45); R. F. Evans, 'Pelagius, Fastidius and the Pseudo-Augustinian *De Vita Christiana*', pp. 72–98; and J. Morris, 'Pelagian Literature', pp. 29–60. Cf. also Norah Chadwick, *SBH*, pp. 211–13.

Cassino MS. of *De VC* and from a reference to him in Gennadius.[1] What Gennadius[2] says of him is this: *Fastidius Britto scripsit ad Fatalem quendam de Vita Christiana librum et alium De Viduitate Servanda, sana et Deo digna doctrina.* A later hand in the best manuscript of Gennadius's book added the word *episcopus* before *Britto* in the sentence just quoted. Gennadius was a semi-Pelagian who wrote this work about the year 480. Two difficulties immediately present themselves. Gennadius clearly thought that the work on the Christian life was addressed to a man (*quendam*) whereas the *De VC* is addressed to a widow who is not named, and the work has a decidedly Pelagian tone about it which even a semi-Pelagian could hardly describe as 'teaching that was wholesome and worthy of God'. The suggestion that in the *De VC* we have the second work of Fastidius mentioned by Gennadius encounters the difficulty that the *De VC* does not particularly stress the importance of widows not remarrying. According to Gennadius's order, the period at which Fastidius wrote his two works must have been 420 to 430.[3]

But there is further evidence about the *De VC* which complicates the question. In one chapter (cap. 11) of the work, the author recommends the widow to whom he is writing to use a prayer remarkable for the Pelagian quality of its doctrine. It runs thus:

ille autem ad Deum merito extollit manus, ille preces bona conscientia fundit qui potest dicere, Tu nosti, Domine, quam sanctae, quam innocentes, quam purae sint ab omni fraude et iniuria et rapina quas ad te expando manus; quam

---

[1] The following scholars have uncritically accepted this ascription: K. Jackson, *LHB*, pp. 110, 114; Collingwood and Myres, *RBES*, pp. 309–10 (though Myres in a later article, 'Pelagius and the End of Roman Rule', pp. 26–27, rejected this view); Bieler, 'Das Bibeltext des heiligen Patrick', p. 258, at least in comparing Patrick's biblical text with the text of this work; Simpson, *Ninian and Origins*, p. 36; and J. Bulloch, *The Life of the Celtic Church*, pp. 109 and 120, on the latter of which he produces the curious solecism 'Fastidius of Lerins'. Norah Chadwick gives a useful but brief summary of the question, *SBH*, pp. 211–12, but later in *ASCC* (pp. 39–40) apparently accepted the attribution to Fastidius. Morris accepts the authorship of Fastidius tentatively ('Pelagian Literature', pp. 32–36). Plinval (*Pélage*, pp. 27–30, 46) and R. F. Evans ('Pelagius, Fastidius, etc.') decisively reject the attribution of this work to Fastidius. R. S. T. Haslehurst attempted without marked success to edit the works of Fastidius, with an English translation, in 1927.

[2] *De Viris Illustribus*, 56.

[3] It should perhaps be noted that the other manuscripts of *De VC* attribute the work to Augustine.

iusta, quam immaculata labia et ab omni mendacio libera quibus tibi, ut miserearis, preces fundo.

Jerome (*Dialogus* 3. 14) refers to this prayer, quotes it and the sentence that introduces it, and attributes it confidently to Pelagius. At the Synod of Diospolis held in December 415 Pelagius was accused of having written this work and this prayer in it, and also another work in which he flattered a widow as being uniquely virtuous. Pelagius at Diospolis firmly denied having written the works or the prayer, and was on this ground (and others) acquitted by the Synod. Jerome disbelieved Pelagius, and insisted that the style of the work was his. Augustine (*De Gestis Pelagii*, 6 (16)), who recorded, and indeed translated into Latin from Greek, the Synod's proceedings, left the verdict open, and admitted that the Synod was justified in accepting Pelagius's denial at its face value. He adds that he has discovered that some 'holy brethren' still believed that Pelagius had written these works, since they had known them for the last four years, but they had never heard Pelagius admit their authorship. This means that the book must have been known to these men at least as early as 413, and that it must have been written no later than 412. A further difficulty is that Augustine introduces his reference to this prayer by the words *post orationem Domini et salvatoris nostri, docens quem ad modum debeant sancti orare*, but there is no reference in *De VC* before this passage, nor after it, to the Lord's Prayer, nor to the Lord praying. Some think that Pelagius quoted the Lord's Prayer and then introduced this prayer in another, lost, work, to which both Jerome and Augustine were referring; or that Augustine confused this prayer with a part of Tertullian's *De Oratione* (13) (which, with Psalm 25, forms the main source of the prayer in *De VC*), and forgot that though Tertullian had mentioned the Lord's Prayer the author of the *De VC* had not.[1] But the most likely explanation is that Augustus did not mean that the prayer came in the *De VC* after a passage quoting or referring to the Lord's Prayer, but meant that *in spite of* the example set by the Lord's Prayer of the necessity for acknowledging sin and seeking forgiveness, the author obtusely encouraged his correspondent to pray this altogether too self-confident prayer. His comment in the same

---

[1] So Plinval, *Pélage*, pp. 410–12.

chapter of *De Gestis Pelagii* on the prayer is *Christiani est haec, an Pharisaei superbientis oratio?*

In spite of the arguments of Plinval and of R. F. Evans, it is impossible not to agree with Morris that this work *De VC* is not by Pelagius. We know that Pelagius himself denied its authorship; we have no evidence strong enough to overturn this, certainly not the opinion of the prejudiced and malevolent Jerome. The style of *De VC* is not like the style of Pelagius's two acknowledged works. The author of the *De VC* calls himself *peccator et ultimus, insipientior ceteris et imperitior universis,* he disowns skill in learning (*sapientiae peritia*) or reputation for knowledge (*scientiae gloria*), and refers to 'our elementary exhortations' (*rudibus admonitionibus nostris*)[1] Pelagius could have written these words, but they would have sounded insincere had he done so. And if we accept Pelagius's word that this work was not by him, there is no reason to doubt the accuracy of Augustine's statement that men known to him had read this work in 413, nor to disagree with Morris when he dates it to 412 at latest. Morris, indeed, believes that he can directly connect this work with Britain from internal evidence, quite apart from the question of whether it is by Fastidius or not. There is a passage in the *De VC* describing the punishment meted out by God to unjust judges, who themslves had put to death innocent men in large numbers and had then robbed their widows and orphans.[2] Morris is particularly impressed by the fact that the writer describes these men only as *iudices* and not by such epithets as *tyranni* or *rebelles*. He believes that, as we are to place this work in 412, this reference can only be to the conduct of the governing authorities left in Britain when the usurper Constantine III had departed and the British *civitates* had declared themselves independent of the Roman government. But this is very frail evidence indeed on which to found a theory of British authorship. We do not know how the authorities in Britain about 412 styled themselves. Any Roman civil magistrate at any time could justly have been called a *iudex*, and the context is one which particularly calls for the consideration of men as *judges* (whatever else they may have been), because the author is reflecting upon the judgement which they received from God. It is in fact possible to compile an imposing list of people to whom this

[1] Preface (1031, 1032).   [2] 3 (1035).

author might have been referring, such as Carausius, Allectus, Valens, Magnentius, Magnus Maximus, Eugenius, Argobast, Stilicho, Rufinus, Gainas, Constantius III, his son Constans, and Attalus. It is not necessary for the author to have lived in Britain in order to refer to any of these. And anyway, if the author is writing in Britain in 412 (or perhaps in 411, for we must allow time for the book to reach Sicily from Britain), the state of affairs must have been *very* chaotic for so many awful examples as are envisaged by this author *within one or two years* to have run the course of unjust oppression followed by punishment, which took the varying forms of lack of burial, or bankruptcy, or the reduction of their wives and children to beggary. Besides, the author suggests that he is adducing cases which occurred over a considerable space of time—*per diversa tempora diversorum iudicum impie scelerateque conversantium . . . interitum.* The rest of the work, too, gives no impression of having been written at a time when atrocities and social strife and dislocation were being experienced. On the contrary, it breathes a spirit of solid and almost *bourgeois* stability that allows rich women (*aliquae divites nobiles et potentes*) to enjoy luscious food, and to entertain (or refuse to entertain) travellers and the indigent.[1] It is, indeed, most unlikely that this author is Pelagius, though we may be sure that he is a Pelagian. But the evidence that he is a British Pelagian is quite insufficient. The *De VC* does not correspond exactly to either of the works attributed by Gennadius to Fastidius, and if we reject this attribution almost the last trace of a British origin for *De VC* disappears.[2] Fastidius has never been much more than a 'fantôme indécis', as Plinval calls him,[3] and it does not seem possible to conjure this ghost into more substantial existence.

Morris, in his long, useful, and able discussion of the list of works mentioned above,[4] attempts to establish certain links between them and to prove that the same author wrote all Caspari's first six tracts. Much of his argument carries conviction, but the only points that concern us here are those where he endeavours to connect these works and their authors with Britain. The first of these is *De Virg.* Gildas (*De Excidio* 38)

---

[1] 15 (1045, 1046).
[2] We are left with the heading of the Monte Cassino MS. of the *De VC*.
[3] *Pélage*, p. 46.　　　　　　　　　　　　　　　[4] p. 40, n 1.

quotes a sentence from this work in the following way: *ut bene quidam nostrum ait, non agitur de qualitate peccati, sed de transgressione mandati*. This sentiment occurs in the same words in *De Virg* 6, and in much the same form in *Letter I* and in *De Op* 13. They could be regarded as an extension of Pelagius's comment in his *Expositions on Romans* 5, 14. Whom did Gildas mean by the term *quidam nostrum*? Morris believes that Gildas would not have deliberately preserved a saying of Pelagius, and that he would probably not have known that Pelagius was a Briton. Morris therefore concludes that this work must be by some other writer than Pelagius, a Briton. But this conclusion is very weakly grounded. It is quite possible that Gildas knew that this work was by Pelagius, and that is why he called him 'one of us' without naming him. He could well have observed that *De Virg* is a Pelagian work. Pelagianism in fifth-century Britain gained a considerable following: Morris himself suggests that 'from the outset, Pelagianism was British', and that in Britain Pelagianism never became heretical but was absorbed in orthodox thought.[1] We should also remember how popular were Pelagius's works in early medieval Ireland, as Zimmer showed in his *Pelagius in Ireland*. Gildas in fact never mentions Pelagianism.[2] It could be that Gildas obtained this quotation from *Letter I* (which, it is worth remembering, Plinval regarded, with *Letter II*, as a late cento of passages taken from the other works) or from *De Op*, and that these went under the name of Pelagius. On any of these hypotheses the proof that *De Virg* or the other two documents came from a British writer other than Pelagius falls to the ground. Another work of this corpus which Morris tries to connect with Britain is *Letter I*, on the grounds that the author equates the expression *in Francia et in Saxonia* with *in omni barbaria*, and that the writer envisages his return home as involving a difficult and dangerous sea voyage.[3] The *Letter* purports to be written from Sicily. Morris admits that both these expressions could apply equally well to Gaul. The journey from Sicily across the Straits of Messina, or up the coast of Italy to Puteoli

[1] 'Pelagian Literature', pp. 55–56.
[2] Haddan and Stubbs (*Councils, etc.*, vol. i, p. 16) state that he does, quoting *De Excidio* (nine according to their text in *Monumenta Historica Brittaniae*, twelve in Williams's edition), but this is a mere error, for this passage refers to Arianism only and in other expressions is entirely general.
[3] 'Pelagian Literature', pp. 37–40.

or Ostia or a more northern port could be as difficult and dangerous as the Channel crossing, and a Briton would not be likely to omit from the list of 'all barbarian territory' the Picts and the Scots, and would not necessarily include the Franks, whereas a Gallic writer would be likely to mention just these two races, Saxons and Franks. Both *Letter I* and *Letter II* address their recipient as *Honorificentia tua*, which Morris describes as 'all but unique in Latin literature'. *Letter II* ends with the sentence *Opto te semper Deo vivere et perpetui consulatus honore gaudere*; Morris suggests that this 'perpetual consulate', which can be paralleled nowhere in fourth- or fifth-century history, represents a title assumed by some ruler in Britain after the withdrawal of Roman rule, and that the flamboyant *Honorificentia tua* has a similar origin.[1] But the fact that we cannot find these titles anywhere else constitutes no proof whatever that they occurred in Britain. In short, the suggestion that in the group of documents to which Caspari attracted the attention of scholars we have a nest or treasury of writings of ecclesiastics of the British Church at the beginning of the fifth century, appealing though it may be to British scholars, must be rejected through lack of evidence. Morris's attempt to show that *De Div* was written by a British writer depends upon the baseless assumption that Caelestius came from Britain, and upon its affinity to the other documents whose British origin we have found so questionable. But Morris's analysis of the radical attitude towards wealth evident in this work is useful and illuminating. He may well be right in his conjecture that it was this levelling tendency in Pelagianism which caused the unusual sharpness in the Imperial reaction against it.[2] Though the career of Pelagius demonstrates that fourth-century Britain could produce a writer of great ability and a thinker of great influence, the fact that he left his native country so early in his life precludes us from drawing any significant inferences about the British Church from his works.

We can, however, be sure that the British Church in the fifth century appreciated the doctrines of its native son. We have the direct testimony of a contemporary author that Pelagianism had taken a strong hold in the British Church. Prosper of Aquitaine in his *Chronicle* records against the year 413 that *hac tempestate Pelagius Brito dogma nominis sui contra gratiam Christi, Caelestio et*

[1] 'Pelagian Literature', p. 39.   [2] Ibid., pp. 40–57.

Juliano adiutoribus, exeruit. And later in the same work, against the year 429, he writes: *Agricola Pelagianus Severiani Pelagiani episcopi filius ecclesias Britanniae dogmatis sui insinuatione corrupit. Sed ad actionem Palladii diaconi papa Coelestinus Germanum Antissiodorensem episcopum vice sua mittit et deturbatis haereticis Britannos ad catholicam fidem dirigit*. Again, in his work *Contra Collatorem* (21. 2), a work written in 433 or 434, after Celestine's death, he describes how Pope Celestine ordered Pelagians to be expelled entirely from Italy, and then adds *nec vero segniore cura ab hoc eode morbo Britannias liberavit, quando quosdam inimicos gratiae solum suae originis occupantes etiam ab illo secreto exclusit Oceani, et ordinato Scotis episcopo dum Romanam insulam studet servare catholicam fecit etiam barbaram Christianam*. What precisely happened in order to rid the island of Pelagianism we shall be considering shortly. But there can be little doubt that Pelagianism was popular in Britain if the Pope himself felt it necessary to send a mission there to extirpate the heresy. It is perhaps significant that it is only in the later part of the third decade of the century that Prosper places the spread of these doctrines in Britain, i.e. after the exile of Pelagius decreed by Honorius. Some scholars (e.g. Caspari) have identified Agricola as the author of *De Div*, but this can be nothing but conjecture. Certainly we can conclude that a Church which could at this period afford the luxury of fostering a heresy and fostering it in episcopal minds cannot have been greatly reduced or afflicted by civil disturbances. This is only one more indication that the British Church in the first half of the fifth century was growing in numbers and in influence.

We have already seen that Prosper recorded a visit paid by Germanus, Bishop of Auxerre, to Britain in the year 429 in order to suppress Pelagianism there. Besides the reference to him here, the only other significant information dating from the fifth century which we possess about Germanus derives from a *Vita Germani* written by a monk of Lyons about 480, and dedicated to Patiens, Bishop of Lyons and Censurinus, Bishop of Auxerre. The monk's name was Constantius. There are two versions of this *Vita*, a longer and a shorter; the longer is less reliable and more stuffed with miracles. It is the text of the shorter version that is followed here. Constantius describes the career of Germanus in the legal profession and in the Imperial civil service before he was made Bishop of Auxerre in 418. The climax of this career Constantius calls the *ducatus culmen*,[1] but the civil and military sides of the Imperial service had long been separate, so that it is difficult to regard this as anything but a mistake.[2] Constantius tells us that Germanus and Lupus, Bishop of Troyes, were chosen to travel to Britain to combat Pelagianism, after a deputation from Britain had appealed to the bishops of Gaul, who held a synod about the matter. There is no doubt about the date of this visit; Prosper fixes it for us as 429. But Prosper in his account makes no mention of Lupus of Troyes, nor of a deputation from Britain, nor of a Gallic synod, but ascribes the whole initiative to Pope Celestine, prompted by the deacon Palladius. It would be easy to dismiss Constantius's account, were it not for the fact that it is known that Bishop Lupus of Troyes was alive when the work was written, and that a *Vita Lupi* written shortly after the death of its subject mentions his visit to Britain.[3] There is no other record of a Gallic council at that time. It might be conjectured that Germanus went as the representative of Pope Celestine and Lupus as the envoy of the Gallic Church. The account given by Constantius of this first visit by Germanus to Britain is couched in such vague and inflated terms as to render almost all its details uncertain. 'The biographers of early saints', says Norah Chadwick, 'were engaged, not upon historical research, but upon the creation of an impressive and edifying portrait.'[4] The two bishops, whose itinerary is accompanied by a continuous shower of miracles, engage in a public disputation with the Pelagians, who arrive *conspicui divitiis . . . circumdati adsentatione multorum*, but owing to the exertions of the two bishops the champions of Pelagianism find themselves deserted on all sides.[5] No mention is made at any point of Agricola, son of Severianus. Later they meet a *vir*

---

[1] *Vita Germani* 1.

[2] The theory of Norah Chadwick which assigns a military career to Germanus as *dux Armoricani et Nervicani* and Prefect of the Gauls, simply on the strength of the phrase *ducatus culmen* and the coincidence in name between Palladius the deacon and Palladius son of Exuperantius, who was Prefect of the Gauls in 424, is too flimsy to be sustained (*PLG*, p. 250, *SBC*, p. 223).

[3] H. Williams, *CEB*, pp. 223, 224. Plinval (*Pélage*, pp. 348–50) and Norah Chadwick (*PLG*, pp. 255–9) also discuss this point. For other references to this visit see K. Jackson, *LHB*, p. 15; Collingwood and Myres, *RBES*, pp. 311–12; A. H. M. Jones, *Later Roman Empire*, vol. i, p. 191.

[4] *PLG*, p. 120.   [5] *Vita Germani* 14.

tribuniciae potestatis in connexion with whom Germanus performs a miracle.[1] Attempts have been made to identify this official,[2] but without obvious success. During the course of their visit the two bishops are described by Constantius as having won a victory against the Saxons and Picts, at the season of Easter. A large number of the British army were baptized before the battle, the bishops (or at least Germanus) are alleged to have taken charge of the army, and a bloodless victory is supposed to have been won because the cries of 'Alleluia' given by the British before engaging battle so terrified the enemy that they ran away.[3] Some scholars can accept this account as sober history, or something like it.[4] But others regard it as mere fantasy.[5] The likelihood of a soldier being allowed to turn bishop in the late Roman Empire was very small. The likelihood of a bishop turning soldier was even smaller. We may perhaps cite Synesius as an example, but the case of Synesius was rather that of a squire arming his tenants than that of a prince–bishop of Durham winning the battle of Neville's Cross or of Bishop Compton putting himself at the head of a volunteer army of rebels in 1689. The days when bishops would lead British armies had not yet dawned in the fifth century. Constantius records a second visit of Germanus to Britain, on this occasion accompanied by a Bishop Severus of Treves, about whom virtually nothing is known. All that Constantius says concerning Germanus's motive in this second visit is: *Interea ex Britannis nuntiatur Pelagianam perversitatem iterato, paucis auctoribus, dilatari. Rursumque ad beatissimum Germanum preces omnium deferuntur ut causam Dei quam prius obtinuerat, tutaretur.*[6] The bishops harangue a multitude, and accompany their doctrine by a convincing miracle of healing. The people spontaneously arrest the authors

---

[1] Ibid. 15.

[2] e.g. by P. Grosjean, 'Notes d'Hagiographie Celtique' (1957), pp. 174–80; he also attempts to give content to the vague phrase *regionis illius primus* of *Vita* 26.

[3] *Vita Germani* 17.

[4] e.g. Morris ('Dark Age Dates', pp. 162–3), who brings the episcopal pair and the British army to Wales for this purpose. It is difficult to see on what grounds Meissner can assert of these two bishops, 'We know they visited the northern part of the province and the region of Hadrian's wall' (*History of the Church of Ireland*, vol. i, p. 84).

[5] e.g. Norah Chadwick, *PLG*, p. 254; P. Hunter Blair, *Roman Britain and Early England*, pp. 159–60.

[6] *Vita Germani* 25.

of the heresy, and hand them over to the bishops. The culprits are expelled from the island, *sacerdotibus adducuntur ad mediterranea deferendi*,[1] presumably to be escorted to Rome. The result is that the Christian faith has remained intact in Britain up to the writer's own day.

This account is clearly legendary; in fact it may be doubted if Constantius knew anything about this second visit, except that it took place. But can we be sure that he even knew that? Some scholars have regarded the account of the second visit as a mere doublet of the account of the first.[2] Prosper does not mention it. But then, Prosper mentions no Gallic affairs after 440.[3] Though the account of the second visit is extremely vague, it is not a mere repetition of the account of the first. Both accounts mention miracles in plenty, to be sure, and both involve an harangue by Germanus and his companions directed towards the people. But in other respects the second visit is different from the first. The crossing of the Channel in both directions is calm, whereas during the first visit a fierce storm was encountered on the way across to Britain. In the second visit there is no 'Alleluia victory', in the first no arrest and deportation of the offending Pelagians. It is difficult to account for the two names peculiar to the second account, Severus and Elafius, if it is a mere doublet. So it is better to assume that the second visit did take place, though Constantius knew almost no details about it. E. A. Thompson has been able to make a very shrewd guess in dating it.[4] According to Constantius's account, Germanus had scarcely arrived home from this visit when he became involved in an Armorican revolt, and Aetius's measures to suppress this had only just begun. This revolt had been suppressed by the time that Aetius had entered on his third consulate, in 446. Germanus's second visit, then, can hardly have been as late as 446, but must be dated 444–5. Incidentally, this means that we cannot assume that at that period any very serious civic disturbance could have been troubling Britain, not only because Constantius gives no sign of Germanus and Severus having

---

[1] *Vita Germani* 27.
[2] So Norah Chadwick, *PLG*, 255–9; *SBC*, p. 23; *CB*, p. 142.
[3] H. Williams, *CEB*, p. 228. But Williams's conjecture that it was semi-Pelagianism with which Germanus was concerned on his second visit to Britain seems unnecessary (ibid., pp. 240–2).
[4] 'Zosimus on the End of Roman Britain', p. 167.

encountered such conditions, but because it is unusual for people to show enthusiasm for heresy-hunting in the middle of invasions or civil war.

Much speculation has been expended on the visits of Germanus. The first visit has been connected with the mission of Palladius to Ireland,[1] with which we shall deal later. The suggestion is an attractive one, and we shall return to it soon. At the moment, however, we should simply note that Prosper does not connect the mission of Germanus with the mission of Palladius. He simply tells us that the purpose of Germanus's visit was to stem the tide of Pelagianism, and that he succeeded in doing so.

Like Magnus Maximus, Germanus left a lasting impression upon the British folk-memory. Norah Chadwick has argued that a *Book of Germanus* had been composed in south-west Scotland or north Wales at some period not later than the seventh century, 'the period at which . . . the supporters of the Anglo-Roman party in the Celtic Church were beginning to write the Vitae of important saints'.[2] The Life of St. Germanus in Latin hexameters was written by Heiric, monk of St. Germain-in-Auxerre, at the request of Lothair, abbot of that monastery, and finished in 865. Heiric added two books in prose, *De Miraculis Germani*. He derived much of his information from a British bishop called Marcus who had settled at Soissons, with the approval of Charles the Bald (Abbot Lothair's father). Marcus told Heiric about the miracles of St. Germanus, which were still preserved in Britain in Marcus's day in written form.

---

[1] So Ryan, *Irish Monasticism*, pp. 70–74; Binchy, *PB*, pp. 134–5; so also Morris (see below, pp. 52–56), L. Bieler, *Life and Legend of St. Patrick*, p. 70, and McNeill (*St. Patrick*, p. 66). J. H. Todd (*Patrick, Apostle*, pp. 270–6), inimical though he was to the thought that St. Patrick had been sent to Ireland by Pope Celestine, was quite ready to accept the conclusion that this Pope had sent both Germanus and Lupus to Britain (in addition to a Gallic synod's sending them) and Palladius to Ireland. It is perhaps worth remarking in this context that the sectarian bias of Todd has been greatly exaggerated by many later writers on Patrick. He has perhaps an obsession about Celestine's alleged sending of Patrick, but he had good reasons for rejecting this theory, though he may have overstressed them. A much more serious example of sectarian bias is the feeble and uncritical essay of Newport White on 'The Teaching of St. Patrick' in cap. IV of *The History of the Church of Ireland*.

[2] *SBC*, p. 113. In *CS* (p. 329) she suggests that this life may have been based on a nucleus composed by Rhun, son of Urbgen or Urien, early in the seventh century.

This written book of miracles may have been the *Life of Germanus*, already mentioned, deriving from the seventh century. It formed one of the sources of Nennius's *Historia Brittonum*.[1] Nennius's narrative, of course, represents Germanus as having extensive dealings with Vortigern, his son Guorthemir, and the Saxon leader Henghist, and in particular it delineates the unrelenting pursuit of Vortigern, the wicked ruler, by Germanus, the righteous bishop.[2] Some scholars[3] have been ready to see in this an historical reminiscence of a genuine opposition between Vortigern the Pelagian and Germanus the anti-Pelagian. But this seems quite fantastic, if only because it reverses the historical roles of the two men. Vortigern was presumably an aristocratic despot or monarch, who would not be in the least inclined to adopt a moral and intellectual movement which could have disturbing and unpleasant results for the rich and powerful, and which had perhaps for this very reason been banished by a Roman Emperor. Germanus, the ascetic, popular bishop in the democratic tradition of Martin, who was apparently involved in some way with the welfare of the people of Armorica, a people who had such a penchant for initiating revolutionary 'Bacaudae', opposed Pelagianism surely on doctrinal rather than on social or political grounds. It is much better to conclude with Norah Chadwick that originally Germanus had no connexion with Vortigern, and that his mission to Britain was religious rather than political. His cult in the fifth, sixth, and seventh centuries was a popular one; it rivalled that of St. Martin. He was a saint who had been connected with Britain, and consequently Nennius and his immediate source, Bishop Elvodug of Bangor, found him a useful hero in their strategy of bringing the Welsh Church at the turn of the eighth and ninth centuries under the newly introduced Roman order.[4]

The figure of Palladius is one that naturally comes to mind in connexion with Germanus, for Prosper mentions them both. We have seen[5] that Prosper records that Celestine sent Germanus to Britain *ad actionem Palladii diaconi*. The best translation (if we follow Lewis and Short, and Blaise) of this sentence is

---

[1] Norah Chadwick, *PLG*, pp. 267–8; *SBC*, pp. 111–13.
[2] Nennius, *Historia Brittonum* 32 ff. (172 ff.), where a story from Heiric's collection of miracles is also printed by Mommsen.
[3] e.g. P. Hunter Blair, *Roman Britain and Early England*, p. 160.
[4] *PLG*, pp. 268–71.   [5] See above, p. 47.

'at the suit of Palladius the (or a) deacon'. This would suggest either that Palladius was one of the deacons of Rome and that he induced his papal master to send Germanus, or that he was a deacon of Auxerre and that he induced Celestine to commission Germanus. Later, in the same work, the *Chronicle*, under the year 431 Prosper writes: *Ad Scotos in Christum credentes ordinatus a papa Caelestino Palladius primus episcopus mittitur.* And we have seen already that in his later *Contra Collatorem* Prosper refers to the same event.[1] Bede's references to Palladius are wholly dependent upon Prosper.[2] Bury points out that the Irish must have asked for a bishop, or at least have been ready for one, because Pope Celestine in one of his letters expressly lays down *nullus invitis detur episcopus*.[3] Binchy reminds us that we have another reference to Palladius in the statement of Columbanus in the year 513 to the effect that the Irish received their Christianity from Rome.[4] Celestine died in 432. Prosper and his friend Hilary visited Rome in 432 to solicit the aid of Pope Celestine against the semi-Pelagians, and about 434 Prosper settled in Rome and eventually entered the service of Pope Leo I (440–61).[5] The question of what exactly happened to Palladius in Ireland, how his career ended, and his relation to Patrick (if any) will be dealt with in a later chapter.[6] But it certainly seems curious that Prosper, writing after Celestine's death, should in the *Contra Collatorem* eulogize the late pope for converting the Irish to Christianity, if by that time the late pope's emissary in Ireland had either died or for some reason abandoned his mission (as the later tradition suggests that he did).[7] We should also ask ourselves whether we can envisage a pope in the fourth decade of the fifth century sending one of his deacons, who presumably would be an indispensable official in the administration of a rudimentary *Curia*, to a part of the world which was everywhere regarded as the very last and remotest country in Europe, situated in a sea-girt corner literally (as Patrick frequently reminds us) at the ends of the earth; or, indeed, whether we can

---

[1] See above, p. 47.   [2] *Historia Ecclesiastica* i. 13; v. 24.
[3] Bury, *LP*, pp. 52, n. 1, and 65. Celestine's words will be found in *PL* 50. 434, *Epistles* 4.
[4] Binchy, *PB*, pp. 11, 12; cf. 97.
[5] Gennadius, *De Vir. Ill.* 85. *CEB*, p. 198; Bindy, *PB*, p. 142.
[6] See below, pp. 192–4.
[7] So O'Rahilly, *The Two Patricks*, pp. 20–21.

imagine such an official having so lively a care for the island of
Britain, now no longer even a part of the Roman Empire, as to
arrange that Germanus should be sent there to extirpate heresy.
It is very difficult to envisage this, and it is therefore reasonable
to conclude, with several scholars, that Palladius was a deacon
of the Church of Auxerre and that he had made the journey to
Rome about the year 428 to gain papal approval for Germanus's
visit to Britain. Some authority wider than the merely diocesan
or metropolitan was necessary in order to obtain sanction for an
action which could have been represented as interfering in the
affairs of other bishops, a misdemeanour for which Victricius of
Rouen had received a papal rebuke about thirty years earlier.
Celestine's own Letter 4 gives the impression that one of its
aims is to prevent bishops meddling with episcopal elections
in sees where they have no business to do so.[1] The conjecture of
O'Rahilly may therefore be correct that Palladius accompanied
Germanus on his first visit to Britain, and then on his return
reported the result of the mission to Rome, was there detained by
the Pope, and not long afterwards sent by him to the Irish as
their bishop.[2]

We have sufficient assurance that there were Christians in
Ireland before Palladius arrived there from Prosper's words—*ad
Scotos in Christum credentes*. Besides, it was entirely unknown in the
ancient Church for a bishop to be sent to a place where there
was no flock for him to minister to.[3] Some scholars have refused
to admit the force of this argument,[4] but it is one difficult to

---

[1] *PL* 50. 431 (*Ep.* 4. 5).

[2] O'Rahilly, *The Two Patricks*, p. 19. There is no need to follow H. Williams in
his conjecture that Palladius was originally British (*CEB*, p. 210), and still less to
accept the curious notion of Morris that Celestine's chief object in sending Palladius to Ireland was to keep *Britain* orthodox by establishing a bishop in a nearby
see to keep a watch on British bishops ('The Celtic Saints', pp. 356–7). Unless
Palladius could make direct contact with the Pope, he would have no authority
whatever over British bishops, and the prospects of easy communications between
Ireland and Rome in those days were nil. No less curious is the theory of Norah
Chadwick (*ASCC*, pp. 34–35) that Palladius was sent to suppress monasticism—
in a country where there were probably no monks!

[3] This point is made by M. Esposito, 'The Patrician Problem', p. 145, and
Norah Chadwick, *ASCC*, p. 17. See also E. A. Thompson, *The Visigoths in the Time
of Ulfilas*, p. xvii, for the invariable custom in this matter.

[4] e.g. Ryan (*Monasticism*, p. 76), and Bieler (*Life and Legend*, p. 73). Esposito
maintains that there were no Christians in Ireland before Patrick ('The Patrician
Problem', p. 152), but then he believes that Patrick reached Ireland *before* Palladius.

resist, and is, moreover, supported by other evidence. Zimmer had marshalled a few pieces of linguistic evidence designed to show that loan-words in Old Irish from ecclesiastical Latin were pre-Patrician, because they appear to have been borrowed not direct from Latin but through the British language.[1] Zimmer's theory has been abandoned in its original form, but it may be true that two different strata of words can be detected, an earlier and a later, derived from Latin pronounced in two different ways, the earlier from Latin as spoken in Britain. Binchy refers to this list of early Latin loan-words in Old Irish also, as evidence of Christianity's existence there before Patrick (and therefore, of course, before Palladius). He notes that this list does not contain a word for 'bishop', and thinks this points to the fact that there had been no bishop in Ireland before Palladius or Patrick.[2] A century ago Todd, after an exhaustive survey of all the evidence for pre-Patrician Christianity in Ireland provided by later tradition, had concluded very wisely that Prosper's words are the only reliable piece of evidence for this.[3] Perhaps the most striking of all the later traditions on this subject is that to which Kuno Meyer called attention more than fifty years ago. This is an extract, not consistent nor continuous with its context, from the Leyden Glossary, written probably 'not later than the sixth century, in the West of Gaul'. It refers to the invasions of the Huns, Goths, Vandals, and Alans, and continues: *sub quorum vastatione omnes sapientes cismarini fugam ceperunt et in transmarinis videlicet in Hiberia et quocumque se receperunt maximum profectum sapientiae incolis illarum regionum adhibuerunt.* Meyer thought that this statement was given independent support by the occurrence of the word *Bordgal*, the Irish form of Burdigala = Bordeaux, as a place-name in Westmeath and Kilkenny. He argued that this could only mean that in the fifth century Ireland was full of learned men. But Patrick certainly was not learned. Therefore this learning was not imported by the Church. So it must have arrived before Patrick, and Patrick

---

[1] So Bury, *LP*, pp. 349–52, and Meissner, *History of the Church of Ireland*, vol. i, p. 47. Christine Mohrmann, *Latin*, p. 31, points out that clearly Patrick was unable to draw upon an already developed Christian Irish Latin. But this is not inconsistent with there being some Christians in Ireland before his day.

[2] *PB*, pp. 166–73. For a further discussion of this point, see below, p. 153.

[3] J. H. Todd, *Patrick, Apostle*, pp. 189–226.

must have found plenty of Christians there when he arrived in Ireland. This would equally apply to Palladius.[1]

This rather naïve argument can best be estimated by bringing it to the test of Patrick's own words. Bury thought that the words *ad plebem nuper venientem ad credulitatem*[2] suggested a people converted in Patrick's own day, in contrast to others converted earlier. The words which Patrick attributes to those who deprecated his going to Ireland as bishop, *Iste quare se mittit in periculo inter hostes qui Deum non noverunt?*,[3] need mean no more than that Patrick intended to go to hitherto unevangelized parts of Ireland, and not that no Irish knew God. The obscure phrase at *Confession* 42, *virgines, viduae et continentes de genere nostro qui ibi nati sunt*, could, indeed probably does, refer to British Christians domiciled in Ireland.[4] Finally, a very strong confirmation for the view that there were other Christians in Ireland besides those for whom Patrick was caring, and that they had been there before his arrival as bishop, is conveyed by the words *pergebam... usque ad exteras partes, ubi nemo ultra erat et ubi numquam aliquis pervenerat qui baptizaret aut clericos ordinaret aut populos consummaret.*[5] The inference to be drawn from the natural sense of this passage is that though Patrick had penetrated to unevangelized parts, others (apparently including another bishop) had baptized, ordained, and confirmed somewhere else. It is difficult to avoid the conclusion that there were Christians in Ireland before Patrick and before Palladius, and that when Patrick was there as bishop he not only knew of the existence of these Christians but knew that a bishop (presumably Palladius) had ministered to them, perhaps, even, had been doing so during Patrick's ministry. But that the country was full of learned refugees spreading culture there is little or no evidence.

Having glanced at the very first appearance of the Christian faith in Ireland in the fifth century, we shall now look at its first appearance in another distant part of the British Isles in the same

---

[1] K. Meyer, *Learning in Ireland in the Fifth Century*. See also a summary of this lecture in Kenney, *Sources*, p. 142. Norah Chadwick's theory that Christianity 'had reached southern Ireland from the Mediterranean areas, perhaps through Aquitania and Spain' before Patrick's day (*ASCC*, pp. 50–60, the quotation from p. 50) is too far-fetched and slender in its argumentation to be convincing.

[2] *Confession* 38. Bury, *LP*, pp. 349–52.

[3] *Confession* 46.   [4] See below, pp. 138–9.

[5] *Confession* 51. The words *sicut indulsit et ceteris amantibus se* (*Conf.* 57) could refer to Palladius, but are so general as to be of little value as evidence.

period. Bede in the third book of his *Ecclesiastical History* begins the fourth chapter with an account of the appearance among the northern Picts in the year 565 of a missionary from Ireland, Columba. He remarks that the southern Picts had already become Christians a long (but indefinite) time before this:

... by the preaching of the word to them of Bishop Nynia, a most venerable and holy man, of the nation of the Britons, who had been instructed properly in the faith and the mysteries of the truth at Rome. His episcopal see is famous for the name and the church of saint Martin, where he himself lies in the body along with many holy men; this see the nation of the Angles now possesses. This place belongs to the province of the Bernicians, and is popularly called 'At the White House', because he built there a church of stone in a manner to which the Britons were not accustomed.[1]

The face value of this account has been sufficient for several scholars.[2] But ever since W. Levison published an article in 1940 on 'An Eighth-century Poem on St. Ninian', Bede's account has been open to considerable doubt. Levison details the sources of our knowledge of Ninian apart from this account of Bede.[3] Ailred of Rievaulx (*c.* 1110–67), a Cistercian abbot who knew Bishop Christian (*fl.* 1154–86)[4] of Whithorn (a see which had been revived within his own lifetime), wrote a *Vita Niniani*. Ailred had certainly visited Scotland. He used what he called 'a book on Ninian's life and miracles, written in a barbarous style', now lost, of unknown date. His life of Ninian adds very little of value to what we know from Bede. He says that Ninian was the son of a king, that he visited Tours and obtained from Martin masons who built the church at Whithorn, and that this

---

[1] Bede, *Ecc. Hist.* iii. 4: *praedicante eis verbum Nynia episcopo reverentissimo et sanctissimo viro, de natione Brettonum, qui erat Romae regulariter fidem et mysteria veritatis edoctus; cuius sedem episcopalem sancti Martini episcopi nomine et ecclesia insignem, ubi ipse etiam corpore una cum pluribus sanctis requiescit, iam nunc Anglorum gens obtinet. Qui locus, ad provinciam Berniciorum pertinens, vulgo vocatur ad candidam Casam, eo quod ibi ecclesiam de lapide insolito Brettonibus more fecerit.*

[2] e.g. Collingwood and Myres, *RBES*, p. 310; Bury, *LP*, pp. 187, 313; Ryan, *Irish Monasticism*, pp. 105–6; Simpson, *Ninian and Origins, passim*; K. Jackson, *LHB*, p. 164; J. A. Duke, *The Columban Church*, pp. 24, 25; and, at least as regards Ninian's training in Rome, J. A. Bulloch, *Celtic Church*, p. 51.

[3] 'An Eighth-century Poem', pp. 281–91. Bury, of course, knew about Ailred's life of Ninian; see *LP*, p. 313.

[4] Ailred had been brought up at the Court of King David I of Scotland, and was a Cistercian monk who later became Abbot of Rievaulx (Duke, *The Columban Church*, p. 22).

church was dedicated to Martin, who had died before it was dedicated to him. Levison then describes a poem (or rather two poems, one of which is so artificial as to be irrelevant) about St. Ninian, now to be found edited in the *Poetae Latini Aevi Carolini*. This poem (though not the copy we have of it) was known to Alcuin, for he mentions it as having been sent to him by his pupils, the scholars of the Church of York, in a letter written to the monks of Candida Casa at some point between 777 and 790. In form the poem imitates Aldhelm's works and Bede's metrical *Life of St. Cuthbert* (705–16), and it also follows the headings of the chapters of that *Life*. Levison confidently dates it to the eighth century. The author clearly wrote in Whithorn. There can be no doubt from the resemblance between this poem and Ailred's *Vita* that it too used the old 'barbarous' *Life of Ninian* employed by Ailred. We can deduce from these facts, first that this old *Life of Ninian* was of the eighth century,[1] and second that it would have added very little to our knowledge of Ninian's career had it survived, for the poem tells us little more of Ninian than the *Vita* of Ailred does. But we can by comparison with this poem detect what is peculiar to Ailred (and therefore likely to be legendary or just invented by Ailred for effect), by noting details in Ailred's *Vita* which are not reproduced in this poem. The poem makes no mention of Ninian's having visited Tours on returning from Rome. We may therefore conclude that this is a detail elaborated by Ailred, and neither original nor historical; perhaps it was an imitation of Sulpicius Severus's reference to his own stay with Martin. Hitherto it had been usual to date the beginning of Ninian's activity by the date of the death of Martin, 397. We therefore must detach Ninian from Martin, and regard the usual date assigned to him as uncertain.

What Levison began Grosjean finished. He contended[2] that we cannot rely upon Bede's statement that Ninian was consecrated at Rome, nor upon his account of Ninian dedicating a church to St. Martin, for both Bede and Picthelm, who was

---

[1] From the fact that Bede did not know this *Life*, Levison deduces that it was written 'in the middle or second part of the eighth century' ('An Eighth-Century Poem', p. 290).

[2] 'Les Pictes Apostats dans l'Épître de S. Patrice', pp. 354–63. The question of Ninian's contact with St. Martin is discussed in Chapter V, see below, pp. 145–8, as is the question whether Ninian was a monk. Morris deals with the subject of dedications, 'Celtic Saints', p. 354, n. 2.

Bishop of Whithorn in his day, and from whom he no doubt derived his information about Ninian, were champions of Roman authority and Roman diocesan and metropolitan organization, and they were only interested in the Celtic Church in as far as it supported or complied with these. This, for instance, is the reason, in Grosjean's opinion, why Bede does mention Palladius but does not mention Patrick. Further, Grosjean declared that it is totally unprecedented, indeed anachronistic, that in the last years of the fourth or the beginning of the fifth century an altar or a church should have been dedicated to a saint who was a confessor, and neither a martyr nor an original New Testament figure, outside the place where his body lay. The first example of this known to Grosjean was the dedication of a church in Rome to St. Martin by Pope Symmachus (498–514). Had Ninian dedicated a church to St. Martin he would have had to go to Tours to fetch Martin's bones. It is wholly improbable that he did this.

Levison and Grosjean between them, therefore, separated Martin entirely from any literary evidence by which he might be dated. He might have come to Whithorn as late as 500, or later.[1] But where literary evidence has proved unreliable, archaeological evidence has come to the rescue. We can come to the point immediately by pointing out that there is to be found on the site of the cathedral at Whithorn, which archaeological investigation has proved decisively to be the original Whithorn of antiquity (and not the Isle of Whithorn lying just off the coast near it), an ancient stone slab with an incised *Chi-Rho* monogram and an inscription whose lettering can be dated to about the middle of the fifth century. The inscription reads thus:

(T)E DOMINU(M) / LAUDAMUS / LATINUS / ANNORU(M) / XXXV ET / FILIA SUA / ANN(ORUM) IV / (H)IC SI(G)NUM / FECERUT / NEPUS / BARROVA / DI

The exact meaning is not clear. If this is a monument to Latinus and his daughter, the 'grandson' (*nepus*) cannot be the grandson

---

[1] Grosjean did not deny that a church may well have existed at Whithorn early in the fifth century. Norah Chadwick has expressed her agreement with the conclusions of both Levison and Grosjean (*SBC*, pp. 26–27). The latest authority on Ninian, J. MacQueen, accepts these conclusions also. His contribution to the subject is discussed below, pp. 61–62.

of Latinus who died aged 35. But presumably 'the grandson of
Barrovadi' (Latinus's father?) put it up, or 'the grandson [but
of whom?] named Barrovadi'. At any rate, here are Christians
about the year 450 erecting Christian funerary monuments to
the generation that went before them (and perhaps the generation that went before that), who were themselves Christians.
We are brought back well into the first half of the fifth century
for a date at which Christianity existed in Whithorn. Another
stone in the nearby cemetery of Kirkmadrine commemorates
praecipue sacerdotes Ides Viventius et Mavortius, and this dates from
the fifth century also; and there is another in the same place, to
be dated at the end of the fifth century, with a fragmentary
inscription ending . . . *s et Florentius*.[1] *Sacerdotes* in this context
certainly means 'bishops', as the word invariably does in
Patrick's writings, and not 'presbyters'. It would be absurd to
suggest that the existence of Christianity in Whithorn quite
early in the fifth century owes its origin to anybody but Ninian;
his name, and his name alone, is associated with the beginning
of Christianity there. Even if we cannot date him by an association with St. Martin (and, as will be shown later, this association is by no means put out of court),[2] we can with confidence
assign his activity in Whithorn to the first half of the fifth century,
and probably not to a late period within that half-century.

Archaeological investigation has also explored the ecclesiastical buildings at Whithorn.[3] The earliest church which can be
traced on the site, at the easternmost part of the nexus of
buildings on the site of the priory or cathedral, was a rectangu-
lar building fifteen feet wide, with walls three feet four inches
thick, of which only the foundations survive. It was made of
'roughly split, undressed blocks of local stone set in clay.

---

[1] C. Ralegh Radford and G. Donaldson, *Whithorn Official Guide*, pp. 10, 38, and
45–46. Françoise Henry interestingly compares with this stone a pillar stone which
now lies at Arraglen, on the slopes of Mt. Brandon in Kerry, and which has on
one side a Greek cross inscribed in a circle and on the other a *Chi-Rho* surrounded
by the inscription (in oghams) 'Ronan the priest son of Comgall' (*Irish Art in the
Early Christian Period to A.D. 800*, pp. 56–57 and Plate 14).

[2] See below, pp. 145–8.

[3] The main authorities on St. Ninian are Simpson, *Ninian and Origins*; Duke,
The Columban Church; Bulloch, *Celtic Church*; Ralegh Radford and Donaldson,
Whithorn Official Guide; and J. MacQueen, *St. Nynia*. Simpson and Duke did not
have an opportunity of learning from the results of the archaeological investigation.

Outside, the masonry had been daubed with a cream-coloured plaster, portions of which were still found adhering to the base of the wall face.' The site of this building must have been near the centre of the Celtic monastery, and it was near this that a number of Christian inscribed stones were found. The plaster suggests the origin of the title attributed to the spot by Bede, *Ad Candidam Casam*. Those who conducted the excavation concluded that this church was in fact the church built by Ninian.[1] This identification has been challenged by MacQueen,[2] who produces evidence to suggest that the word *casa* could not possibly mean a building as substantial as a stone church, but could only mean a hut or a temporary or frail construction, made of boughs or wattles or some materials unlikely to last. On this argument *Candida Casa* must have been built by Ninian, but built of mud and wattles or wood, and the epithet *candida* must refer to some such quality as spiritual or moral purity; the stone church must have been built after Ninian's day. None of MacQueen's examples of the use of *casa* are taken from Vulgar Latin, and until we can establish the use of *casa* in that type of Latin we cannot estimate their value. Patrick, who certainly is writing Vulgar Latin, when he wants to indicate a little hut does not use *casa* but *tegoriolum*.[3] Blaise gives two instances of *casa*, one meaning 'farm' or 'property', from Cassiodorus (fifth century to sixth), and one from Augustine, where *casa* means 'brothel'. It should be remembered that *casa* in modern Spanish and modern Italian, both derived directly from Vulgar Latin, means 'house'. For the expression *Ad Candidam Casam* there is a mid fourth-century parallel in Ammianus Marcellinus (27. 7. 5), who describes how two Roman Imperial officials who were Christians had been unjustly executed by Valentinian I, and were commemorated in a place near Milan called *Ad Innocentes*. It may be that in Vulgar Latin, which these two titles may well reflect, *casa* could mean a substantial building like a stone church.

The question of what people precisely it was among whom Ninian's work lay is an interesting one. Bede says that it was the

---

[1] Ralegh Radford and Donaldson, *Whithorn Official Guide*, p. 34 (including the quotation). So also Bulloch, *Celtic Church*, pp. 37–38.

[2] *St. Nynia*, pp. 13–17. MacQueen's attempt to date Ninian by Tutwal (mentioned in the poem and by Aelred (pp. 8–12) is so hypothetical) as to be of little real value.

[3] *Confession* 18.

southern Picts, who lived *intra montes*, and high and difficult mountains at that;[1] and this can only mean on this side, Bede's side, the southern side, of the mountains. In his short study MacQueen shows that these mountains must mean not the hilly parts of Galloway (as had been suggested) but the mountain mass which is today called the Grampians, and that these southern Picts must not be thought of as living in Galloway, nor on the shore of the Solway estuary, but in what would today be called Forfar, the Mearns, Perth, Stirling, and Fife. Ninian himself lived and founded his see among people who were Britons, of the same race as himself. At one point[2] MacQueen even suggests that the Britons in the region of Whithorn were already Christians when Ninian arrived among them early in the fifth century. His main evidence for this seems to be that Bede represents Ninian as evangelizing the southern Picts, but not the Britons. It would be unwise to take Bede's words as literally as this, in view of the evidence for the condition of the British Church about the year 400 which we have already considered. Though MacQueen can find little satisfactory evidence that Ninian did actually evangelize, or found churches among, the southern Picts, it would be difficult to dissociate him from them. If the British inhabitants of the Kingdom of Strathclyde, north of Galloway were, with their ruler, Christian or mainly Christian in the time of Patrick, it is unlikely that the southern Picts, living to the south of them, were untouched by Christianity, on the very probable assumption that Christianity reached Strathclyde from the south. We may finally refer to the suggestion of J. Wall[3] that there is a connexion between the Christian tombstone at *Brocavum* (Brougham), which may date from the fourth century, and the dedication to Ninian at Nynekirks, only one and a half miles away. In short, it is not unreasonable to see Ninian as an example of the missionary activity of the British Church in the fifth century, and his mission in many ways as an earlier version of Patrick's mission. In this case certainly we need not introduce Celestine or Germanus to explain the origin of his work. We can also note that Ninian's activity is yet another indication that the British Church in the first half of the fifth

---

[1] *Ecc. Hist.* iii. 4.
[2] *St. Nynia*, p. 20.
[3] *Christian Evidences in the Roman Period*, pp. 205, 206.

century was growing—even growing rapidly—in numbers and in influence.

We shall now return to consider two more figures connected with the British Church in the middle of the fifth century. The first is Faustus of Riez.[1] He was born about the year 405. Avitus, Bishop of Vienne, writing about the year 500, describes him as *ortu Britannum*.[2] He became a monk in St. Honoratus's monastery at Lerins at some point between 426 and 433 (earlier, probably, rather than later in that period). He was Abbot of Lerins from 433 until some point before 462, by which time he is known to have been Bishop of Riez. It has often been stated that his mother was of British race, purely (as far as can be ascertained) on the basis of one ambiguous reference in Sidonius Apollinaris's *Carmen Eucharisticum*, addressed to Faustus at some date after the year 462, and perhaps much later than that date. The reference runs thus: Sidonius has been describing how he approached the house of Faustus (who is already Bishop of Riez), and how Faustus's wish was achieved:

> *ut sanctae matris sanctum quoque limen adirem,*
> *derigui, fateor mihi conscius atque repente*
> *tinxit adorantem pavido reverentia vultum;*
> *nec secus intremui quam si me forte Rebeccae*
> *Israel aut Samuel crinitus duceret Annae.*[3]

It has been suggested that Sidonius Apollinaris is here not referring to Faustus's mother, but to the Church of Riez, the mother of the Christians of the place, or to the Church as representing the Catholic Church, Mother Church. Such a conceit is not beyond the possibilities of Sidonius's far from brilliant poetical talent, but it must be admitted that the passage is much more naturally explained as referring to Faustus's actual mother, who was living with him in the episcopal house at Riez. Norah Chadwick

---

[1] See H. Williams, *CEB*, pp. 238–42; Bury, *LP*, p. 40; Ryan, *Irish Monasticism*, pp. 108–10.

[2] *Aviti epistula ad Gundobadum*, ed. R. Peiper (*MGH* vi. 2, p. 30).

[3] 'That I should approach the holy threshold of the mother who is holy too. I became stiff with self-consciousness, I confess, and suddenly a sense of awe brought a blush of fear to my cheek. I trembled no less than if Israel had brought me to Rebecca or curly-haired Samuel to Hanna' (Sidonius Apollinaris, *Epistulae et Carmina* (*MGH* viii, ed. C. Luetjohann, Berlin, 1887), p. 241, 84–87 of the *Carmen Eucharisticum*).

has produced a curious theory that Faustus was of aristocratic birth, the son of Vortigern by the daughter of Magnus Maximus,[1] basing her argument on the occurrence in old Welsh genealogies of a Britu, son of Vortigern. Quite apart from the slenderness of the evidence thus produced, we encounter here a serious difficulty in chronology. If Magnus Maximus's daughter married Vortigern before her father fell from power (an assumption which seems unavoidable), she would have been at least 15 by at latest 388, and probably older. This means that she would have been at least 32 at the time of Faustus's birth and probably older, perhaps ten years older, and at the time that Sidonius greeted her with such reverence at least 91 and probably 101 or older! If we date Sidonius's *Carmen Eucharisticum* later than 464, then Faustus's mother's age advances steadily up the nineties, even on the most favourable interpretation. In short, this theory of Faustus's origin is so unlikely as to be impossible.

Faustus was a very prominent leader of the semi-Pelagian school of thought. It is not surprising, therefore, that he came from Britain. Perhaps it is significant that he did not seek a monastic life in Britain itself, but with this point we shall deal later.[2] We can infer little more about the British Church in which he was brought up from a consideration of his life. But there is an interesting incident, of which Sidonius Apollinaris is again our informant, which introduces both Faustus and the other British figure to whom we have already attended. There is a letter written from Sidonius Apollinaris to Faustus of Riez in which Sidonius says that he has read a book written by Faustus which a certain Riochatus, a British monk and bishop, had brought with him. Riochatus had brought Sidonius gifts from Faustus, but had concealed the fact that he had Faustus's book in his possession. However, a few months after Riochatus's arrival Sidonius discovered that he had this book, followed him (for he had just left the city), read the book, had certain extracts copied out, and then sent Riochatus on his way. Some of Sidonius's sentences must be looked at more closely. Of the book, he says: *legi volumina tua quae Riochatus antistes et monachus atque istius mundi bis peregrinus Britannis tuis te reportat.* He describes the movements of Riochatus thus: *ipse venerabilis apud oppidum nostrum cum moraretur donec gentium concitatarum procella defremeret,*

---

[1] See *SBH*, pp. 26–33, 254–63.   [2] See below, pp. 152–3.

cuius immanis hinc et hinc turbo inhorruerat.[1] It is clear that Sidonius is writing from his villa at Avitacum in Auvergne, and that Avitacum is the town in which Riochatus lingered because of the movements of barbarians. Most authorities therefore date this letter to 475 or just before, because in 475 Euric the Visigoth took possession of Auvergne and drove Sidonius temporarily out of it. It is clear too that Riochatus is travelling from Faustus to *Britannis tuis*, i.e. to Faustus's Britons. The name Riochatus looks very like a Celtic one, and his existence gives us unmistakable proof of the existence of monasticism in Britain, not only by 475 but for some time before it, say back to at least 450, for Riochatus must have been a monk before he was a bishop.[2] But where was Riochatus going, and why? The second question, we may conjecture, is connected with Faustus's interest in semi-Pelagianism; this is probably why Faustus and Riochatus did not want Sidonius to see the book. Was Riochatus going to Britain? If we could be sure of this, we could say with some confidence that the British Church was still able to make contact with the Gallic Church as late as 475.[3] But unfortunately we cannot be sure of this. In the first place, Sidonius does not say that Riochatus was going to Britain but to Britons. In the second place, Sidonius calls Riochatus *istius mundi bis peregrinus*. Why was Riochatus *twice* an exile from this world? Once as a bishop and once as a monk? Monks might indeed be called exiles or aliens from this world, but hardly bishops. Is it not likely that what Sidonius in his allusive style, full of *double entendre*, meant was that Riochatus was twice an exile from this world, once as a monk and once as an exile from his native land, Britain, among the Britons in Armorica? This interpretation would preclude us from assuming that Faustus was communicating with the British Church as late as 475; it would mean that he was keeping in touch with the British settlers in Armorica, whose existence in the country north of the Loire we have already seen reason to assume by about this period.[4] On this hypothesis we should be able to range Riochatus with Mansuetus, *episcopus Britannorum*, who attended the small Council of

---

[1] Sidonius Apollinaris, *Epistulae et Carmina* ix. 6 (p. 157), which contains all the information given here.

[2] For the whole question of monasticism in the British Church, see below, cap. vi, pp. 20–21.

[3] So Williams, *CEB*, p. 316.   [4] See above, pp. 20–21.

Tours in 361.[1] This would mean that the local Gallic Church accommodated itself readily to the existence in its midst, or on its fringes, of clergy from the British Church. Perhaps it is significant that it was to celebrate the feast of St. Martin that this Council originally met. Martin was perhaps by then a saint whose cult had advanced some way in the British Church.[2]

There is one more intricate but useful subject which throws some light upon the British Church in the middle of the fifth century. This is the subject of the Paschal Cycle, that is to say the method of calculating (necessarily cyclic) the date of Easter in any given year or series of years. It is a well-known fact that in the seventh and eighth centuries this question became a burning issue between the Celtic Church in the British Isles and the Anglian Church founded by Augustine of Canterbury. Cummian, Abbot of Durrow, wrote to Segene, Bishop of Iona, in 632 or 633 on the subject, describing the current Roman Cycle as *cyclo illo quem sanctus Patricius, papa noster, tulit et fecit*.[3] It was this Paschal controversy which probably accounted for the extension of the cult of Patrick in Ireland in the seventh century and the beginning of the eighth. The champions of the old, less accurate, calculation were the tribes and monasteries called by Binchy 'the Columban federation', who possessed influence and property in parts of Scotland as well as of Ireland. The uí Neíll dynasty, though they were of Columba's kin, sided against the 'Columban' view in favour of the uniform practice of the rest of the Western Church. They probably revived and championed the cult of Patrick as their patron saint in order to outweigh the influence of Columba as the patron saint of the other party. The temporal claims of the uí Neíll dynasty for overlordship extending over all Ireland, centred at the royal headquarters of Tara, went along with the spiritual claim of Armagh as the place favoured by Patrick, its 'érlam' (patron saint and founder).[4] This was the controversy whose issue was decided at the Synod of Whitby in 664, and it was to the Roman side of this cause that

[1] See above, p. 20–21; cf. Williams, *CEB*, p. 282.

[2] For further evidence on this point, see below, pp. 145–8.

[3] Whitley Stokes, *TL* ii, p. 493 (*PL* 87, 96 & ff.); see Norah Chadwick, *ASCC*, pp. 130–1; in *SBH*, p. 14, she dated this letter *c*. 627, but in *SBC*, p. 51, she dated it 632/3, without giving reasons for the change.

[4] Binchy, *PB*, pp. 170–1; Kathleen Hughes, *The Church in Early Irish Society*, pp. 111–20.

Adomnan at the end of the seventh century devoted much energy. It may therefore be instructive to look at the origins of this controversy and see how the matter stood in the middle of the fifth century.[1]

The need for an Easter Cycle arises from the fact that the Passover is based on lunar reckoning, and the ordinary calendar on solar reckoning. The Cycle is an attempt to find a period of time when two series of years, as reckoned by these two calendars, will begin on the same day. None of the cycles is exactly correct; they differ by a day or a day and a quarter, differences remedied by minute intercalations of Epacts and months. There was room for variance, even if a single cycle were agreed upon, about the correct procedure when the Passover Day, on any reckoning, fell on a Sunday. The Quartodeciman issue, as to whether Easter was to be celebrated on the Passover Day or on the Sunday after the Passover Day, was not in dispute. It had been settled by the Council of Nicaea in 325.

Eusebius (*Hist. Ecc.* 7. 20) mentions the Cycle of Dionysius of Alexandria, produced *c.* 268, which was an eight-year cycle. But he also tells us of Anatolius, an Alexandrian Christian mathematician who, about the year 280, introduced, or rather reintroduced, an old (originally Attic) cycle of nineteen years. It was called a Metonic Cycle, for it had originally been drawn up in Athens (for purposes other than deciding the Passover, of course), when Meton was Archon. But in 312 an earlier cycle, based on eighty-four years, which had originally been drawn up to cover the years 213–312, called the *Laterculus* of Augustalis, was emended and formally accepted by the Church of Rome, under the title of the *Supputatio Romana*. It had been widely used in the provinces. This was the Cycle which the British delegates to the Council of Arles in 314 no doubt carried back to the British Church. It continued to be used till 342, when it was further modified. This modified version was the Cycle adopted by the British Church and retained by it until the

---

[1] Bury (*LP*, pp. 371–4) and Bulloch (*Celtic Church*, p. 152) deal with this subject. But by far the most informative and illuminating account is that of Williams, *CEB*, pp. 152–4, 191–2, 406–10, 438, and 463–73. Williams's account is followed here. See also P. Grosjean, 'Recherches sur les débuts de la controverse pascale chez les Celtes'; vol. iv of the *Annals of Ulster*, separately issued by B. Mac-Carthy in the year 1901, Introduction, pp. xiv–clxxvii, which is a mine of information; and Kathleen Hughes, *The Church in Early Irish Society*, pp. 103–11.

seventh century, and it was this Cycle that Augustine of Canterbury found the British Christians using when the course of his missionary work brought him into contact with them. In 457 Victorius, a learned man of Aquitaine, introduced a new Paschal Table for calculating Easter, called the *Cursus Paschalis*; it was based on a cycle of 532 years (84 × 19), combining the older Cycle with the Metonic one. Finally, in 525 the Table of Dionysius Exiguus, based on a return to the old, Alexandrian, nineteen-year Metonic cycle, was adopted in Rome.[1] Now for the first time Rome and Alexandria (which had followed this Cycle ever since about the year 300) were agreed upon their Paschal Table. This was the Cycle which Augustine of Canterbury brought with him to England, calling it 'Roman', 'Petrine', and 'Catholic'. This was the first table to use the calculation B.C.–A.D. The various cycles can be set out in tabular form:

1. *Laterculus* of Augustalis, used in Roman Church *c.* 268–312.
2. *Supputatio Romana*, prepared for 312–42.
3. The later *Supputatio*, which lasted from 342 to 444.
4. The *Cursus Paschalis* of Victorius, adopted by the Roman Church in 457.
5. The *Table* of Dionysius Exiguus, adopted by the Roman Church in 525.

It had been the custom since the Council of Nicaea in 325 that the Bishop of Rome should annually inform the Western Church in advance of the date of Easter (as the Bishop of Alexandria informed the Eastern Church). The *Annales Cambriae* record against the year 455 that a change of Easter was made by the Britons in conformity with Leo, Bishop of Rome, and there is evidence in the *Annals of Ulster* and the *Annals of Innisfallen* that Leo's instructions on the date of Easter for 454 (which fell on 24 April in that year) were known in Ireland. In the years 441, 451, and 453 Leo had engaged in correspondence variously with the Bishop of Alexandria, Paschasinus, Bishop of Lilybaeum, and the Byzantine Emperor about the date of Easter, which would fall on the occasion foreseen in these letters outside the limits traditionally observed by the Roman see (i.e. earlier or

---

[1] Or rather, was drawn up for the benefit of the Roman see. It was not then officially adopted, owing to the death of Pope John I. See Grosjean, 'Recherches sur les débuts de la controverse pascale chez les Celtes'.

later than was customary). He obtained no concessions from his correspondents and finally admitted that their dates must be observed. But the result of these negotiations was that in 454 Leo asked Victorius of Aquitaine to produce an Easter Cycle. Victorius produced this in time for it to become the official Cycle of the Roman Church in 457. It is clear that the British and the Irish Churches did not know of Victorius's Cycle until some centuries later, and did not adopt it until a period later still.[1] Williams thinks that Leo's instructions of the year 454 represent the last formal contact between the Church of Britain and the Church of Rome until the seventh century. This is not to say, of course, that the Church of Britain was thenceforth totally shut off from the Continent. The Welsh Church of Nennius (and perhaps of some of his sources) knew the *Cursus Paschalis* of Victorius (though they did not use it),[2] and it was observance of Victorius's cycle, not that of Dionysius Exiguus, which was pressed so strongly upon Columbanus when he was working on the Continent in the early years of the seventh century. But the fact remains that the Cycle of Victorius was not adopted by the British Church, and we may safely conclude from this that by the year 457, when Leo adopted Victorius's Cycle, communications between the British Church and the see of Rome, and therefore probably between the British Church and the Church on the Continent, had been broken off by circumstances. By the time knowledge of Victorius's *Cursus Paschalis* reached the British Church the observance of the older calculation had become so much a matter of ancient tradition and corporate pride that even the sense of allegiance to the Roman see felt by that Church (a sentiment whose existence we need not doubt) was not strong enough to break the old bonds.

Our picture of the British Church in the fifth century must necessarily be composed of faint lines and scattered pieces. But it leaves us with two lasting and definite impressions. In the first place, the British Church in the first half of the century, though we can make little progress in reconstructing its life in detail, and none in tracing a continuous history for it, was clearly a

---

[1] B. MacCarthy, *Annals of Ulster* vol. iv, Introduction, pp. cix–cxv; Williams, *CEB*, pp. 191, 192, 410, and 438. The Paschal Table known as that of Zeitz in Switzerland (where the manuscript of the Table is kept) was apparently tried by Leo from 447 to 455, when it proved unsatisfactory.

[2] So Williams, and Hunter Blair, *Studies in Early British History*, p. 138, n. 4.

vigorous and successful Church, claiming the loyalty of great numbers of people, probably of the majority of the population, pushing its evangelizing activity northwards and westwards, patronized and valued by those who were in authority. It was capable of producing men eminent for learning and for piety, like Pelagius and Faustus. It was not a mere dependant of the Church of Gaul nor a mere puppet of the Roman see. It was capable of fostering a very independent outlook upon the Pelagian question. If we think it right to give substance to Fastidius, we can believe that it was producing literature of its own. It had initiated the monastic life at least as early as 450, and we shall see reason later to decide that the date when monasticism reached Britain must be placed earlier than this.[1] It had nourished a cult of its native martyr, St. Alban. It had apparently welcomed Germanus when he arrived, but we may doubt whether it had acquiesced as readily in banishing Pelagianism as Constantius represents it as doing. We shall see later that there is some evidence that it had shown a particular interest in the cult of St. Martin.[2] We know from Lullingstone and from Whithorn and Kirkmadrine that the *Chi-Rho* monogram was one of its favourite forms of Christian device.

The other impression we derive from this survey of the British Church in the fifth century is that of a curtain falling, an interruption of normal life shortly after the middle of the century. The situation was not that Britain was finally cut off from the Continent, for archaeological evidence shows that communications were maintained and trade continued between Gaul and Western Britain.[3] But for some considerable period ecclesiastical contact at least seems to have been lost. The literary evidence dies out. The Gaulish Chronicler could gain the impression that the Saxons had virtually enslaved all Britain. A large-scale migration from Britain to Armorica took place. The British Church, which had hitherto shown no disinclination to adopt Papal or Continental customs concerning Easter, failed to assimilate Leo's recommendation of Victorius's Paschal Cycle. All these facts tell the same tale. This can hardly be mere chance. It is reasonable to assume that from about the year 460 onwards the British Church began to face vicissitudes and

[1] See below, pp. 140–58.   [2] See below, pp. 145–8.
[3] See Kathleen Hughes, *The Church in Early Irish Society*, pp. 31–32.

dangers which arrested the current of its normal life, precluded it from influences which might have brought it into the larger history of the Western Church as a whole, and prevented its full and natural development. Once again, we are reminded that the efforts to fit the career of Patrick into the second half of the fifth century which have recently been made (e.g. by O'Rahilly and Carney, and even tentatively by Binchy) are bound to meet peculiar difficulties from which theories that place his career in the first half of the century are free.

III

ASSESSMENT OF THE SOURCES

SOURCES of information about St. Patrick fall readily into three classes: 1. The writings of Patrick himself; 2. Later Traditions about St. Patrick;[1] 3. Entries about St. Patrick in the Irish Annals. No proper account of Patrick can be given until clear and distinct ideas are reached about the methods and criteria for assessing the relative worth and reliability of these sources. We shall therefore begin this chapter with a brief enumeration of them.

1. *Writings of St. Patrick himself*

The only two surviving works which all scholars today confidently believe to have been written by Patrick in the fifth century are the *Confession* and the *Epistula ad Coroticum*, both written in Latin. The first is an account in sixty-two short chapters of Patrick's own spiritual conversion, struggles, and development; and a thanksgiving to God for the unfailing support supplied him throughout his life. The second is a letter, of twenty-one short chapters, written by Patrick in order to rebuke a certain Coroticus, who with his soldiers had shortly before the writing of the letter massacred a number of newly baptized and newly confirmed Irish Christians, and kidnapped others with the intention of selling them into slavery; Patrick excommunicates Coroticus and his men, and summons them to repentance and restitution. Both these works are extant in several manuscripts; they mostly appear together, but the *Confession* appears alone in a curiously abridged form in the famous *Book of Armagh*, a manuscript written in Armagh about the year 807.[2] Bieler has shown reasons for believing that all

---

[1] For classes 1 and 2 the short work of L. Bieler, *Codices Patriciani Latini, A Descriptive Catalogue of Latin Manuscripts relating to St. Patrick*, is almost indispensable.

[2] For suggestions why the *Confession* should appear in this abridged form here see P. Grosjean, 'The Confession of Saint Patrick', chap. vi in *St. Patrick*

the copies of both the *Confession* and the *Epistula* derive from an early seventh-century exemplar made in Ireland, and that a copy of this manuscript was made in the north of France by a continental scribe of the eighth or ninth century. The Irish exemplar of this manuscript may have passed through Péronne in the seventh century.[1]

Several other works have been ascribed to Patrick, but none of them have been universally accepted by scholars as authentic. They have all for one reason or another had suspicion cast upon their genuineness. There is a list of isolated sayings attributed to Patrick, called the *Dicta Patricii*; they run as follows:

1. *Timorem Dei habui ducem itineris mei per Gallias et Italiam, etiam in insolis quae sunt in mari Terreno.*

2. *De saeculo requissistis*[2] *ad Paradisum. Deo gratias.*

3. *Aeclessia Scotorum, immo Romanorum, ut Christiani, ita ut Romani sitis, ut decantetur oportet omni hora orationis vox illa laudabilis, Curie lession, Christe lession. Omnis aeclessia quae sequitur me cantet, Curie lession, Christi lession. Deo gratias.*[3]

The Latin of these *Dicta*, though by no means elegant, is rather too concise and straightforward to suggest Patrick's laboured and cumbrous style. And the exhortation to use the formula 'Christe eleison' suggests a later period than Patrick's, for this phrase was first introduced into the liturgy of the Western Church by Pope Gelasius (492–6). This leaves the genuineness of the mention of Patrick's journey to Gaul, Italy, and the islands of the Tyrrhenian Sea questionable. Some canonical literature has been ascribed either directly to the hand or indirectly to the inspiration of St. Patrick: a circular letter alleged to be from Patrick, Auxilius, and Iserninus; a 'Canon of

---

(ed. J. Ryan); Binchy, *PB*, pp. 41–42, 171; and Carney, *The Problem of St. Patrick*, pp. 92–94; the last two do not find Grosjean's ingenious theory of the origin of this abridgement convincing. For further information about the *Book of Armagh* see below, pp. 75 ff.

[1] For accounts of this hypothesis see Grosjean, 'Les Pictes Apostats', pp. 364–5, and Carney, *The Problem of St. Patrick*, pp. 115–16. Most unfortunately, all editions of these two works of Patrick and all English translations of them are out of print, though not completely unobtainable. For the editions of the texts by Newport White and by Bieler see the Bibliography of this book. The two most recent English translations are those of Newport White and of Bieler.

[2] i.e. *recessistis*, a reminiscence of *Epistle* 17.

[3] The text of this is from the *Book of Armagh* (Stokes, *TL* ii. 301, 9 a 1; Gwynn 17).

St. Patrick' from Armagh (found in the *Book of Armagh*); a document known as the *Synodus II S. Patricii*; and a number of canons attributed to St. Patrick in the collection known as *Collectio Canonum Hibernensis*.[1] The authenticity of some of these has been defended by some recent scholars, such as Bury, McNeill, and Bieler, but the verdict of Binchy that they all bear the clear marks of having been composed to meet the needs and serve in the controversies of the Irish Church of the seventh or later centuries is very hard to refute.[2] It is significant that these ecclesiastical decisions are not mentioned in the seventh-century traditions about Patrick. A few fragments in Latin include a reference to a letter sent by Patrick to two bishops who ordained clergy without his consent in Mag Ai, in the north of Co. Roscommon, with a prophecy that as a result of their disobedience (I quote) 'your churches will not be big'.[3] As Binchy remarks,[4] this last sentence betrays the atmosphere of the seventh-century stories of Patrick the prophet and wonder-worker, and of the much later situation when monastic churches founded by some famous saint had a number of lesser churches and monasteries under their influence. The whole question of whether Patrick consecrated other bishops in Ireland is an open one.[5] These fragments must be judged with the rest of those stories. Finally, there is the famous *Breastplate of St. Patrick* (Latin *Lorica*, Irish *Faeth Fiada*, 'Deer's Cry'). This is a hymn in the form of an invocation of God, or charm, against a list of dangers, in Old Irish, which is certainly of great antiquity. This form of 'breastplate' invocation is known elsewhere both in Irish and Welsh sources, and probably had a pagan prototype.

---

[1] For descriptions of these see Bieler, *Codices Patriciani*, pp. 4–8.

[2] Binchy, *PB*, pp. 45–52. A number of works originally ascribed to Patrick but now universally acknowledged to be spurious are here ignored. They are listed by Bieler, op. cit., pp. 8–16. Bieler has recently attempted a defence of the Circular Letter in *Mélanges offerts à Mademoiselle Christine Mohrmann*, to my mind unconvincingly. He has not attempted to explain the silence of Patrick himself about any bishops working with him, which constitutes the most serious objection to this document. Bieler has printed a translation of the Circular Letter in *ACW*. No recent scholar has attempted to vindicate the authenticity of the Second Synod of St. Patrick. Kathleen Hughes has recently given good reasons for placing the Circular Letter in the middle of the sixth century (*The Church in Early Irish Society*, pp. 44–50).

[3] A translation of the text of these fragments will be found in Bieler, *ACW*, p. 48.

[4] *PB*, pp. 43–45.   [5] See below, pp. 137–8.

Many authorities (Newport White, Bury, Meissner, Bieler) have been ready to attribute it to Patrick. But opinion among scholars who are experts in ancient Irish is decidedly against this view, and this is a matter in which linguistic arguments must be paramount. Binchy, for instance, produces arguments which make it very difficult to take Patrick's authorship of this hymn seriously.[1] We must now turn to the assessment of later traditions about Patrick.

2. *Later Traditions about St. Patrick*

The most important later traditions about Patrick date from the second half of the seventh century and are contained in the remarkable manuscript, the *Book of Armagh*, to which reference has already been made. This manuscript was copied in the year 807 (when Torbach was Abbot of Armagh) by a scribe called Ferdomnach, who is known to have died in 845. The complete book contains a number of documents relating to Patrick, the whole of the New Testament in the Vulgate version (the only entire copy of the New Testament which survives from the ancient Irish Church), the *Life of St. Martin* by Sulpicius Severus, and the same author's *Dialogues*, which also deal with St. Martin.[2] The material about St. Patrick includes a memoir or biography by a certain Muirchu Moccu Machteni, a life, or notes for a life, of Patrick by a Bishop Tirechan (both of which are in Latin), some miscellaneous *Additions* to Tirechan's material (partly in Latin but mainly in Irish), a curious section apparently consisting of a number of headings in Irish, with a few Latin words interspersed, almost all proper names, and then a connected narrative called the *Liber Angueli*, in Latin, purporting to be an account of what an angel revealed to Patrick, but in fact an early medieval list of the ecclesiastical and territorial claims made by the monastery of Armagh, whose head regarded himself as St. Patrick's successor. Then follows the abridged copy of Patrick's *Confession*.[3] There also survive, though not in the *Book of Armagh*,

---

[1] *Ériu* xx (1966), 234–7.

[2] See the Introduction to J. Gwynn's edn. of the *Book of Armagh*, pp. xiii–xv.

[3] There is one other manuscript for Tirechan's memoirs of Patrick (in the Bodleian Library, Oxford), and two others for Muirchu's *Life* (one in Brussels, and one in Novara which differs in interesting ways from the other two).

two ancient hymns about St. Patrick, one in Latin, attributed to St. Secundinus, who is alleged to have been a companion of Patrick and (if we are to trust the Irish Annals) to have died before him, and one in Irish called Fiacc's Hymn or the *Génair Patraic* (The Birth of Patrick). We must also reckon with a number of later Lives of Patrick, written in the eighth or ninth centuries, printed by Colgan in his *Acta Sanctorum Hiberniae* (1647), which are also known from other manuscripts,[1] and a few medieval Lives of Patrick, such as those of John of Tinmouth (*ob.* 1348 or 1349), a Life by an otherwise unknown Probus (*c.* tenth century), and the Lives of William of Malmesbury (*ob. c.* 1142) and of Jocelin of Furness (written *c.* 1185–6).[2] These later Lives are valuable for the light they may cast upon the times in which they were written and on the text of Patrick's works, or of the works of Muirchu and Tirechan which they may have used, rather than for any evidence concerning the historical Patrick. Finally, there is the *Vita Patricii* in Nennius's *Historia Brittonum*, which we have encountered already,[3] and a remarkable document extant in Irish, with Latin sections amounting to perhaps one-tenth of the whole, called the *Vita Tripartita*. This homily on St. Patrick has been dated variously: to the eleventh century, or a little earlier (Whitley Stokes); to a period between 894 and 901 (Kenney and Bieler);[4] and (in its earliest form) most recently to about the years 700–10 (McNeill and Grosjean).[5]

The authenticity of Secundinus's Hymn as a document contemporary with Patrick has been accepted by several scholars (Todd, Bury, McNeill, O'Rahilly, Newport White, Meissner, Grosjean, and Bieler).[6] But several weighty reasons make this very unlikely. It is clear that the language of this *Hymn* has either borrowed from the *Confession* of Patrick or has been borrowed by Patrick in his *Confession*. If this Hymn is by a

---

[1] For descriptions of them see Bieler, *Codices Patriciani*, pp. 22–30.
[2] For descriptions of all these see Bieler, op. cit., pp. 30–36, 37–41. Bieler gives descriptions of late medieval Lives of Patrick, pp. 41–48.
[3] See above, pp. 16, 17.   [4] *Codices Patriciani*, p. 36.
[5] See below, pp. 84–85. For a description of the manuscripts see W. F. Skene, *Chronicles of the Picts and Scots*, Preface, pp. xxix–xxx, and Bieler, *Codices Patriciani*.
[6] J. H. Bernard and R. Atkinson issued a critical edition of this hymn in *The Irish 'Liber Hymnorum'* in 1898 (pp. 36–37); a translation of it into English can be found in Newport White's *The Writings of St. Patrick* and Bieler's *ACW*. The Latin text can also be found in Whitley Stokes, *TL* vol. ii, pp. 386–9.

contemporary of Patrick called Secundinus then it was written before the *Confession*, for Secundinus is recorded as having died before Patrick. This would mean that Patrick borrowed eulogistic words about himself from a Hymn written in praise of him by his friend during his lifetime, without acknowledgement, to insert into his last solemn public utterance—something which it is almost impossible to imagine for those who have read with care the *Confession* and sensed in it Patrick's almost obsessional self-depreciation. Again, the Hymn suggests a Patrick without trials and without set-backs or vicissitudes, an effortlessly successful saint; this is the Patrick of later legend.[1] The hymn appears in the *Bangor Antiphonary* (680–91), but not ascribed to Secundinus. The earliest documents ascribing it to Secundinus are the *Martyrology of Oengus* (ninth century) and the *Vita Tripartita*. We may attribute it to the sixth century (perhaps the late sixth century) and regard it as 'the earliest extant testimony to a cult of Patrick'.[2] MacNeill in his book *St. Patrick* attempted to prove that the Irish Hymn *Génair Patraic* (Fiacc's Hymn) was written by Bishop Aedh of Sletty (in modern Carlow), who was the patron of Muirchu and died about 700. The Hymn clearly is heavily indebted to Patrick's *Confession*. But it assumes that Patrick's period of slavery was spent with Milliuc at Slemish in Antrim, that he had studied with Germanus, that 'in the isles of the Tyrrhene sea he fasted', that he encountered King Loeghaire, that his ministry in Ireland lasted sixty years, and that he established the primacy in Armagh, but was not buried there.[3] The deciding factor in determining the date of this document also must be linguistic, and scholars well versed in Old Irish, such as O'Rahilly and Binchy, find it impossible to place this hymn as early as *c.* 680, and prefer to date it at least a century later.

We may dismiss the later Lives and the Hymns briefly, but we must look more closely at the material provided by Muirchu and Tirechan, at Nennius's *Vita Patricii*, and at the *Vita Tripartita*. Muirchu describes his work in these words: *Haec*

---

[1] The arguments against the authenticity of the Hymn as Secundinus's are those of Binchy (*PB*, pp. 53–54). But Esposito, Kenney, and Carney have also rejected Secundinus's authorship.

[2] Binchy, *PB*, p. 55.

[3] The Irish text of the Hymn, with an English translation, is printed in Stokes, *TL* ii. 402–11.

pauca de sancti Patricii peritia et virtutibus Muirchu maccu Machteni dictante Aiduo Slebtensis civitatis episcopo conscripsit.[1] From this we can gather that Muirchu was son, or spiritual son, of the Cogitosus (the Latin form of the Irish Machten) who wrote a very legendary and miracle-laden *Life of St. Bridget* in the seventh century, and that Aedh, Bishop of Sletty, encouraged Muirchu to write. Muirchu also tells us that nobody before him, except his father Cogitosus, had attempted to write a *Life of Patrick*, and complains of *incertis auctoribus* and *memoria labili*.[2] From time to time in his narrative he refers to *periti* as his source.[3] The early chapters of Muirchu survive only in the Brussels codex.[4] They follow the *Confession* closely in their account of Patrick's early life, only adding the following details: Patrick's other name was Sochet, his mother was called Concessa. After spending some years with his parents, on returning from captivity in Ireland, at the age of thirty he visited the see of Rome to study there. Then he made his way to Bishop Germanus *Alsiodori civitate*, and spent some time studying with him. Muirchu goes on to narrate that Patrick left Gaul without being ordained by Germanus, that Palladius (whom he calls Archdeacon of Celestine in Rome) was ordained and sent to Ireland, but that, deterred by the hostility of the inhabitants and by homesickness, he started on his journey home, but died *in Britonum finibus*.[5] On receiving the news of Palladius's death, Patrick and his companions (who had already been sent by Germanus on the road to Ireland from Gaul) turned aside to a bishop called Amatorige, who consecrated Patrick, Auxilius, and Iserninus as bishops, and sent them off to Ireland, via Britain.[6] Then Muirchu brings Patrick ashore at Inver Dea on the coast of Wicklow, causes him to re-embark, and to sail up the coast of Ireland to Co. Down, where he lands near Saul, and seeks his old master, Milliuc, at Slemish. Muirchu also brings Patrick into contact with King Loeghaire at Tara. But on the whole in his description of Patrick's movements he tends

---

[1] Stokes, *TL* ii. 271, 20 b 1 (Gwynn 40).
[2] Ibid. ii. 272, 20 a 1 (Gwynn 39).
[3] e.g. 292, 7 a 2 (Gwynn 13).
[4] *Analecta Bollandiana*, t. i, pp. 549–52, 575–7; Stokes, *TL* ii, pp. 494–8.
[5] Ibid. 272, 2 a 7 (Gwynn 3).
[6] Ibid. 273, 2 a 2 (Gwynn 3). For a more detailed treatment of this account see below, pp. 90–91.

to confine him to a comparatively small area in the north-east of Ireland. In his account Patrick is an invariably successful, wonder-working saint, who constantly prophesies the future destinies of people and churches, fully in the tradition of early medieval hagiography, and especially of Irish hagiography. He records the foundation of Armagh as Patrick's chief church, but does not seem to be concerned to extend Armagh's claim over the whole of Ireland. It is possible that Gwynn is correct in seeing in Muirchu a desire to advocate the claim of Down-patrick to possess the grave of Patrick, as a counterweight to the importance of Armagh.[1]

Tirechan begins his account of Patrick with the following words: *Tirechan episcopus haec scripsit ex ore vel libro ultani episcopi cuius ipse alumnus vel discipulus fuit.*[2] Tirechan says that he learnt from Bishop Ultan the four names of Patrick—Magonus, Succetus, Patricius, and Cothirthiacus; that the master whom he served in his period of slavery was Milliuc of Slemish; that an angel called Victor conducted him during his escape; and that after his escape he wandered for seven years *in campistribus locis et in conuallibus montanis per Gallias atque Italiam totam atque in insulis quae sunt in mari Terreno, ut ipse dixit in commemoratione laborum* (apparently a reference to the *Dicta Patricii*). Ultan also informed Tirechan that Patrick *erat in una ex insolis quae dicitur Aralanensis* [? *Lerinensis,* ? *Arelatensis*] for thirty years.[3] Tirechan then launches into a narrative which brings Patrick to Ireland with a large escort of 'bishops, presbyters, deacons, exorcists, ostiaries, readers and boys whom he had ordained',[4] causes him during the course of his ministry to ordain 350 bishops (the names of forty-one of whom Tirechan records), including Benignus, Miserneus (? Iserninus), Secundinus, Auxilius, and Victorius,[5] and then conducts him on a carefully planned round tour of Ireland, during which the saint, always master of the situation, founds a great number of churches, performs several miracles, and shows a remarkable interest in the future disposition of Church properties. He secures a safe conduct from Loeghaire, but does not convert him, and he discomforts Loeghaire's magicians by

[1] Gwynn, *Book of Armagh*, Introd. xii.
[2] Stokes *TL* ii, 303, 9 a 2 (Gwynn 17).
[3] Ibid. 302, 9 a 2 (Gwynn 17).   [4] Ibid. 303, 9 a 2 (Gwynn 17, 18).
[5] Ibid. 304, 9 b 1 (Gwynn 18).

means of a miracle. There can be no doubt that Tirechan had an ideological motive in writing. He was concerned to claim the hegemony of Armagh over all the monasteries of Ireland, and his claim ran parallel to the claim of the dynasty of the Uí Neíll to provide high-kings (or, to be more accurate, kings of Ireland) who would exercise hegemony over all the kings in Ireland. He explicitly says at one point that there are those who oppose and dislike the *paruchia Patricii* and are anxious to draw what is Patrick's away from him, but that in fact everything in Ireland belongs to Patrick, *quia Deus dedit illi totam insulam cum hominibus*.[1] It is likely that Tirechan had in mind those whom Binchy calls 'the Columban federation', the authorities, ecclesiastical and secular, who supported the hegemony of Iona, of Columba and his foundations and successors. They were during the seventh century the champions of the old, British, Paschal Cycle deriving from the amended *Supputatio Romana*.[2] Tirechan and his friends and the foundation at Armagh were championing the more recent, Roman, *Cursus Paschalis* of Victorius, and were using the cult of Patrick as their means of claiming authority for the rule and the customs of Armagh.[3]

At the end of Tirechan's memoirs there occurs a passage which runs thus:

Tertio decimo anno Teothosii imperatoris a Celestino episcopo papa Romae Patricius episcopus ad doctrinam Scottorum mittitur . . . Paladius episcopus primo mittitur, qui Patricius alio nomine appellabatur, qui martyrium passus est apud Scottos, ut tradunt sancti antiqui. Deinde Patricius secundus ab anguelo dei, Victor nomine, et a Celestino papa mittitur, cui Hibernia tota credidit, qui eam pene totam babtizavit.

The only reference to Germanus in Tirechan's work occurs in a Latin passage in the *Additions*, which are otherwise wholly concerned with describing encounters of Patrick with individuals, and foundations of churches and grants of land by the saint. This reference runs thus:

[1] Stokes, *TL* ii. 311, 312, 11 a 1–11 a 2 (Gwynn 21).
[2] See above, pp. 68–69.
[3] See O'Rahilly, *The Two Patricks*, p. 4 and pp. 49–50 (n. 8); Binchy, *PB*, pp. 58–68, 170–1. It is an ironical fact that the Paschal Controversy in the Irish Church was fought over the calculation of Victorius, presented as the true and catholic one, which was already at the time of the controversy being rendered obsolete by Dionysius Exiguus's Paschal Cycle.

Patricius et Iserninus[1] cum Germano fuerunt in Olsiodra civitate. Germanus vero Isernino dixit ut praedicare in Hiberniam veniret. Atque prumptus fuit oboedire etiam in quamcumque partem mitteretur nisi in Hiberniam. Germanus dixit Patricio, 'Et tu an oboediens eris?' Patricius dixit, 'Fiat si vis'. Germanus dixit: 'Hoc inter vos erit et non potuerit Iserninus in Hiberniam non transire.' Patricius venit in Hiberniam, Iserninus vero missus est in aliam regionem, sed ventus contrarius detulit illum in dexteram partem Hiberniae.[2]

At the end of the *Additions* there occurs a note written either by Ferdomnach or by Tirechan indicating that he had left these passages in the Irish tongue because he found the meaning of the stories (which he calls *fabulae*) difficult to understand, and because the Irish names were difficult to reproduce in Latin.[3]

The *Vita Tripartita* represents the legend of Patrick in a full state of embroidery. Here Patrick moves triumphantly through Ireland confounding foes (among them Loeghaire and his wizards), founding churches, making prophecies, and scattering miracles (many of them lethal). It places Patrick's birth in a place called *Nemthor* (which occurs also in the *Génair Patraic*), among the Britons of Ail-Cluaide (i.e. Dumbarton).[4] It records that Patrick was given one name by Germanus, and another by Celestine.[5] Pilgrimages were made in the time of the author to Slemish in order to visit the place where Patrick's angel Victor ascended into heaven.[6] Not only is Patrick placed as a disciple under Germanus in Rome, but he is also brought to Tours, to be made a monk under Martin.[7] He also is represented as spending a long time with Germanus at Auxerre.[8] Palladius is allowed to land in Ireland, at Inver Dea, before Patrick, but he is described as having been frightened off by Nathi, son of Garrchu, after having founded three churches and baptized a few people; he then died (on his way home) of a sickness in the land of the Picts.[9] Patrick is later said to have made three journeys to Rome.[10] There are several references throughout the work to the community of Columbcille having encroached upon property which properly should belong to

---

[1] An interlinear gloss in Irish over this word says 'i. epscop Fith'—'that is, Bishop Fith'.

[2] Stokes, *TL* ii. 342, 18 b 1 (Gwynn 35).

[3] Ibid. 348, 18 b 2 (Gwynn 36).
[4] *TL* i. 8 (Irish)–9 (English).

[5] Stokes, *TL* i. 16–17.
[6] Ibid. 18–19.

[7] Ibid. 25 (Latin only, extant).
[8] Ibid. 26 (Latin only, extant).

[9] Ibid. 30–31.
[10] Ibid. 74–75.

Patrick. At the end of the work an angel forbids that Patrick should be buried in Armagh and directs that he shall be buried in Saul.[1] But the narrative relates that in fact he was buried in Downpatrick.[2]

The account of St. Patrick to be found in caps. 50–55 of Nennius's *Historia Brittonum* looks very like a later version of some of the documents we have been considering, and also of Patrick's own *Confession* and Prosper's *Chronicle*.[3] Patrick's master in slavery is named as Milchu, and on escaping from slavery Patrick went to Rome to be educated in the mysteries of Christianity. Meanwhile, Palladius was sent to Ireland by Celestine, but God prevented him by stormy weather and he departed from Ireland, went to Britain, and died in the land of the Picts. When the news of Palladius's death became known Patrick was sent *a Celestino papa Romano, et angelo Dei cui nomen erat Victor, monente et suadente sancto Germano episcopo*. Germanus sent a presbyter called Segerus with Patrick *ad quemdam hominem mirabilem summum episcopum Amatheum regem in propinquo habitantem*. There Patrick was consecrated bishop by 'Amatheus the King' and received the name Patricius, having previously been called Maun. Auxilius, Iserninus, and some others were consecrated with him. He first went to Britain and then to Ireland, where he landed in the reign of Loeghaire. He then began a career of successful evangelism accompanied by miracles, briefly summarized in the language of conventional early medieval hagiography. A final reference is made to his being ordained *ab Amatheo sancto episcopo*. The author admits that he had has to omit many details for the sake of brevity.

Such is the information that can be gleaned from later tradition about Patrick. It has been very diversely estimated by different scholars. Bury thought that he could reconstruct Patrick's career out of these materials, and those supplied by Patrick's own writings, and in his famous *Life of Patrick* set the fashion for Patrician scholarship for many years after its publication. He was followed by a large number of later scholars in his type of approach.[4] Bury accepted a surprising amount of

---

[1] Stokes, *TL* ii. 252–3.   [2] Ibid. 254–5.

[3] It can be found in Nennius, *Historia Brittonum*, ed. Mommsen, pp. 194–8, and also in Stokes, *TL* ii. 498–500.

[4] Bury may be said to have been followed in outline or in detail by J. Gwynn, Newport White, Meissner, Collingwood and Myres, K. Jackson, Kenney,

the later tradition as genuine: the residence of Patrick in Gaul (he thought that Lérins was the monastery where he was educated), his visit to Rome, and his encounters with Loeghaire. He accepted as authentic most of the *Dicta Patricii*, many of the canons attributed to Patrick, and Secundinus's authorship of the Hymn. Those who have followed his main line since have tended to shift the place of Patrick's education as a monk from Lérins to Auxerre. Few of Bury's disciples have cared to go so far as Gwynn, who was ready to correct a statement in the *Confession* by the light of information found in Tirechan and Muirchu.[1] But Bieler does openly avow that in his critical work on Patrick he has thought it right to 'accept as probable all traditions which existed at the end of the seventh century unless they are demonstrably false',[2] and to assume that 'unless a later piece of evidence is in itself suspect, or runs counter to fifth-century evidence that is unequivocal, it ought to be accepted'.[3] Others, such as Esposito and Binchy, have taken a sceptical line and rejected almost all the later tradition. O'Rahilly and Carney have been suspicious of the later tradition, but have regarded the Annals as trustworthy. Each scholar has produced a different account of Patrick's career in accordance with his presuppositions about the later traditions.

Many scholars have attempted to reach a better understanding of some of the documents involved in the problem. McNeill and some others in their work on the *Book of Armagh* and the *Vita Tripartita* have shown themselves anxious to demonstrate that Muirchu's work was probably written later, in Aedh's

Grosjean, Ryan, Williams, Duke, Bulloch, McNeill, Christine Mohrmann, Bieler, and Ralegh Radford. For succinct accounts of the history of Patrician scholarship see Esposito, 'The Problem of the Two Patricks' (in *St. Patrick*, ed. Ryan), the first part of Binchy's *PB*, and R. P. C. Hanson, *St. Patrick, a British Missionary Bishop*, pp. 1–11.

[1] *Book of Armagh*, Introd. lxxxiii, n. 3, where, on the sentence 'Come and walk among us as before' (*Conf.* 23), said in Patrick's vision to Patrick by the children of the wood of Foclut, Gwynn remarks that we cannot accept the (obvious and natural) meaning of the words that the wood of Foclut had been the place of Patrick's captivity, because Muirchu and Tirechan tell us that he had spent his captivity at Slemish. But Olden (*The Church of Ireland*, p. 15) follows the same principle when he says that Patrick's original name was not Patrick, relying on the *Vita Tripartita* and Nennius.

[2] *Life and Legend*, p. 102; and see the whole passage.

[3] 'The Lives of St. Patrick and the Book of Armagh' (in *St. Patrick*, ed. Ryan) p. 62; and see the whole passage on pp. 61 and 62.

lifetime, and that it was based on a document about Patrick, but not a connected life of him, by Aedh himself. Tirechan's memoirs, it was thought, were probably written later than Muirchu's work, but not much later. McNeill thought that the chapters in Irish in the *Book of Armagh* relating to Leinster were written by Bishop Aedh, and the *Additions* to Tirechan's work were not written by the scribe Ferdomnach, but represent material complied by Tirechan himself, though not framed into a narrative, in order to complete his account of Patrick. Tirechan can be dated from a reference he makes to *mortalitates novissimas*, which probably means the bubonic plague of 664–5.[1] McNeill's own research and that of others was designed to demonstrate that the *Vita Tripartita* derives from a period perhaps as early as 700. The spelling of the present text was thought to have been altered to accord with that of a later day, but the older text behind it was probably written by Tirechan himself, early in the eighth century. The *Vita Tripartita* is, on this view, largely an expansion and continuation of Tirechan's earlier memoirs.[2]

Grosjean tried to improve and refine upon these findings. He concluded that when the scribe Ferdomnach at the beginning of the *Book of Armagh* refers to the *Libri Sancti Patricii* he meant all the ancient documents preserved during the seventh or eighth centuries in the archives of Armagh, except the *Vita Tripartita*, which, as the official account of the saint's life, would be preserved in a different manuscript suitable for reading aloud in its three parts on the three days of the annual commemoration of St. Patrick.[3] Though much of the *Vita Tripartita* is in Irish, he thought that it was originally written in Latin, and the Irish was a translation of the Latin.[4] Grosjean enforced with arguments the conjecture originally made by Gwynn

---

[1] McNeill, *St. Patrick*, essay on 'The Earliest Lives of Patrick', especially pp. 118–19 and 126–34, and Part iii, 'Dates of Texts in the Book of Armagh relating to Patrick'. For Tirechan's reference to the plague see Stokes, *TL* ii. 314, 12 a 7 (Gwynn 23). But it is possible that the plague should be dated to about 700. Tirechan was a pupil of Bishop Ultan, who is known to have died in the pestilence of 664–5.

[2] McNeill, *St. Patrick*, Part iv, 'The Origins of the Tripartite Life of St. Patrick'; and Part v, 'Later Accretions to the *Vita Tripartita*'. There are some additions to the *Vita Tripartita* later than Tirechan's time, and McNeill details them.

[3] 'Notes sur les Documents Anciens concernant S. Patrice', p. 51.

[4] Ibid., p. 59.

that the *Notulae*, or headings, which follow the *Additions* to Tirechan's work in the *Book of Armagh* were indices made by Tirechan himself to assist in sorting the material included in the *Vita Tripartita*, and were included by Ferdomnach because he was ordered to copy *all* the documents about Patrick in the archives of Armagh, except the *Vita Tripartita*. Our *Vita Tripartita* is not Ferdomnach's, which was at Armagh, but another (later and modified) copy coming from some other centre.[1]

Analysis of the material in the *Book of Armagh* and the *Vita Tripartita* along these lines, which explains their relationship to each other as almost contemporary documents, has nevertheless to face serious obstacles. It is very difficult to allow the contention of McNeill and Grosjean that the Irish of the *Vita Tripartita* is contemporary with the careers of Muirchu and Tirechan, and quite as difficult to accept Grosjean's view that the Irish of the *Vita Tripartita* is a translation from an original Latin. In fact both O'Rahilly and Binchy confidently dismiss such ideas. O'Rahilly says that the *Vita* could not have been composed before the second half of the ninth century,[2] and Binchy dates it two centuries later than the narratives of Muirchu and Tirechan.[3] It certainly gives the impression, even to a superficial observer, that its version of the Patrick legend is considerably more developed, and therefore presumably later, than that of these two writers. For the theory that it represents a translation from the Irish there is really no solid evidence, and Grosjean scarcely offers any. Again, we have seen that the theory that Bishop Aedh of Sletty composed the *Génair Patraic* in the second half of the seventh century has been strongly challenged. It cannot be said that the work of McNeill, Grosjean, and those who have adopted their point of view on the *Book of Armagh* and the *Vita Tripartita*, has carried the question of the historical worth of the later traditions about Patrick much nearer solution.

Study of the material in the *Book of Armagh* and the *Vita Tripartita* may eventually help towards answering the question which must next be investigated, whether we can identify

---

[1] Ibid., pp. 66–70.
[2] *Early Irish History and Mythology*, p. 409.
[3] 'The Fair of Tailtu and the Feast of Tara', p. 128.

among these later traditions an early connected *Life of Patrick*,
or any similar piece of literature, embodied in a single document of the sixth, or even of the fifth, century, which could
justify us in trusting the reliability of some or most of the facts
alleged in these stones, or whether we can confidently assume
its existence, even though we cannot now recover or reconstruct it. It must be admitted, however, that the analysis of
the contents of these two books does not encourage the discerning reader to hope that such a document can be found or
assumed. But this has not deterred several scholars from finding
such a source. Ryan, referring, it is true, to the Annals and not
to the later tradition, has spoken of 'an old Irish chronicle
reaching from A.D. 437 to 661'.[1] Meissner thought that a
'British source' lay behind the Lives of Patrick.[2] O'Rahilly
believed that some of the facts related by Muirchu and Tirechan 'must ultimately go back to a written document embodying information obtained in Gaul not later than the seventh
century, by some monk who had visited Auxerre and had had
access to the church records preserved there'.[3] If this is so, it is
curious that the monk Constantius, who wrote his *Vita Germani*
before 480, and who must have had access to the church
records of Auxerre, either did not know of any records of
Germanus's contact with Patrick, or did not make use of them.
Carney has been anxious to see behind Tirechan's narrative a
source of information deriving in unbroken continuity from
Patrick himself. Tirechan relied upon the narrative of Bishop
Ultan. Ultan (according to the *Martyrology of Oengus*, under
4 September) was Abbot of the monastery of Louth in 630. This
monastery had, according to tradition, been founded by St.
Mochtae or Mocteus, who (according to tradition) was a
disciple of St. Patrick and died in 535.[4] As an addition to this
rather frail argument there could be added the reference to
St. Mochtae in Adomnan's *Vita Columbae*:

    [1] *Irish Monasticism*, p. 75. He also believes that Muirchu's and Tirechan's
accounts 'go back to a common, but distant, source, which can hardly be placed
later than the middle of the sixth century and may be many years earlier' (ibid.,
p. 74, following Gwynn, *Book of Armagh*, Introd. lii).
    [2] So Grosjean, 'Notes d'hagiographie celtique' (1945), pp. 112–22; Grosjean in
these pages shows how unlikely this theory is.
    [3] *The Two Patricks*, pp. 18–19.
    [4] *The Problem of Patrick*, pp. 26–27; see also pp. 155–6.

nam quidam proselytus brito homo sanctus sancti Patricii episcopi discipulus Maucteus nomine ita de nostro profetizavit patrono sicuti nobis ab antiquis traditum expertis conpertum habetur. 'In novissimis', ait, 'saeculi temporibus filius nasciturus est cuius nomen Columba per omnes insularum ociani provincias devulgabitur notum, novissimaque orbis tempora clare inlustrabit. Mei et ipsius duorum monasteriolorum agelluli unius sepisculae [hedge] intervallo disterminabuntur. Homo valde deo carus et grandis coram ipso meriti.'[1]

It must at the same time be pointed out that if this is a quotation from a document by (or alleged to be by) Mochtae, the quotation is very reminiscent of the type of hagiography represented by Tirechan's *Breviarium* and the *Vita Tripartita*.

The latest attempt to detect a reliable source among the later traditions concerning Patrick has been made by J. Morris in an article, which has already been referred to, called 'The Dates of the Celtic Saints', and if we examine it in some detail we shall be able, perhaps, to reach firmer ground for our conclusions about this point. Morris begins by laying down clear and consistent principles for dealing with this kind of material. The general criterion is 'common sense, and its first precept is that overriding priority must go to the interpretation of contemporary statements, second priority to those which link events in the British Isles with datable and intelligible events in Europe'.[2] A little later he quotes Fustel de Coulanges, the French scholar, to the effect that, though saints' lives have, of course, been elaborated and developed, they are not invented *de novo*: 'We may be certain that the author did not invent, though he added virtues to his hero, he did not imagine the small details of his life. . . . What interests us is not the miracle, but the details that surround it. . . . What we need to look for are the . . . facts that the hagiographer had no incentive to change.'[3]

Later in his article he applies these principles to the work of Muirchu.[4] He distinguishes sharply between the first part of Muirchu's narrative (which is delimited in the *Book of Armagh* by a heading *Finit Primus, Incipit Secundus Liber*), and the

---

[1] Adomnan's *Life of Columba*, ed. A. O. and M. O. Anderson, Second Preface, 3a, p. 182. Incidentally, this is the only mention of Patrick in this work.
[2] 'Celtic Saints', p. 342; see also the whole discussion of criteria, pp. 342-7.
[3] Ibid., p. 347.
[4] Ibid., pp. 365-9.

Second Part.[1] For the Second Part, and for all that Tirechan has to relate, he has little respect, but he values highly the earlier material in Muirchu's work. He describes Muirchu's reproduction of information from the *Confession* and *Epistle* of Patrick as 'sober' and 'scholarly'. He says that in the middle of the matter drawn from these two works Muirchu places 'an equally sober account of Patrick's life in Gaul, at Auxerre, under Amator, whom he did not know to be either Bishop of Auxerre or Germanus's predecessor, and under Germanus, an account which may well derive from the lost writings of Patrick; and a collection of stories drawn from Irish tradition cited on the authority of unreliable authors and fallible memory'.[2] In this part of Muirchu's work Patrick's activity is almost confined to Ulidia (Ulster); Patrick is not described as consecrating any bishops (though he is accompanied by two), except for a muddled story involving bishops in the Isle of Man; and there is no hint that Armagh is his principal church.[3] Finally, Morris writes: 'Muirchu's account is wholly consistent with the *Confessio*; what it adds contains nothing improbable save a wonder-working virtue, that is noticeably less extravagant than that which Adomnan claims for Columba.'[4]

This quotation from the work of Fustel de Coulanges (which was published in 1888) seems to have a strange fascination about it, because it was reproduced by Whitley Stokes in 1890 in the Introduction to his *Lives of the Saints from the Book of Lismore* (pp. xci–xcii), and also by Meissner, in Chapter V, Volume I, of *The History of the Church of Ireland* (pp. 156–7) in 1933. If one reads a number of lives of the Irish saints, such as those to be found in Stokes's work and Plummer's *Vitae Sanctorum Hiberniae*, one can see what de Coulanges means. The background to the lives of the saints mentioned can be reconstructed, as the editors of the lives in their introductions usually do reconstruct it. But this task demands much material and a broad canvas. There is nothing like enough material in the first part of Muirchu's narrative to justify our applying the rule in this case. For his account of Patrick's sojourn on the Continent, at Rome, and

[1] The First Part covers Stokes, *TL* ii. 269–71, 20 a 1–20 a 2 (Gwynn 39–40) and 271–93, 2 a 7–7 a 2 (Gwynn 3–13). The Second Part covers the rest of the work of Muirchu, *TL* ii. 293–301 (Gwynn 14–17). Morris also uses the beginning of Muirchu's narrative, extant only in the Brussels codex.

[2] 'Celtic Saints', p. 366.   [3] Ibid., p. 367.   [4] Ibid., p. 367.

at Auxerre, there is no background material whatever. For his account of Patrick's early life the background is simply the *Confession*. Muirchu does indeed, as Morris says, treat the *Confession*, where it provides a narrative, soberly, but this is clearly because he has no other information. He certainly does not give the impression of supplementing the *Confession* with a continuous source of any sort.

Properly to assess Morris's suggestion, however, we must first note the difficulties that Muirchu himself admits he encountered in discovering satisfactory sources for an account of Patrick. Modelling himself on the evangelist Luke, he begins:

> *Quoniam quidem, mi domine Aido* [Aedh], *multi conati sunt ordinare narrationem utique istam secundum quod patres eorum et qui ministri initio fuerunt sermonis tradiderunt illis, sed propter difficillimum narrationis opus diversasque opiniones et plurimorum plurimas suspiciones, numquam ad unum certumque historiae tramitem pervenierunt; ideo, ni fallor, iuxta hoc nostrum proverbium, ut deducuntur pueri in ambitheatrum, in hoc periculosum et profundum narrationis sanctae pylagus, surgentibus proterve gurgitum aggeribus, inter acutissimos carubdes per ignota aequora insitos, a nullis adhuc lintibus, excepto tantum uno patris mei Coguitosi expertum atque occupatum, ingenoli mei puerilem remi cymbam deduxi.*[1]

And he goes on, as Morris reminds us and as we already have had occasion to note, to complain of 'uncertain sources and defective memory'.[2] This opening does not encourage us to imagine that Muirchu had at his disposal a document or documents that gave clear and early information about the details of the life of Patrick which he is about to relate. If we are to judge by Cogitosus's *Life of St. Bridget*, this is the last thing we could expect of the writings of Muirchu's father (or father in God), and as for 'lost' writings of Patrick himself, not only is there no evidence at all that they ever existed, but the difficulty and embarrassment which Patrick plainly experienced in expressing himself in Latin in his two surviving works do not encourage us to think that he is likely to have written more than these.[3]

---

[1] Stokes, *TL* ii. 269, 20 a 7 (Gwynn 39).

[2] See above, p. 88. Todd had already noticed the unsatisfactory nature of Muirchu's sources (*Patrick, Apostle*, p. 402).

[3] For Cogitosus's *Sanctae Brigidae Virginis Vita* see *PL* 72. 775–90. There are lives of Bridget in the *Book of Lismore* and in the *Acta Sanctorum Hiberniae*, but they are clearly later than that of Cogitosus.

If we go on to analyse Muirchu's account of Palladius and Patrick, we shall find in them a number of glaring inconsistencies. Why, for instance, should Palladius have abandoned his mission to Ireland simply because *neque hii feri et inmites homines facile receperunt doctrinam eius, neque et ipse voluit transegere tempus in terra non sua?*[1] If Palladius did not want to spend his time in a foreign land, why did he set out at all? Again, Muirchu tells us that Patrick and his companions had already set out (apparently for Ireland) under Germanus's inspiration, but that on hearing the news of Palladius's death in *Ebmoria* (wherever that may be) they turned aside and successfully sought ordination at the hands of someone who should probably be recognized as Amator (Germanus's predecessor in the see of Auxerre, *ob.* 418), and that Patrick went to Ireland, accompanied by two other bishops, Auxilius and Iserninus.[2] Even if we rationalize this into assuming that Amator ordained Patrick deacon or presbyter, and Germanus later consecrated him bishop, how are we to imagine that a bishop in Auxerre, a not very large town in the middle of Gaul, should consecrate a bishop for Ireland, which was nowhere near his own see and was manifestly within the sphere of missionary activity of the Church of Britain? Neither Amator nor Germanus was a pope of Rome, who could do such things. Besides, it is quite clear from Patrick's *Confession* that he was consecrated a bishop and sent to Ireland from Britain, and not from Gaul.[3] It is equally clear from both *Confession* and *Epistle* that Patrick after many years as a bishop in Ireland had no other bishops with him. The best that we can say is that this jumbled narrative somehow connects Patrick, not with Auxerre, but with the names of Amator and his successor Germanus. But it is not difficult to explain this fact without positing the existence of 'lost' writings of Patrick from which knowledge of this association could stem. The names of Amator and of Germanus were widely current in folk-lore, and not least in British folk-lore, of the sixth and seventh centuries. We have seen how great a figure Germanus cut in this milieu.[4] There is extant a wholly legendary life of Amator, to be dated to the end of the sixth century. All that

---

[1] Stokes, 272, 20 a 1 (Gwynn 3).
[2] Ibid., 272, 273, 20 a 1 and 3 (Gwynn 3).
[3] See below, pp. 128–35.   [4] See above, pp. 47–52.

we have in Muirchu is a development on Irish soil of the legends of the two men.[1] If we resume Muirchu's narrative,[2] we find that Patrick puts in first at Inver Dea near the modern Wicklow and then, no reason for the sudden change of plan being given, decides to visit his old master, Milchu, in Ulster, and so sets off again by boat and lands at Saul. After meeting the swineherd *Dichu*, Patrick sets out for Slemish. This is the place where he had seen the angel Victor while he was in captivity, *presso vestigio in petra alterius montis*.[3] Here we have a clear contradiction of the *Confession*, for if Muirchu and Tirechan had not described Patrick's placed of captivity as Slemish, in Co. Antrim, it would never have occurred to anybody that the place was not 'the wood of Foclut, near the western sea', which is the place from which, in Patrick's vision described in his *Confession*, the people of Ireland were calling him to 'come and walk *again*[4] among us' (23). Wherever the wood of Foclut was (and there is no reason to doubt Tirechan's statement that it was in Tirawley, on the borders of Sligo and Mayo),[5] if it was 'near the western sea', it was not in Co. Antrim. If we are to say that there was a local tradition at Inver Dea that Patrick had landed there, and another at Saul that he had landed near there, and that a natural depression in some rock on Slieve Miss (which probably had had its aetiological legend long before Patrick's day) had attracted a story about Patrick's angel having stood there, we shall be nearer the mark. Finally, we shall look briefly at the story of how Daire came to

---

[1] 'His method of proceeding was very simple. It was to follow the *Confession* a certain way, and then tack on the legendary matter' (Olden, *The Church of Ireland*, p. 412).

[2] I omit in the text a treatment of Muirchu's account of Loeghaire as *imperator barbarorum regnans in Temoria*, i.e. Tara, Stokes, *TL* ii. 3 b 1, 273–4 (Gwynn 3–4), though I believe it to be inconsistent with the *Confession*, which knows of *reges* and *reguli* and a British *tyrannus*, but of no single *rex Hiberniae* or *imperator Hiberionacum*. I believe, too, that we must accept the verdict of experts such as O'Rahilly and Binchy that no regularly recurring festival held at Tara existed in the fifth century, and that Tara was not the headquarters of a King of Ireland in that period.

[3] Stokes, *TL* ii. 275, 276, 2 b 1 (Gwynn 4, 5). Todd had already remarked upon the suspicious similarity between Palladius's brief visit to Wicklow and that of Patrick (*Patrick, Apostle*, pp. 338–9).

[4] *Adhuc*, of which 'once again' is a perfectly well-attested meaning in Blaise; cf. *Confession* 21 *et iterum post annos multos* adhuc [again] *capturam dedi*.

[5] Stokes, *TL* ii. 326, 14 b 2 (Gwynn 28).

give Patrick land at Armagh, as Muirchu tells it.[1] It is difficult to see how the details of this account of a miraculous killing by Patrick of Daire and his horse, and their miraculous restitution to life again, followed by a grant to Patrick by Daire of the particular piece of elevated ground upon which he wanted to build a church at Armagh, could be described as historical as far as the details surrounding the miracle are concerned. On the contrary, Patrick is here represented as overbearing, self-confident, truculent, and irritable, whereas his writing reveals him as very anxious not to give offence or cause persecution for the Church. By far the most likely explanation is that this is a typical piece of folk-lore, like most of the other stories in Muirchu or Tirechan's *Breviarium* and the *Vita Tripartita*, and that there lies behind it a (quite possibly authentic) local tradition at Armagh that Patrick founded a church there and that Daire gave the land for it. There is no need to call in a 'lost' writing of Patrick to explain this story, or any other part of Muirchu's narrative, for that matter.

One significant fact has, however, emerged from this examination of Morris's theory, and this is the importance of local traditions in supplying the material for the later stories about Patrick. Tirechan seems to have derived his information, about Patrick's life before he reached Ireland, from the compilation of a Bishop Ultan,[2] where he was not using Patrick's own works. Ultan, according to Gwynn,[3] can hardly have written before the year 657, and the information which is derived from him appears to be nothing more than the sort of embroidery of facts to be found in the *Confession* which we have already encountered in the Hymn *Génair Patraic* and in Muirchu. From the moment in Tirechan's account that Patrick reaches Ireland as a bishop it looks very much as if the source of his information, apart from Patrick's *Confession* and *Epistle* (if, indeed, he knew the latter) was simply local tradition.

---

[1] Stokes, *TL* ii. 290–2, 6 b 2–7 a 2 (Gwynn 12–13).

[2] See above, p. 79. Cf. also Tirechan's words at the beginning of his Second Book, *pauca quae inveni in utilitatem laboris mei a senioribus multis ac ab illo Ultano*: Stokes, *TL* ii. 311, 11 a 1 (Gwynn 21).

[3] *Book of Armagh*, Introd. xlv. Gwynn did not think Tirechan had any connected account of Patrick's itinerary before him (Introd. lix). For other estimates of Tirechan's sources, see Esposito, 'The Patrician Problem and a Possible Solution', p. 133, and Binchy, *PB*, p. 67.

No reconstruction of the process of composition of the Patrician material in the *Book of Armagh* and the *Vita Tripartita* is likely seriously to contradict this conclusion.

Those who have devoted some time to the study of the New Testament will be familiar with the technique of Form Criticism, employed by scholars who are investigating the history of the transmission of the material that finally appeared in the Synoptic Gospels. These scholars ask themselves the question, In what form did the material circulate when it was being transmitted orally, before it was written down? And they also ask the question, What motives caused the early Christian community to select for preservation the material which did ultimately survive? To the first question the answer they return is that at any rate a large part of the material during the oral period survived in separate, independent units that all tended to have a common form, or a relatively small number of common forms. And to the second question they answer that the criterion for preserving the material used, consciously or unconsciously, by the early Christian community was the *Sitz im Leben* of that community, the circumstances and requirements of the life which it found itself living. It is possible that we can with advantage employ a not dissimilar technique of Form Criticism to the later traditions about Patrick. We must, of course, allow for a difference between the two cases. The lapse of time between the alleged events and the writing down of them is far longer in the case of the Patrician material, two hundred years, instead of the two or three decades in the case of the Synoptic Gospels material, and in the case of the Gospels there is nothing corresponding to the *Confession* and *Epistle* written by Patrick himself. These two documents must from the very beginning have played a part both in fostering the memory and the cult of Patrick and in controlling the later tradition about him. But for the Patrician material we have a period at which the material was written down and we have an earlier period when it was circulating in oral form, and it is possible to identify two of the forms in which that oral tradition was circulating. If, as seems very likely, the search for an early connected reliable document about the details of Patrick's life apart from the *Confession* and *Epistle* is a search for a will-o'-the-wisp, then we can identify the seventh century as the period when the tradition was

written down, largely in response to contemporary ecclesiastical
and even political needs, and regard the period 450–650 as
the time during which the material was circulating in oral
form. And we can identify the two forms in which it is likely to
have circulated, the form of isolated traditions about Patrick
associated with different churches, and the form of folk-lore
stories connecting Patrick with some great person who had
left an impression on the popular mind—Amator or Germanus
or Pope Celestine or Loeghaire. It was these isolated units of
tradition, circulating in such forms as those outlined here, that
were available for weaving into a connected narrative, with
the aid of the *Confession* and *Letters*, for these writers who in the
seventh century essayed the task of producing a *Vita Patricii*,
Aedh or Ultan or Cogitosus or Muirchu or Tirechan. But our
analysis of the subject suggests plainly that we must agree with
Binchy that these were the only materials available to these
writers.[1]

That the seventh century witnessed a movement to put in
written form the lives of saints and of some of the heroes of the
earlier history of the Celtic nations in the British Isles in more
than one centre, and not in Ireland only, is strongly suggested
by the work done on Nennius's history and on the *Annales
Cambriae* in recent years by such scholars as Norah Chadwick
and K. Jackson.[2] Norah Chadwick can write of the seventh
century as 'the period at which . . . the supporters of the
Anglo-Roman party in the Celtic Church were beginning to
write the *Vitae* of important saints'.[3] Again and again information sieved from Nennius or some similar source goes back to the
seventh century. It appears to have been a period of intensive
writing after a period of about 150 years of comparative
silence, broken only by such rare voices as those of Gildas.
This may well account for the curious silence about Patrick
which follows immediately upon his death and lasts for well over
a century, a silence commented upon by more than one writer.[4]

---

[1] Binchy, *PB*, pp. 9, 67, 75, 157.

[2] See *SBH*, *SBC*, *CS*, and *CB*, and in particular K. Jackson's essay in *CS* on 'The
Northern British Section in Nennius'.

[3] *SBC*, p. 113. A parallel can be observed in the history of the material for a *Life
of Ninian*, though it occurs over a different time-schedule, according to MacQueen;
see *St. Nynia*, p. 85.

[4] e.g. Binchy, *PB*, pp. 178–9.

The question of where exactly this material circulated in the period of its oral transmission, and of its historical value, is a very difficult one to decide. In the composite volume she edited, called *Celt and Saxon*, Norah Chadwick, after remarking that, in the case of Nennius's *Historia Brittonum* it is not until the seventh century that we can detect written Latin sources, observes that among Celtic peoples the vernacular hardly appears to have been written before that century, 'except for lapidary funeral inscriptions of the briefest nature'. All information was carried by oral transmission. As far as the centres in Wales and north Britain from which the information in Nennius's compilation ultimately derives are concerned, Norah Chadwick thinks (no doubt justly) that the main transmitters must have been a class of professional bards, and that the value of the tradition thus transmitted was relatively high.[1] But the nature of the Patrician traditional material does not suggest that it was preserved by a class of professional bards. There are not many long genealogies; there are very few old poems or fragments of verse; there are virtually no descriptions of battles or of their results; there are not even many kings involved in these stories. The genre of literature into which the Patrician material falls is hagiography, which is not likely to have been extensively handled by professional bards, but was no doubt preserved and transmitted in ecclesiastical circles. Now, this genre of literature, though it has great literary charm and is often useful as a reflection of the social and religious ideas of the age in which it circulated, is notoriously a stranger to historical accuracy or historical perspective. 'With the luminous exception of Adomnan,' says Binchy, 'no biographer of an Irish saint can be regarded as a genuine historical witness.'[2] From the *Catalogus Sanctorum Hiberniae*[3] onwards most early medieval saints' lives, and especially Irish saints' lives, are almost

---

[1] *CS*, p. 2.

[2] *PB*, p. 56. For a brilliant description of the methods, assumptions, and rationale of Irish saints' lives, see Kenney, *Sources*, pp. 291–304.

[3] For a recent and very useful edition of this short but interesting document, see Grosjean, 'Édition et commentaire du *Catalogus Sanctorum Hiberniae secundum diversa tempora* ou *De Tribus Ordinibus Sanctorum Hiberniae*'. Grosjean (in sharp contrast to Ryan, *Irish Monasticism*, p. 185) does not rate the historical value of this work at all highly, and gives good reason for thinking that it should be dated to the ninth or tenth century rather than to the eighth, where Todd and Haddan and Stubbs had placed it.

worthless as sources of historical information.[1] We must not, of course, dismiss such material out of hand. Even Binchy allows that 'Tirechan's work is least likely to have been contaminated by folk-lore where he cites the names of these local kings and magnates who granted land to Patrick or his helpers on which to found a church; among a people so steeped in genealogical lore the memory of events associated with the ancestors of their rulers would long survive'.[2] And oral tradition of a very elementary sort associated with places tends to survive intact longer than other forms of oral tradition.[3] But still it remains an extremely difficult and delicate operation to compare the later traditions about Patrick with the information which can be gleaned from his authentic works, for the two are not strictly comparable, certainly not in such a way that statements made, for instance, by Muirchu and Tirechan can usually be put side by side with statements made by Patrick himself, in order to supplement or explain or even to correct Patrick's words, which is the method used by the great majority of Patrician scholars hitherto. It is time for another method, using different criteria, to be tried.

3. *Entries about St. Patrick in the Irish Annals*

Muirchu makes no attempt to give an absolute dating to Patrick's career, but only gives internal indications of time in his account of various stages in Patrick's life; and he tells us that Patrick died at the age of 111.[4] But Tirechan does make this attempt. He tells us, first, that Patrick died 436 years after the Lord's Passion, by which he apparently intends the date 461,[5] and later, in a curious addition at the end of the second division of his material, he tells us *Tertio decimo anno Teothosii imperatoris a Celestino episcopo papa Romae Patricius episcopus ad doctrinam Scottorum mittitur.* Two sentences later, this passage continues: *Paladius episcopus primus mittitur, qui Patricius alio nomine appellabatur, qui martyrium passus est apud Scottos, ut tradunt*

---

[1] For a list of the sources for these Irish medieval saints' lives see Meissner, *History of the Church of Ireland*, vol. i, pp. 155–7, and Morris, 'Celtic Saints', p. 345, n. 1.   [2] *PB*, p. 67.

[3] See R. P. C. Hanson, *Tradition in the Early Church*, p. 21.

[4] Stokes, *TL* ii. 300, 8 b 2 (Gwynn 16).

[5] Ibid., 302, 9 a 2 (Gwynn 17).

sancti antiqui. Deinde Patricius secundus ab anguelo Dei, Victor nomine, et a Celestino papa mittitur, cui Hibernia tota credidit, qui eam pene totam baptizavit.[1] Most scholars emend *tertio decimo* to *octavo decimo*, on the assumption that when these numbers were in Roman numerals in the manuscript the figure xiii was mistakenly written for xviii, though if Ferdomnach was copying Tirechan's original manuscript this seems difficult to believe. Tirechan tells us that Patrick died aged 120 years.[2] It seems likely that his absolute dating for Patrick was taken from some contemporary annalistic source.[3] The *Vita Tripartita*, though it agrees that Pope Celestine sent Patrick, and that he lived for 120 years, does not essay any other absolute dating for his career.

That there were in existence in Tirechan's day annals giving the dates of important events in Irish history, secular and ecclesiastical, in which occasional links with historical events on the continent were provided, is certain, for we have considerable remains of the later successors of these annals in our hands.[4] Those of them that date Patrick's arrival in Ireland as a bishop unanimously give the year 432. Most of them record that he lived to be 120, but they differ considerably about the date of Patrick's death, not only among themselves, but sometimes a single source differs within itself. For instance, the *Chronicum Scottorum* records against 457 *Dormitatio sancti senis Patricii, id est Glosdoniensis* (Glastonbury) *ecclesiae*, against 465 *Quies Benigni successoris Patricii*, and against 489 the death of *Patricius Archiepiscopus et Apostolus Hibernensium*, but it subjoins to this a verse in Irish which dates Patrick's death to 493. The Annals from the *Book of Leinster* record against the year 457 *Secundinus et senex Patricius quieverunt*, and against the year 507 *Patricius Scottorum episcopus quievit*. The *Annals of Ulster* have against the year 457 *Quies senis Patricii ut alii libri dicunt*, and against 461 *Hic alii quietem Patricii dicunt*, but against the year 493 they record the death of 'Patrick archbishop of the Irish'

---

[1] Stokes, 332, 15 b 2 (Gwynn 31). For remarks on the subject of the 'second Patrick' see below, pp. 189–92.   [2] Stokes, *TL* ii. 331, 15 b 1 (Gwynn 30).

[3] The *Luxeuil Calendar*, which dates from the end of the seventh century and is therefore contemporary with Tirechan, has the following entry: *xvi Cal. Apr. Depositio S. Patricii episcopi.*

[4] See the Appendix, pp. 210-14 below, for an account of these Annals and a reproduction of the material in them relevant to Patrick.

again, in solemn form. Tigernach's *Annals* also place his death in 493. Most of the entries in the Irish Annals concerned with Patrick are in Latin, though a few are in Irish. There are, too, entries which mention names alleged by the later tradition to be associated with Patrick, such as Secundus, Auxilius, Iserninus, and Benignus. The compilers of all these Annals certainly had at their disposal some ecclesiastical histories composed by early Fathers, such as those of Jerome and the *Chronicle* of Prosper.

It is not easy to conjecture how reliable are the entries in these annals relating to the fifth, or the sixth, century, nor from what precise sources the annalists can have gained their information. Some scholars have claimed that annalistic writing was actually taking place in the fifth century. Bury had thought that behind some of the Annals was a calendar primarily designed to calculate the date of Easter, with records of various events added to the calendrical material, and that this calendar derived from one which Patrick himself had brought to Ireland. In support of this view he cited the words of Abbot Cummian to Abbot Segene in 632 or 634: *cyclo illo quem sanctus Patricius, papa noster, tulit et fecit.*[1] Ryan, as we have seen, appears to suggest that the source of the *Annals of Ulster* may derive from that period.[2] O'Rahilly was not as optimistic as this; he believed that all Irish Annals dealing with the fifth and sixth centuries go back to a common original, 'which was a compilation made *ca* 740 by an unknown monk, possibly in Bangor, Co. Down, from various local records, supplemented by certain foreign chronicles'. But behind this some of the information preserved 'presumably reproduces an entry made in a fifth-century Paschal table or other church record'.[3] Nevertheless, O'Rahilly described the authority of the Annals for reconstructing Patrick's career as 'paramount',[4] Kenney, on the other hand, believed that no entries in the *Annals of Ulster* were written earlier than the eighth century.[5] Norah Chadwick tells us in a recent book that

[1] *LP*, p. 283. For this quotation, see above, p. 66.   [2] See above, p. 86.
[3] *The Two Patricks*, p. 12. See also *Early Irish History and Mythology*, pp. 251–2s 253–9, where he gives his reasons for this belief. He suggested that Palladiu, brought a copy of Prosper's *Chronicle* with him to Ireland. See also Kathleen Hughes, *The Church in Early Irish Society*, pp. 65–68.
[4] Ibid., p. 16. Bieler (*Life and Legend*, pp. 80–91) is much more cautious.
[5] *Sources*, p. 373.

'The earliest part of the *Annales Cambriae* . . . does not represent contemporary annals recorded in Wales, but is believed to have been compiled from a lost chronicle, on which the principal sets of Irish annals are also based—the *Annals of Ulster*, of Tigernach (from Clonmacnoise), and of Innisfallen (from Munster)',[1] but she would hardly place this lost chronicle as early as the fifth, or even as the sixth, century.[2] She is, however, convinced that behind this written annalistic tradition lay an oral tradition. 'Though the compilation of the Irish annals in their present form', she says, 'was no earlier than the seventh century, they are derived in part from oral tradition carefully preserved by a strictly regulated professional class.'[3] Earlier, H. M. Chadwick had similarly believed that though the entries in the Irish Annals relating to the fifth century must be regarded as relying on oral tradition, still this oral tradition should not be lightly disregarded.[4] 'In the fifth century', he wrote, 'the Annals are still largely derived from oral tradition. But from 431–2 there is a considerable ecclesiastical element relating to Ireland which would seem to come from early, though perhaps not strictly contemporary, written records.'[5]

The most recent writer on this subject, Morris, believes that the origin of the Irish Annals is a document or documents in which items taken from native tradition were inserted into a copy of the *Chronicle* of Isidore of Seville, which ends in 612. The important question is, How did the annalists correlate native tradition with the events of Isidore's *Chronicle*? Clearly the date round which all the other dates were orientated was 432, the date of Patrick's arrival in Ireland as bishop.[6] Morris believes that Patrick was sent by Pope Celestine as a successor to Palladius,[7] though he allows that it was at a British synod that

---

[1] *CS*, p. 16.

[2] As a parallel we may cite the conclusion of K. Jackson that behind the Northern Section of Nennius's *Historia Brittonum* there lies some such document as 'the marginal entries of contemporary events made on the pages of a Paschal Table, or some kind of brief chronicle, scarcely to be dignified as "Annals" ' (*CS*, pp. 48–49; cf. pp. 49–54). Jackson suggests that the earliest nucleus of this document may have appeared from the pen of Rhun, son of Urbgen, *c.* 625 or 635.

[3] *CB*, pp. 17–18.　　　　　　　[4] *Early Scotland*, pp. 133–6.

[5] Ibid., p. 135.　　　　　　[6] Morris, 'Celtic Saints', pp. 365, 368–9.

[7] Just as 'the first bishop constituted to the Irish had been appointed by the Pope', so 'it was inconceivable that a later bishop should be consecrated without his approval', ibid., p. 361.

Patrick was appointed bishop. We shall find reason later to regard it as overwhelmingly unlikely that Pope Celestine should have sent Patrick,[1] and we may view with scepticism a theory which in the fifth century brings Patrick, after being chosen as bishop in Britain, to Rome for consecration, or alternatively introduces a papal *congé d'élire* into the appointment of bishops in Britain. And we may ask why Patrick did not introduce into his *Confession*, against those who were impugning his right to be bishop of the Irish, the stunning argument that the pope himself had appointed him. But we must move on to consider the theory which Morris advances, relying partly upon the conclusion that Patrick had been appointed by Pope Celestine, but partly upon some entries in the Irish Annals, because an investigation of this theory will help us towards a better understanding of the value of these Annals. Several of the Annals record an event which they call *Probatio Patricii* in or about the reign of Pope Leo I (440–61).[2] Morris accepts these entries as giving us authentic information: 'The entry is the more significant because there is no attempt to explain its meaning; it plays no part whatever in the Patrician writers, though it is grist to their mill, and could not but have been heavily exploited by them if they had understood what it meant. Its origin is therefore old enough for its purport to have been forgotten by the latter part of the seventh century.'[3] One would think that a much simpler explanation was that those who were compiling tradition about Patrick at the end of the seventh century omitted to mention a *Probatio Patricii* by Pope Leo because the incident had not yet been invented, not because they knew of the entry but could make nothing of it.[4] But Morris thinks that these

[1] See below, pp. 141, 145.

[2] *Annals of Ulster* under the year 441, *Leo ordinatus xiii Romanae ecclesiae episcopus et probatus est in fide Catolica Patricius episcopus*; and under 443, *Patricius episcopus ardore fidei et doctrina Christi florens in nostra provincia*. *Annals of Innisfallen* against the year 442 have *Probatio sancti Patricii in fide Catholica*. The *Annals of Clonmacnoise* record that Patrick was approved in the Catholic religion by Pope Leo (against the year 427), and by the rest of the popes who succeeded in his time. These entries have, of course, also been noticed by earlier scholars, e.g. Todd (*Patrick, Apostle* pp. 469–70), Kenney (*Sources*, p. 168), McNeill (*St. Patrick*, pp. 80, 84), and O'Rahilly (*Early Irish History and Mythology*, pp. 250–1).

[3] Morris, 'Celtic Saints', p. 364. Morris refers to this theory briefly in 'Dark Age Dates', pp. 162–3 and 182.

[4] A further piece of evidence against this view is Patrick's emphasis, visible throughout his *Confession*, that he has been appointed by God and is a representative

entries mean that Patrick, attacked by opponents in Britain, appealed to Leo, and that the appeal, forwarded through Patrick's friends in Gaul, was upheld by Leo, who confirmed him in his episcopate. Leo followed a policy of dealing with individual bishops above the heads of synods and metropolitans. The second visit of Germanus to Britain (dated by Morris 444) and his later visit to Ravenna would have formed an occasion of the appeal's being forwarded.[1] Morris, of course, accepts 432 as the date of Patrick's arrival in Ireland as bishop. The appeal took place after the writing of the *Confession*.

It can at once be pointed out that, on Morris's own chronology for the events of Patrick's career, an appeal to Leo in 441, 442, 444, or even 446 is virtually impossible. In his *Epistle*, Chapter 3, Patrick tells us that he had a few days before writing sent to the soldiers of Coroticus an *epistolam cum sancto presbytero quem ego ex infantia docui*. The presbyter must have been at least thirty years old; thirty-five would be a more likely guess.[2] Patrick must therefore have known him for at least twenty years, and possibly longer; but he can hardly have begun teaching him, or encountered him as a child, until he arrived in Ireland; we cannot assume that Patrick had begun teaching him before his arrival in Ireland as a bishop; clearly the presbyter, first as a boy and then as a young man, was one of the *familia* of Bishop Patrick. This means that the date when Patrick sent this presbyter to the soldiers of Coroticus cannot be earlier than 452, and may well be later, if Patrick reached Ireland as bishop on 432. The vast majority of scholars agree that the *Confession* was written after the *Epistle to Coroticus*, and with good reason, as will be shown later.[3] The alleged appeal

---

of God, e.g. *Conf.* 56 *Deo meo pro quo legationem fungor* (cf. 46). It is not, of course, incompatible with this emphasis that he should have been appointed by the Pope. What is incompatible is that he should not allude to this appointment.

[1] Ibid., pp. 364–5; cf. p. 372.

[2] Pope Siricius in 384 sets out the ages suitable for ordination: acolyte or subdeacon, at least thirty years; deacon, some age later than that; presbyter, five years later (than deacon or subdeacon); bishop ten years later (than subdeacon, deacon, or presbyter); see *Ep.* i. 13. ix (1142–3).

[3] See below, pp. 106–7. If, distinctly against the evidence, the *Epistle* is to be dated after the *Confession*, then we must ask whether it is conceivable that Patrick, who had just had an unpleasant controversy with British bishops, ending with his being confirmed as Bishop of the Irish by Leo, would afterwards have invited fresh trouble by excommunicating Coroticus and his soldiers, who were British

to Leo, therefore, which Morris places, of necessity, after the composition of the *Confession* (for the *Confession* shows not the slightest knowledge of it), must have taken place well after the year 452, probably many years after it. This agrees neither with the dates assigned to the *Probatio Patricii* by the Irish Annals, nor with the date for it designed by Morris to fit in with Germanus's second visit to Britain and later visit to Ravenna.

Next, we must question Morris's translation of the word *Probatio*. The word can mean 'approval' in classical Latin. But Blaise, who gives the uses of it in ecclesiastical and late Latin, gives only the meanings 'testing' and 'proof or demonstration' for it, and not that of 'approval'. For the sense which Morris attributes to it one would expect some such word as *confirmatio* or *vindicatio*. The word *confirmatio* is in fact used by Gregory the Great for the confirmation of a bishop in his see. Morris remarks that the word did not have any significance for those who were compiling traditions about Patrick in the seventh century. It is doubtful if it would have had any significance for writers even in the fifth century, if we are to give it the meaning of 'confirmation'.

But in fact it is not difficult to account both for this entry and for the date to which it is assigned in the Irish Annals. The annalists of the seventh and later centuries certainly had at their disposal the text of Patrick's *Confession*, and also, among other ecclesiastical documents, a list of the Bishops of Rome, with their regnal dates and notes of some of the events which distinguished their reigns. In the thirtieth chapter of Patrick's *Confession* an annalist could have read the words *fides mea probata est coram Deo et hominibus*, and if he wanted to give a general description of the successful emergence of Patrick from the accusations and trials described in this part of the *Confession*, the annalist might well have taken *Probatio Patricii* as a title to describe it. At the same time he might have been anxious to link Patrick with the very eminent Pope Leo I, and have found no better date to assign to this meeting between the two men than the year of Leo's accession to the papacy, or what

Christians under the jurisdiction of British bishops. It is much more likely that it was this excommunication that started the trouble for Patrick, than that it took place after the attack on Patrick's status. It is scarcely conceivable, anyway, that if by the time Patrick wrote *Epistle*, cap. 6 he had been confirmed by Leo, he should have omitted to mention this fact.

the annalist thought was that year. This embroidery upon the text of the *Confession* is exactly in the style of the compilers of the later tradition about Patrick, who, we may confidently conjecture, were much the same sort of people as the compilers of the early Irish Annals. This stage of development of legend must be dated after the period when the works of Muirchu and Tirechan were produced, for they evince no knowledge of it. But the legend that Patrick had visited Rome several times, which appears in the *Vita Tripartita*, would have helped towards the formation of the legend of the *Probatio Patricii* by Leo. Indeed, we may suspect that the assigning of the year 461 for Patrick's death by Tirechan and by the *Annals of Ulster* may arise from a similar desire to make Patrick's death coincide with the date of the death of Pope Leo (461). This may even account for the curious references to the demise of *senex Patricius* under 457 in the *Chronicum Scottorum* and the Annals from the *Book of Leinster*.

This investigation of the legend of the *Probatio Patricii* may afford us a clue to the nature of entries relating to Patrick in the Irish Annals. They were compiled by men who had before them at least the text of the *Confession*, some books relating to the ecclesiastical history of the fifth and later centuries on the Continent, and especially in Rome, and much of the later tradition about Patrick which had begun from the seventh century onwards to find its way into collections such as those of Muirchu and Tirechan. The writers were men who could conduct historical calculations reasonably well, and were anxious as far as possible to produce a presentable account in annalistic form of the chief events in Patrick's career. They could be sure of the year 432, not because they had reliable information that this was the precise year of Patrick's landing in Ireland as bishop, but because they could learn from Prosper's *Chronicle* or some similar source that this was the earliest year that could be assigned to Patrick's arrival, if he was to reach Ireland as bishop after Palladius, and because they knew of several accounts from tradition of Palladius's death. The account varied greatly, but this did not trouble the annalists. In short, the 'considerable ecclesiastical element' observed by H. M. Chadwick in these Annals was only composed by 'a strictly regulated professional class' (in the words of Norah Chadwick), in the sense that it represents the inventions of relatively learned monks instead of the freer and more fantastic inventions of popular folk-lore. On such subjects as fairly recent pestilences these Annals may be trustworthy; the Irish Annals, for instance, record a serious plague between the years 546 and 550, and this can be checked from reference to the gradual approach of this plague across Europe in the years before 546 in Procopius, Gregory of Tours, and other authorities.[1] And there may be incidents in the secular history of Ireland during the fifth century which popular memory had correctly preserved until they reached written form in the Annals, though neither O'Rahilly nor Binchy, as we have seen, give us much reason for thinking so.[2] But we should otherwise view the entries concerning the ecclesiastical history of the fifth century in the Irish Annals with the gravest suspicion.

The investigation of Irish annals is the work of specialists in ancient Celtic studies, and it must not occupy more space in this work. One very eminent specialist in this field, D. A. Binchy, has given excellent reasons for concluding that the whole system of constructing annals based on Paschal Tables could not possibly have existed in Ireland during the fifth century, and can only have been in its infancy during the sixth, if then.[3] This means, of course, that the search for a fifth-century or even a sixth-century *connected source* for the Irish Annals, whether conducted by Bury or by anyone else, is a wild-goose chase.[4] 'I do not believe', says Binchy, 'that there is a single "genuine entry" throughout the whole of the fifth century; and this applies as much to the obit of 461 . . . as to that of 492-3.'[5] If the foregoing discussion of the Annals can be thought to have added a small footnote, explaining how some of those entries could have come about, to Binchy's impressive demolition of

---

[1] So Morris, 'Celtic Saints', pp. 382-3.   [2] See above, pp. 25-27.

[3] *PB*, pp. 70-75. Another, equally eminent, Grosjean, expressed himself in a very similar sense; see *PB*, p. 75, quoting Grosjean, *Analecta Bollandiana*, 63. 110.

[4] Cummian in his letter to Segene would, of course, ascribe to Patrick as traditional author any Paschal Cycle of which he approved and whose immediate origin he could not trace.

[5] *PB*, p. 71. J. V. Kelleher ('Early Irish History and Pseudo-History', p. 122) goes further: 'I believe it can be shewn that everything in the Annals up to about 590 and a large number of entries from thence to 735 (the entry on Bede's death) were either freshly composed or wholly revised not earlier than the latter half of the ninth century.' His theory of the origin of the Annals is well worth study.

existing theories about the Annals, it will have served its purpose.

All literature upon St. Patrick of any considerable extent hitherto has assumed that the evidence to be derived from the *Confession* and the *Epistle* can be handled alongside the evidence from the later tradition and the Annals, so that these last two sources can in some sense and in some particulars supplement and fill out the information coming from Patrick's own hand.[1] In view of the discussion of these last two sources which has occupied this chapter, we shall take a quite different course. We shall try for the next few chapters to look at Patrick entirely without the aid of the later tradition or of the Annals, or, to put the point in another way, we shall divest ourselves of the spectacles through which almost everybody, consciously or unconsciously, has hitherto looked at Patrick. This is not to say that this later information is necessarily worthless in every particular and can be permanently consigned to oblivion. We shall in fact return to it in the last chapter. But the argument here advanced is that in the light of the sources available the Patrician problem is best approached by first considering as carefully as possible those primary documents of whose authenticity we can be sure, studying them without paying any regard to later and less clearly authentic additions to them; and only when this task has been thoroughly tackled returning to look at the information about Patrick which can be gleaned from later tradition and from the Annals. The two collections of information are not comparable in value, and the first must be given an unprejudiced hearing before we listen to the second.

[1] Olden can produce these excellent sentiments: 'It is obvious that the Lives of St. Patrick composed at the present day on the principle of using these religious romances as though of equal authority with the contemporary records must be unsatisfactory. There is no doubt that they preserve many facts of his history, but no criterion has yet been discovered by which the true can be discriminated from the false, and it is, therefore, absolutely necessary to draw a line between them and the original documents' (*The Church of Ireland*, p. 13). But in his subsequent discussion of Patrick he quite fails to observe these principles.

IV

ST. PATRICK'S CAREER

THE first step in any arguments based upon Patrick's own writings, the *Confession* and the *Epistle to Coroticus*, is to decide which of these two works was written first. Some few scholars[1] have suggested that the *Confession* was written before the *Epistle*, but their reasons have all been extrinsic to the two works themselves, because they found it convenient to place the two works in that order, so that they might support their own theories, and were not based upon a careful examination of the documents. Most writers upon Patrick have preferred to assume that the *Confession* was written after the *Epistle*, and for good reasons.[2] In the *Confession* Patrick explicitly says that he is writing at the end of a long and laborious episcopate. The last words are, *et haec est confessio mea antequam moriar* (62). He refers to himself once or twice as an old man,[3] whereas he never describes himself as an old man in the *Epistle*. He has had time to baptize thousands of people.[4] Perhaps most impressive of all are the suggestions to be found in the *Confession* that Patrick has retired from an active life as bishop, even though he is determined to stay in Ireland until his death, by the significant use of the imperfect tense in describing his previous career: he speaks of devout women 'who used to give voluntary gifts and used to throw some of their ornaments on the altar and I used to return them to them and they used to be offended with me because I used to do this'.[5] Or again, 'among you and everywhere I used to travel',[6]

---

[1] e.g. Esposito, 'The Patrician Problem', p. 153.

[2] Among these can be numbered Bieler (*Life and Legend*, pp. 39, 40), Christine Mohrmann, who bases her argument on the rather correcter Latin of the *Epistle* (*Latin*, p. 37), and, as we shall see presently, Grosjean.

[3] *In senectute mea* (10) *post aerumnos et tantas moles, post captivitatem, post annos multos in gentem illam . . . quod ego aliquando in iuventute mea numquam speravi* (15).

[4] *Conf.* 50.

[5] *Conf.* 49, *donabant . . . iactabant . . . reddebam . . . scandalizabantur.*

[6] *Conf.* 51, *inter vos et ubique pergebam.*

'I used to give gifts to kings in addition to the allowance which
I used to give to their sons',[1] 'you yourselves have experienced
how much I paid out to those who used to be judges throughout
all the territories whom I used frequently to visit'.[2] On the
other hand, it is evident that when he wrote the *Epistle* Patrick
had only a few days before baptized and confirmed a large
number of Christians in some neighbouring place, and was
prepared to conduct a vigorous campaign of denunciation
against Coroticus. If we confine ourselves to the evidence of
Patrick's writings, we must conclude that the *Epistle* was
written before the *Confession*. It is tempting to adopt the suggestion of Grosjean that the attack on Patrick from Britain mentioned in the *Confession* (which we shall be considering later)
was motivated by resentment at his action of excommunicating
fromIreland Coro ticus, a British ruler not formally under his
jurisdiction.[3] But certainty here is unattainable.

The next point to determine is the audience for whom his
works were intended. It is easy to see that the *Epistle* was sent to
Coroticus and his soldiers, who are addressed throughout. It
was probably designed to be read out at his court: *legatur coram
cunctis plebibus et praesente ipso Corotico* (*Ep.* 21). These people
were all British. Patrick at one point writes *Indignum est illis
Hiberionaci sumus*, meaning that Coroticus and his men despise
Patrick's authority because they associate him with the Irish.[4]
He calls them *socii Scottorum atque Pictorum apostatarumque* (v. l.
apostatarum),[5] and describes Coroticus as *traditor Christianorum in
manus Scottorum atque Pictorum* (12). He says of Coroticus: *vendis
illos genti exterae et ignoranti Deum* (14), meaning the Picts. If,
as these quotations make clear, Coroticus and his men are
neither Irish nor Pictish, they must be British. Further, it is
quite clear that they are at least nominally Christian. The very
fact that Patrick excommunicates them (7, 21) makes this
certain, quite apart from other references. One passage, which
we have already glanced at, has caused some discussion among

---

[1] *Conf.* 52, *dabam* in both cases.
[2] *Conf.* 53, *iudicabant . . . visitabam*. The last phrase is, indeed, *quos ego frequentius
visitabam*, which, if taken literally, should mean 'more frequently than now', but
we cannot trust the accuracy of Patrick's Latin sufficiently to be sure that this is his
meaning.
[3] Grosjean, 'Notes d'hagiographie celtique', 1945, pp. 100–7.
[4] See the earlier discussion of this point, p. 24.   [5] *Ep.* 2.

scholars, in which Patrick calls Coroticus and his men *socii Scottorum atque Pictorum apostatarumque*;[1] later he applies the same epithet to the Picts again.[2] Some have thought that this implies that the Picts had once been evangelized but had at a later stage formally abandoned Christianity for paganism.[3] But this is to press Patrick's language too far. As Grosjean points out,[4] all that Patrick's language need imply is that the Picts whom he mentions have behaved in such a way as to render themselves equivalent to apostates; their behaviour had been tantamount to abjuring Christianity. Similarly, he can call Coroticus and his men *rebellatores Christi* (*Ep.* 19). His language, does, however, imply that Coroticus and his followers were Christians, that some Picts at any rate were Christians, though some were 'an outsider race who do not know God', and that some Irish were at that point unevangelized. Perhaps we may detect in the *Epistle* a hint that Patrick knows that his words will reach a wider audience, in the words *invidetur mihi* (12) and *etsi contempnor aliquibus* (1) and *et si mei me non cognoscunt* (11). It is difficult to reconcile this evidence with the conclusion of J. MacQueen in his book *St. Nynia* that the activity of St. Ninian among the Picts (as contrasted with the Britons of the area round Whithorn) is badly evidenced and may not have achieved much. The Britons of Strathclyde (if we are to identify Coroticus with the Ceretic mentioned in the Welsh genealogy and with Muirchu's *regem Aloo*)[5] were evangelized by Patrick's time, and so were some of the Picts. Who had done the work of evangelization? It is impossible to eliminate the name of Ninian.

The question of the audience to which the *Confession* was addressed is a rather more complicated one. Most writers believe that the main reading public envisaged by Patrick was in Britain, probably for the most part bishops and other clergy.[6]

---

[1] *Ep.* 2; *apostatarumque* is Bieler's reading; Newport White, *apostatarum*. But, as Bieler points out (*LE*, Part II, *in loc.*), we cannot assume that Patrick distinguished three classes here, Irish, Picts, and apostates; it is far more likely that he meant to designate the Picts as apostates, whether he added the *-que* or not.

[2] *Ep.* 15, *apostatarumque Pictorum*.

[3] So Todd (*Patrick, Apostle*, p. 384) and Duke (*The Columban Church*, p. 28). Bieler (*ACW, in loc.*) does not commit himself.

[4] 'Les Pictes apostats dans l'Épître de S. Patrice', pp. 363–75.

[5] See above, pp. 22–25.

[6] So Bury, *LP*, pp. 200–1; McNeill (*St. Patrick*, p. 59), Christine Mohrmann

As we shall see later,[1] there can be little doubt that Patrick was chosen bishop in Britain, consecrated there, and sent from there. Patrick tells us that he desires in writing this *Confession fratribus et cognatis meis scire qualitatem meam* (6); and later he writes (47, 48):

nunc ergo simpliciter insinuavi fratribus et conservis meis qui mihi crediderunt propter quod praedixi et praedico ad roborandam et confirmandam fidem vestram. . . . Vos scitis et Deus qualiter inter vos conversatus sum a iuventute mea in fide veritatis et in sinceritate cordis. Etiam ad gentes illas inter quas habito, ego fidem illis praestavi et praestabo.

But towards the end of the *Confession* the reader senses that Patrick, without turning his attention wholly from his audience in Britain, associates with them his friends, converts, and supporters in Ireland: *et inter vos et ubique pergebam causa vestra in multis periculis etiam usque ad exteras partes* (51), and *vos autem experti estis quantum ego erogavi illis qui iudicabant per omnes regiones quos ego frequentius visitabam* (53) can only refer to readers in Ireland. There is no hint in either work that Patrick envisages readers in Gaul (in Lérins or in Auxerre), or in Rome.[2]

There is one passage, however, where the type of people addressed is obscure, and it has caused much heart-searching among scholars. Here Patrick directly speaks to his readers (13):

Unde autem ammiramini itaque magni et pusilli qui timetis Deum et vos domini cati rhetorici [gnari P, ignari BCFR] audite et scrutamini. Quis me stultum excitavit de medio eorum qui videntur esse sapientes et legis periti et potentes in sermone et in omni re . . .

Who are these *domini cati rhetorici*? The phrase literally translated means 'masters, cunning ones, rhetoricians'. It is likely that the reading *gnari* of P comes from a gloss on the rare word *cati*, and presumably *ignari* of BCFR is an attempt to amend this.

(*Latin*, pp. 29–31), Carney (*The Problem of Patrick*, p. 96), and Morris ('Dark Age Dates', p. 150).

[1] Below, pp. 131 ff.

[2] Kenney, curiously, regarded the *Confession* as written almost entirely for British people in Ireland (*Sources*, p. 168). Kuno Meyer envisaged the audience as his (visionary) large group of learned refugees; these also were the *dominicati rhetorici*; see *Learning in Ireland in the Fifth Century*, pp. 9, 10, and also above, pp. 55–56.

The passage must have caused the scribes trouble from an early period in the manuscript tradition. K. Jackson took these people to be the schoolmasters, and perhaps teachers of oratory, employed by the romanized British upper classes to teach their sons Latin.[1] But there is no reason to think that Patrick had any occasion to address schoolmasters and teachers of oratory, or to defend himself against them. Bieler[2] printed the phrase as *dominicati rhetorici*, assuming the existence of an adjective, *dominicatus*, meaning 'wealthy', endowed with estates (from *dominicum*, an estate), and interpreting *rhetoricus* to mean a man of letters, as it can. The allusion, he thinks, is to the wealthy landowners of Gaul who were also literary men, like Sidonius Apollinaris. He therefore regards this as a proof that Patrick had a Gallic audience in view. But there are many objections to this theory, and it has found few supporters. It is difficult to imagine that the badly educated Patrick ever came within the range of people like Sidonius Apollinaris. Sidonius might have described him as *bis peregrinus* to the Latin language,[3] but he otherwise would hardly have troubled to attack him. Again, the adjective *dominicatus*[4] is given in Ducange as meaning *ad dominum pertinens*, and (as Bieler admits) there is no parallel for the meaning 'wealthy'. Grosjean dismisses this suggestion as philologically and semantically impossible,[5] and so does Christine Mohrmann.[6] Grosjean himself argued that both *dominicati* and *rhetorici* are later glosses on *legis periti* and *potentes* which occur in the same chapter.[7] But here Grosjean's usual astuteness seems to have deserted him. Not only is his theory a complicated one, but to argue that two rare and obscure words were added as glosses to two perfectly plain and simple terms is to put the cart before the horse. Christine Mohrmann herself wanted to derive *dominicati* from *dominicum*, a word which certainly was in use, meaning a church building, in the fifth century. *Dominicati* would then mean 'churchmen', and *legis periti* a little further on would mean 'skilled in the law of God',

---

[1] *LHB*, p. 110.   [2] *LE, in loc.*   [3] See above, p. 65.

[4] As Esposito pointed out as early as 1918 ('Notes on the Latin Writings of St. Patrick', p. 344).

[5] 'Dominicati Rhetorici', pp. 41–46.

[6] *Latin*, pp. 29–31. Carney (*The Problem of Patrick*, pp. 97–98), and Binchy (*PB*, p. 22) agree with Christine Mohrmann.

[7] 'Dominicati Rhetorici', pp. 41–46.

i.e. the Old Testament Law or the Bible.[1] But it is illegitimate
to assume that *dominicati* can mean 'churchmen' in the sense of
'men belonging to the people of God'; *dominicum* cannot mean
'people of God', but only 'church building', and there is no
reason why Patrick should have addressed men associated with
church buildings. There is no more parallel for this meaning
of *dominicati* than there is for the meaning which Bieler attached
to it. Besides, it is perverse to interpret *legis periti* as referring to
Scripture or a part of it when Patrick has only a few chapters
before used the phrase *qui optime itaque iura et sacras litteras utraque
pari modo combiberunt* (*Confession* 9) of the same group of people;
here *iura* cannot refer to Scripture but must mean secular
laws. It is obvious that in the expression *domini cati rhetorici*,
or whatever lies behind it, Patrick is intending a class of
people who have got what he has not got, and who therefore
despise him for the lack of it. They are trained in oratory and
they are trained in civil law. They are also trained in sacred
Scripture, but here Patrick can compete with them, for
Chapter 9 suggests that his difficulty is that he cannot display
both *utraque pari modo*. His writings confirm this. He has a
remarkable knowledge of the Latin Bible, but his Latin prose is
almost unique in the whole range of Latin Patristic literature,
in that it is destitute of any artificial rhetoric whatever. This is
what gives his prose its clumsiness but also its note of sincerity
and its directness of appeal. This is what makes his prose at
once so difficult to interpret and so worth while studying. We
can easily imagine that well-educated clergy in Britain, like
Pelagius and Faustus of Riez, would not only have derived a
knowledge of rhetoric from their higher education but also
some knowledge of law. Indeed, as the example of Augustine
shows, these two subjects formed the staple of higher education
in the later Roman Empire. It seems necessary to abandon the
attempt to read an adjective *dominicati* into this *crux interpretum
Patricianorum*, for to do so is to explain an obscure phrase by a
word which probably did not exist in the fifth century. We
must either take the phrase as *domini cati rhetorici*, translating it

---

[1] *Latin*, pp. 29–31. Binchy agreed with this interpretation (*PB*, p. 22). Carney
(*The Problem of Patrick*, pp. 97–98) wants to read *domini gnari cati rhetorici*, 'lordly
fellows, wise, judicial and eloquent'; from the point of view of textual criticism this
looks like trying to have his cake and eat it.

as 'skilled master-rhetoricians',[1] very clumsy indeed though the expression is in Latin, or we must emend. If we are to emend, I suggest that we could do worse than read *domini cata rhetorica* or *domini cata rhetoricen*. The word *cata* meaning 'according to', always with the accusative, is widely used in the Latin Old Testament (and therefore must have been known to Patrick), and appears in the Vulgar Latin of Etheria's *Peregrinatio*.[2] *Rhetoricus* is quite a common adjective, used (e.g.) by Quintilian, *rhetorica* (neut. pl.) is used by Cicero to mean 'rhetoric', and the same word (fem. sg.) or *rhetorice* means 'the art of rhetoric'. If we follow this emendation, we translate by some such expression as 'masters in the domain of rhetoric'. At all events, this phrase places us under no obligation to conclude that Patrick was addressing an audience in Gaul. Clearly he was here writing for well-educated British persons, probably clergy, who were casting aspersions on his education and suggesting that it was not fitting that so ill-educated a person as Patrick should be a bishop in Ireland.

Let us now turn to consider the details which Patrick's two works supply about himself and his career. The facts about his ancestry and native place can be easily summarized. He begins his *Confession* by telling us:

patrem habui Calpornium diaconum filium quendam Potiti presbyteri, qui fuit uico bannauem taburniae: villulam enim prope habuit, ubi ego capturam dedi. Annorum eram tunc fere sedecim.

He divulges a few important facts in the *Epistle* too (10):

Numquid a me piam misericordiam quod ago erga gentem illam qui me aliquando ceperunt et devastaverunt servos et ancillas domus patris mei. Ingenuus fui secundum carnem; decorione patre nascor. Vendidi enim nobilitatem meam—non erubesco neque paenitet—pro utilitate aliorum.[3]

It should, however, be noted that *ingenuus* in Patrick's usage need mean no more than 'freeborn', as a later passage in the *Epistle* shows, *ibi venundati ingenui homines, Christiani in servitute*

---

[1] Which is Newport White's 'ye clever sirs, ye rhetoricians' taken out of Wardour Street and clothed in modern English.

[2] *Peregrinatio*, 1. 7. 2 *et alibi*.

[3] Cf. his other reference to his *ingenuitas, Conf.* 37, *ut darem ingenuitatem meam pro utilitate aliorum*.

redacti sunt (15). It is scarcely necessary to add that he tells us several times in the *Confession* that his native land was Britain, e.g. *ut pergens in Britannis—et libentissime paratus eram quasi ad patriam et parentes* (43), *et iterum post paucos annos in Brittannis eram cum parentibus meis* (23).

The first among these facts to examine is the name and the whereabouts of Patrick's father's village. The name is either *bannavem taburniae* or *bannaventa burniae*. Bury prefers the latter.[1] We know of at least two place-names in Roman Britain called *Venta*. No one has ever succeeded in identifying Patrick's father's *vicus* definitely. Haverfield and others in the last century were strongly in favour of identifying it with a station in Watling Street, a few miles north of Daventry, called *Bannaventa* in the *Itinerarium Antonini*.[2] And de Labriolle in the *Histoire de l'Église* edited by Fliche and Martin adopted this suggestion.[3] Bury rejected this on the unsatisfactory ground that it would clash with Muirchu's information about the place.[4] But we may dismiss it for the simpler and more compelling reason that Irish pirates are not in the least likely to have attacked a village in Northamptonshire near no navigable river and situated at least fifty miles from the nearest sea, and that the North Sea. Considerations of British geography apparently do not trouble French historians. Muirchu alleges that *Bannavem Taburnie* was *haut procul a mari nostro quem vicum constanter indubitanterque comperimus esse Nemtrie.*[5] If we assume that the original reading here was *ventre* or something like it, we could identify Patrick's village with Caerwent in South Wales (*Venta*). Geographically, this would be much preferable to Northamptonshire as a target

---

[1] *LP*, Appendix C, p. 322. Bieler (*Life and Legend*, pp. 51–53) discusses this place-name very learnedly but to little effect. He prefers *Bannaventa taburniae* or *Bannaventa Burniae.*

[2] Ibid., p. 322. E. B. Nicholson in *Academy* for May 1895 warmly advocated this view.

[3] Vol. 4, cap. V, p. 387. In dealing with Patrick's career (pp. 387–8) de Labriolle appears to be wholly guided by other authorities.

[4] *LP*, p. 323.

[5] This information occurs in the early chapters of Muirchu, which only appear in the Brussels Codex; Stokes, *TL* ii. 494. The reading *Nemtrie* is not certain. Stokes's footnote reads 'MS ventre prius venitre (?), Hogan. So Probus (Tr. Th. p. 47, misprinted 51): de vico Bannave Tiburniae regionis, haud procul a mari occidentali: quem vicum indubitanter comperimus esse Nentriae [*sic* Neutriae, p. 62] provinciae, in qua olim gigantes habitasse dicuntur. *Nemtria* is probably formed from *Nemtor*, supra, p. 405.'

I

for Irish raiders, but there are two serious objections. A possible emendation of a document embodying much later tradition about Patrick is very slender authority. And, as we have seen,[1] it is likely that in the fifth century the south-west of Wales was occupied by a kingdom where the population was of mixed Irish and British stock and the language was similarly mixed. If Patrick came from this kingdom, or from anywhere near it, it is not at all likely that he would regard the Irish as an alien race, among whom he is an exile, as he certainly does. If we take Muirchu's reading as *Nemtrie*, we may identify the place with the Nemthur of the Irish of Fiacc's Hymn, *Génair Patraic*,[2] which is repeated in the statement of the *Vita Tripartita* that Patrick was born in *Nemthor* among the Britons of Ail-Cluaide (i.e. Dumbarton),[3] and this statement is repeated in various forms in several later lives of Patrick. This fairly consistent later tradition that Patrick's village was in the kingdom of Strathclyde or of Rheged has won the agreement of several scholars.[4] It has been thought that Patrick in his *Epistle* supports this theory by implying that Coroticus and his men had been his fellow-citizens—*militibus mittenda Coroci, non dico civibus meis neque civibus sanctorum Romanorum sed civibus daemoniorum* (2). But there is no reason to suppose that Patrick confined the word *cives* to the inhabitants of the part of Britain from which he came. He applied it to all Christians, whom he regarded as civilized adherents of a complex of the Christian Church and the Roman Empire; all Christians automatically entered Romania (though he does not use that word). Gildas similarly called all his Christian fellow-Britons *cives* and Latin *nostra lingua*.[5] However, the siting of *Bannavem Taburniae* in Strathclyde or Rheged faces one fatal difficulty. Patrick's father owned a *villula* which employed a number (indeed Patrick implies a large number) of menservants and maidservants. This was not merely 'a farm-house on the estate of Calpornius',[6] because the diminutive has

---

[1] See above, p. 12. Morris calls it 'a bi-lingual state' ('Celtic Saints', p. 365).

[2] See above, pp. 76, 77.

[3] Stokes, *TL* i. 8–9; see also above, p. 81.

[4] Meissner (*History of the Church of Ireland*, vol. i, cap. iii), Simpson (*Ninian and Origins*, p. 21), Bulloch (*Celtic Church*, pp. 43–44), Norah Chadwick (*CB*, p. 143).

[5] So H. Williams *CEB*, p. 3. The *et si mei non cognuscunt* of *Ep.* 11 means that Patrick is a Briton, but not necessarily from Strathclyde.

[6] Bury, *LP*, p. 322; Bury takes surprisingly little notice of Patrick's Latin.

lost its force in Vulgar Latin and we must give *villula* the full meaning of *villa*. Now there is no evidence whatever that Roman villas ever existed in the area which later became the kingdom of Strathclyde, and very little evidence of any in the district further south which later became the kingdom of Rheged. In fact the evidence strongly suggests that during the first half of the fifth century villa-life was decaying in Roman Britain. Of the villas hitherto discovered, not one appears to have ended its existence by violence, but rather economic decay overtook them.[1] These facts tell heavily against any attempt to place Patrick's home in northern Britain, and, we may add, should incline us to place his birth in the fourth rather than in the fifth century. It is impossible to imagine a large villa near a *vicus* as far north as Strathclyde. One other attempt has been made to identify *Bannavem Taburniae*. Grosjean suggested that we should emend to *Glannaventa*, which was the Roman name for the town of Ravenglas on the coast of Cumberland, where it is known that a unit of the Roman fleet was stationed, and that Patrick's father was not a civil *decurio* but a military *decurio*, a rank which is known to have existed among the *auxilia* in the Roman army.[2] But this theory in its turn encounters insurmountable obstacles. It seems likely that with very few exceptions the romanized civil population had disappeared from most places in northern Britain after the *barbarica conspiratio* of 367.[3] An examination of the Roman remains at Ravenglas does not encourage any theory of the existence of a substantial Roman villa in the vicinity.[4] If Calpornius was a military *decurio* and also a land-owner he must have been an exception, for the class of troops called *limitanei* in the late Roman Empire, though they remained in more or less the same area permanently, were not a peasant militia, living on the land and taking up arms when need arose.[5] Salway points out that the Theodosian Code records arrangements for the payment of *annonae* to garrisons

[1] See K. Jackson, *LHB*, p. 233.

[2] 'Notes d'hagiographie celtique', 1945, pp. 64–72; 'Les Pictes apostats dans l'Épître de S. Patrice', pp. 354–78. We have already dismissed his romantic reconstruction, whereby the Roman fleet stationed at Ravenglas was ordered by Coroticus to sail to the Clyde and on the way massacred Patrick's converts. See above, p. 25, n. 1.

[3] P. Salway, *The Frontier People*, p. 15.

[4] Ibid., pp. 125–6.

[5] Bulloch makes this mistaken assumption, *Celtic Church*, p. 34.

in kind, implying that they were not supporting themselves on the land. Provisions in the late legal sources for allotments of frontier land are to *gentiles* (barbarians), or to veterans, not to serving troops.[1] Further, there are very few examples in the late Roman Empire of soldiers being ordained as clergy;[2] if Calpornius had been a soldier he would be exceptional not only as a landowner but also as a deacon. We may add as another objection to Grosjean's theory that it was difficult in the late Roman Empire for the son of a soldier to avoid following his father's profession; the story of Martin illustrates this point.[3] But Patrick never suggests that there was any difficulty about his taking holy orders, though there was opposition from his family to his becoming a bishop. Finally, we may point out the absurdity of imagining that Irish raiders would choose as the object of their attack and plunder a place they knew to be garrisoned by Roman troops. In short, Grosjean's theory is so unlikely as to be incredible. The fact is that we do not know where *Bannavem Taburniae* was, and, short of an archaeological miracle, we probably never shall. But the probability is strongly in favour of locating it in the Lowland Zone of Roman Britain, and in the south-western part of that zone, in Somerset or Dorset or Devon.[4] There is no reason to assume that Muirchu or the Hymn *Génair Patraic* had access to more reliable information on the subject than we have. The statement that it was near the Irish Sea no doubt represents someone's intelligent guess.

Some confident conclusions can be drawn from what Patrick tells us about his father.[5] The word *decurio* does not appear among the Latin loan-words taken into the British language;[6] though a few Latin titles can be recovered from early Celtic

[1] *The Frontier People*, p. 199.

[2] See A. H. M. Jones, *The Later Roman Empire*, vol. i, p. 922.

[3] See Sulpicius Severus, *De Vita Beati Martini (PL* 20. ii. 161); it was the Emperor's decree that the sons of veterans should be compelled to enter the army, which prevented Martin becoming a teenage monk.

[4] O'Rahilly (*The Two Patricks*, p. 33) suggested that Patrick was born near Glastonbury, and conjectured that *Bannavem Taburniae* was originally *Bannaventa Bruviae*, arguing from the river Brue, on which Glastonbury is situated, and whose name, according to O'Rahilly, is of Celtic origin. But there is no evidence of the existence of this name for the river earlier than the Middle Ages.

[5] For the significance of Calpornius being both a *decurio* and a deacon, see chap. vi, pp. 176–9. See also Bury, *LP*, pp. 19–20.

[6] K. Jackson, *LHB*, pp. 78–79.

inscriptions, it is not found among them.[1] It is possible that the title *tribunus* to designate the chief magistrate of the municipality survived among the British after the departure of the Romans:[2] it could therefore be conjectured that *decurio* similarly survived the Roman withdrawal. Gildas mentions as titles among contemporary British officials *tyranni*, *rectores*, and *speculatores*, and the title *Protector* has been found in a fifth- or sixth-century inscription at Llanfalteg, near Carmarthen, given to a man called Voteporigis or Votecorigas, who may be the Vortiporius mentioned by Gildas (*De Excid. Brit.* 31) as *rex Demetarum*.[3] But actually it is quite unnecessary to speculate about whether the title *decurio* survived the withdrawal from Britain of the Roman government. The word *decurio* was in the later Roman Empire used most widely of a member of a local municipal or territorial council, called the *senatus* or *ordo*; each *civitas* possessed its senate and magistrates, who were called *curiales*, the *civitas* being a centre of population of varying size, with a varying amount of land round it. The officials of these in Roman Britain would in many, perhaps in most, cases, represent the local tribal aristocracy.[4] The next division below the *civitas* was that of the *vicus* or *pagus*. A *vicus* was not large or important enough to have *decuriones* attached to it, though the *cannabae* or civilian suburb of a Roman fort could have them,[5] so that we must not assume that Calpornius was the *decurio* of the *vicus* of *Bannavem Taburniae*. At the period of the withdrawal of Roman rule there can be no reasonable doubt that there were plenty of *decuriones* of *civitates* in Britain.[6] It is therefore perverse to seek for Calpornius the *decurio* in sub-Roman

---

[1] Ibid., p. 165.

[2] So Collingwood and Myres, *RBES*, p. 306; but they are basing their evidence on the *vir tribuniciae potestatis* in Constantius's *Vita Germani* 15 (see above pp. 48–49), that it is rather a frail inference. Why should we accept this title as genuine if we reject that of *Heraclius vir consularis in eadem urbe residens*, of the (?) fifth-century *Vita Sancti Symphoriani*? (See J. Zwicker, *Fontes Historiae Religionis Celticae, Pars Altera*, p. 163.) *Tribunica potestas* by itself suggests, of course, a much more considerable authority than that of the chief official in a municipal council; it was a mark of imperial power. Even the separate Gaulish monarchy of the mid third century (258–73) possessed *tribunicia potestas* (see F. Haverfield, *The Romanization of Roman Britain*, p. 17).

[3] F. Haverfield, in *Ephemeris Epigraphica* ix, p. 532, no. 1030.

[4] P. Hunter Blair, *Roman Britain and Early England*, p. 96.

[5] Salway, *The Frontier People*, pp. 125–6.

[6] So J. N. L. Myres, 'Pelagius and the End of Roman Rule', pp. 32 and 34.

Britain. Unless some insurmountable obstacle exists to the conclusion, we must believe that he was an ordinary civilian *decurio* of an ordinary civilian *civitas*, which included a *vicus* called *Bannavem Taburniae*; that near it he had a substantial estate, and that he had been appointed *decurio* before 408. He was also a deacon. This last office, as we shall see later,[1] is accounted for by the fact that the main and engrossing functions of *decuriones* in the fourth century was the raising of taxes.

Although Patrick's father was the son of a presbyter Potitus (or possibly the son-in-law), and Calpornius himself was in holy orders, Patrick's home cannot have been a very religious one. *Deum enim verum ignorabam . . . A Deo recessimus et praecepta eius non custodivimus et sacerdotibus nostris non oboedientes fuimus qui nos nostram salutem admonebant (Conf.* 1), he says. He speaks of his *incredulitas* and his *delicta* and *ignorantia* before he knew God and *antequam saperem vel distinguerem inter bonum et malum (Conf.* 2); and of his life before his captivity he writes: *Deum vivum non credebam, neque ex infantia mea, sed in morte et in credulitate mansi (Conf.* 27), and later, praising God's goodness to him, *unde mihi haec sapientia quae in me non erat, qui nec numerum dierum noveram neque Deum sapiebam? Unde mihi postmodum donum tam magnum tam salubre Deum agnoscere vel diligere, sed ut patriam et parentes amitterem? (Conf.* 36). Even when we have allowed for the exaggeration of a convert, it is impossible to believe that Patrick learnt in his father's home more than a purely nominal piety.

On the question of what language was spoken in Patrick's home, opinions have differed. K. Jackson is definitely of the opinion that the rural aristocracy of Roman Britain spoke Latin among themselves (though they used British in addressing their servants and employees), and that in places it may have been 'the general middle-class Vulgar Latin lingua franca of the Empire'.[2] O'Rahilly thought that Patrick, unskilled though he was in Latin, calls it *sermo et loquela nostra (Conf.* 9).[3] Christine Mohrmann, on the other hand, who is the only person to have devoted a monograph to Patrick's Latin, concluded

---

[1] See below, pp. 176–7.
[2] In Norah Chadwick's *SBH*, pp. 61–62. But K. Jackson does not think that Patrick spoke Latin in his home (*LHB*, p. 103).
[3] *The Two Patricks*, p. 33.

that Latin was not the language of Patrick's daily intercourse.[1]
We shall be dealing more fully with Patrick's Latin in a later
chapter.[2] For the moment it is enough to note that O'Rahilly's
inference is not a necessary one to draw from the passage he
quotes. The whole context runs thus:

> *Non didici sicut et ceteri, qui optime itaque iura et sacras litteras utraque
> pari modo combiberunt et sermones illorum ex infantia numquam mutarunt,
> sed magis ad perfectum semper addiderunt. Nam sermo et loquela nostra
> translata est in linguam alienam, sicut facile potest probari ex saliva scrip-
> turae meae, qualiter sum ego in sermonibus instructus atque eruditus.*

The *lingua aliena* here might refer to Irish, but it is hard to see
how anyone could be expected to recognize this from the
savour of his writing, for he is not writing in Irish but in Latin.
It is far more natural to interpret this passage to mean that
others had been learning both their native language and Latin
from childhood and had never met Latin as an alien language
to which they suddenly had to change, but that this was
exactly Patrick's situation. For Patrick, Latin was a *lingua aliena*,
and (as he says) it is only necessary to read his written work to
see this. *Sermo et loquela* as a phrase should not be pressed very
closely; it is a Scriptural quotation.[3] It seems much more
reasonable to conclude that on Patrick's own admission Latin
was not spoken in his home, though probably not very successful attempts had been made to teach him Latin.

The first crucial event in Patrick's life was his being kidnapped
on his father's estate *cum tot milia hominum* (*Conf.* 1), when he was
nearly sixteen, by Irish raiders, and brought to Ireland, where
he spent six years in captivity as a slave. The 'thousands of
men' cannot possibly all have been employees on his father's
land, even though he does elsewhere say that the raiders
devastaverunt servos et ancillas domus patris mei (*Ep.* 10). This must
have been an extensive raid, occupying a large body of raiders
and affecting a large area of the countryside, perhaps made at
several different points at the same time. Patrick never tells us
directly of the place of his captivity, but, as we have seen,[4] he in

---

[1] *Latin*, p. 33.   [2] See below, pp. 58–70.
[3] Either Ps. xviii. 4 or John viii. 43, as Bieler observes in his admirable note,
in loc. (*LE*). 'For Patrick', he says, 'to write Latin always meant some effort.'
[4] See above, p. 91.

effect tells us where it was when he relates how, when he had returned to Britain, after some years he had a vision (*Conf.* 23):

et ibi scilicet vidi in visu noctis virum venientem quasi de Hiberione, cui nomen Victoricus, cum epistolis innumerabilibus, et dedit mihi unam ex his et legi principium epistolae continentem, 'Vox Hiberionacum', et cum recitabam principium epistolae putabam ipso momento audire vocem ipsorum qui erant iuxta silvam Vocluti quae est prope mare occidentale, et sic exclamaverunt quasi ex uno ore: Rogamus te, sancte puer, ut venias et adhuc ambulas inter nos.

Efforts have been made by scholars obsessed by the supposed necessity of reconciling this description with later tradition to evade the clear, natural sense of this passage, that the 'wood of Foclut' was the scene of Patrick's captivity.[1] The attempt has been made to refer *ipsorum* to the *Hiberionacum*, so that the cry to Patrick to return would come from the people of Ireland and not specifically from those who were by the wood of Foclut.[2] But Christine Mohrmann has rendered this argument, already frail, no longer possible, by pointing out that *ipsorum* can in Vulgar Latin mean simply *eorum*, even as early as Etheria's *Peregrinatio*, where several examples of this can be found.[3]

Wrenched violently away from his home and family while still a boy in his teens and degraded to a life of slavery, employed in keeping cattle among alien people who spoke another language from his own British, Patrick turned to God for comfort and help. From indifference to religion he was converted to a lifelong practice of piety and self discipline. He used, he tells us, often to make a hundred prayers a day and as many in the night.[4] Then after six years he received a message in a dream at night; it ran: *Bene ieiunas cito iturus ad patriam tuam*, and a little later he received another similar message, *Ecce navis tua parata est*. He ran away from his master and travelled about 200 miles to a place where there was a ship.[5] It must constantly be remembered that in his *Confession* Patrick is not

---

[1] e.g. Bieler, *Life and Legend*, pp. 58–59, and *LE, in loc.* For the evidence that Foclut was in the district of Tirawley, near the modern Killala, see O'Rahilly, *The Two Patricks*, pp. 34–35 and 60.

[2] *LE, in loc.*   [3] *Latin*, p. 19.

[4] All this information is found in *Confession* 16: *pecora pascebam* probably means cattle rather than simply sheep; it does not mean pigs, for later, when Patrick refers to a herd of pigs, he calls them *grex porcorum* (19).

[5] *Conf.* 17.

writing his autobiography. He does not feel under any necessity to give details of time or place or names of people, or even to preserve strict chronological order, except in so far as these may serve his main purpose, which is to express his gratitude to God by recounting the ways and the experiences in which God has helped him. We must therefore be prepared for exasperatingly vague indications and tantalizingly uncertain language as he makes his 'confession'. He does not tell us where this ship was or, when it brought him away from Ireland, where it landed. He does tell us that he made some pact or bargain with the pagan shipmen to carry him, that he refused to suck their nipples (*sugere mamellas*), and that he gained his objective of travelling *in fidem Iesu Christi*.[1] It has been proved[2] that sucking the nipples of a man was a manner, among the ancient Irish, of demonstrating and swearing faith and loyalty to the person whose nipples were sucked. Patrick clearly regarded it as a pagan custom and substituted for it swearing or promising faith and loyalty by Jesus Christ.[3]

The ship made land after three days. For twenty-eight days the company then journeyed through desert country. Food failed them and they were starving. The captain (*gubernator*) then appealed to Patrick to show that his Christian God was powerful. Patrick prayed, and a herd of pigs appeared before their eyes. We continue the narrative from the text of the *Confession*:

ecce grex porcorum in via ante oculos nostros apparavit, et multos ex illis interfecerunt et ibi duas noctes manserunt et bene refecti et canes eorum repleti sunt, quia multi ex illis defecerunt et secus viam semivivi relicti sunt, et post hoc summas gratias egerunt Deo et ego honorificatus sum sub oculis eorum, et ex hac die cibum habundanter habuerunt; etiam mel silvestre invenerunt et mihi partem obtulerunt et unus ex illis dixit, 'immolaticum est'; Deo gratias, exinde nihil gustavi.[4]

This account of the journey of the ship's company has given rise to a theory which claims both to decide Patrick's destination and the date of his journey. It has been conjectured that the dogs

---

[1] *Conf.* 18.
[2] See Ryan in the *Irish Ecclesiastical Review*, lii (1938), 293–9 and M. O'Brien, *Études celtiques*, iii (1938), 372.
[3] So Carney, *The Problem of Patrick*, pp. 60–62, most convincingly.
[4] This description of the journey up to this point is all contained in *Conf.* 19.

who here so unexpectedly appear in the narrative were Irish wolf-hounds who were being brought by traders from Ireland to Gaul. There is considerable evidence that Irish dogs were valued as hunting-dogs in the ancient world. We have had one indication of this already.[1] The shipmen, on this assumption, were traders intending to bring a cargo of dogs to the Continent. The ship, on this theory, landed somewhere on the coast of France, and the deserted state of the country is accounted for by the fact that the immensely destructive invasion of barbarians across the Rhine into Gaul had recently taken place[2] and had left large parts of northern France in a state of ruin and devastation. We can therefore, if we adopt this theory, date Patrick's escape from captivity to the year 406, and at the same time be confident that he had visited Gaul. A refinement of this theory adds that the shipmen offered Patrick a passage because they thought that, having handled cattle for some years, he would be skilful in handling dogs.[3]

But this theory, on closer examination, appears very implausible. In the first place, if we are not preoccupied by a desire to reconcile Patrick's narrative with the later tradition about him and so bring him to Gaul, it would not occur to us that Patrick's account meant anything else than that, in accordance with the words of his dream, *cito iturus ad patriam tuam*, he was travelling to Britain, and that therefore it was to Britain that he came. In the second place, it is difficult to imagine that even after the great barbarian invasion of 406 any part of Gaul could have been so much devastated as to render it possible for a company of people to travel for twenty-eight (or for fourteen) days without meeting men or means of food, whereas if the ship's company had set off through some of

[1] See above, p. 38.   [2] See above, p. 7.

[3] The theory about dogs was first advanced by T. Olden in *The Church of Ireland* (1892), pp. 16–18 and Appendix B (pp. 421–4). It was enthusiastically endorsed by Bury (who regarded Olden's book in other respects with some contempt), *LP*, pp. 339–42. It was Bury who connected the escape of Patrick with the great invasion of 406 and who brought Patrick to France on this occasion. At least as far as dating goes, Olden and Bury have been followed by a very large number of writers whom we may, perhaps, without intending any disrespect, call dog-fanciers: Kenney, *Sources*, p. 168; Meissner, *History of the Church of Ireland*, vol. i, cap. iii, p. 80; McNeill, *St. Patrick*, pp. 53–56; Gwynn, *Book of Armagh*, Introd. lxxxii; Duke, *The Columban Church*, pp. 24–28; Bulloch, *Celtic Church*, pp. 44–45; Bieler, *LE* on *Confession* 18 and 19, and *Life and Legend*, pp. 60–61; Christine Mohrmann, *Latin*, p. 37; Ralegh Radford, in *Dark Age Britain*, pp. 68 and 69.

the vast forests which at that time covered the valleys of Wales and of Scotland it is not impossible to envisage their having this experience; it is perhaps significant that Patrick refers to *mel silvestre*. In the third place, the whole story of the dogs has an air of improbability, not to say absurdity, about it. Would a man, even a deeply religious man, of the fifth century, be enough concerned about the welfare of animals as to record the reviving of fainting dogs by sailors with pork chops? And if the ship's company had been in desperate straits for food, as Patrick represents them, would they not have begun killing and eating the dogs? We can escape this quandary by textual emendation. At the only mention of *canes* two manuscripts read *carnes*, and a corrector of one suggests *carne*.[1] We may accept the correction, and translate 'they [the sailors] were filled with their [i.e. the pigs'] flesh, for many of them had fainted'. The embarrassing wolf-hounds are thus dismissed from Patrick's narrative, Patrick is landed safely in Britain, not Gaul, and we are left to conjecture the date of this incident from other evidence.[2]

Patrick goes on to describe a spiritual experience which he had while he was in the company of the shipmen (*Conf.* 20), and then (*Conf.* 21) comes the following passage: ·

et iterum post annos multos adhuc capturam dedi. Ea nocta prima itaque mansi cum illis. Responsum autem divinum audivi dicentem mihi. Duobus mensibus eris cum illis. Quod ita factum est: nocte illa sexagesima liberavit me Dominus de manibus eorum.

Then in the next chapter (22) Patrick reverts to his journey with the shipmen, saying that after ten days of dry and well-provided travel *pervenimus homines* (presumably 'reached human habitations'), and repeating that the whole expedition had

[1] *Carnes* CP, *carne* F 4 corr. So Newport White, *app. crit.*, *in loc.*

[2] Carney argues well for this point of view, *The Problem of Patrick*, pp. 56, 66–67, 75–77, 168–9. Esposito ('The Patrician Problem', pp. 147–8) and Binchy (*PB*, pp. 78–81) have taken this position too. It is perhaps worth noting that Muirchu, the *Vita Tripartita*, and several other later 'lives' assume that Patrick travelled directly to Britain after his escape, even though they are ready to bring him to the Continent later; they make no mention of dogs. E. A. Thompson in 'A Note on St. Patrick in Gaul' shows how difficult it is to hold the theory of Bury, McNeill, and others that St. Patrick and his companions landed in a part of Gaul devastated by the invaders of 406 or 407, but his solution, that they reached Armorica when it was in the grip of a '*Bacauda*' and deliberately avoided human habitation, is very unlikely and almost contradicts Patrick's account.

taken twenty-eight days. The next chapter (23) begins: *et iterum post paucos annos in Brittanniis eram cum parentibus meis qui me ut filium susceperunt.* . . . These passages have understandably puzzled many students of Patrick's works. What was the occasion of Patrick's second captivity 'after many years'? Carney, who argues well for the view that Patrick's shipmen were raiders, not traders, bound together by a common oath of loyalty to their raiding band (a well-instanced custom), suggests that the twenty-eight days were occupied in a fortnight's journeying into the hinterland and a fortnight's travel back to the ship.[1] He also suggests very ingeniously that in his account of the second captivity Patrick is not switching without warning to some occasion years later than the period of his journey with the shipmen, but is regarding his period with the shipmen as a second captivity, and is explaining why he endured it. He interprets the passage thus: 'And so, after many years of captivity I again became captive to raiders.' The reason why Patrick voluntarily stayed with them was that on the first night of companying with the men he had a vision which told him to stay with them, and so he did. He punctuates *ea prima nocte—itaque mansi cum illis—audivi responsum*, etc., 'On that first night—that is why I stayed with them—I heard an answer.'[2] This certainly is a possible interpretation of Patrick's very obscure expressions. It has to face the serious difficulty that immediately afterwards Patrick uses the words *post paucos annos* of virtually the same length of time that he has just described as *post annos multos*. Carney believes that we must simply accept that Patrick, in dictating his *Confession*, was too much preoccupied with his spiritual experiences to notice this glaring contradiction. But it is hard to believe that even Patrick could have tolerated so flat a contradiction as this. It is better to assume that in Chapter 21, when he begins *et iterum post annos multos*, he is moving without warning to a quite different incident, which occurred long after the episode of the shipmen, when he was a bishop in Ireland. On two other occasions he refers to imprisonments.[3] As he describes his spiritual experience

---

[1] *The Problem of Patrick*, pp. 57–68. Carney was not the first to make this suggestion about the journey of twenty-eight days.

[2] Ibid., pp. 60–62, 66–67.

[3] *Conf.* 37 and 52; the second text tells of an imprisonment of only fourteen days, and could not be that referred to in *Conf.* 21.

in *Confession* 20 he is suddenly reminded of the later imprisonment, which he briefly describes; then he returns in *Confession* 22
to his period with the shipmen, which, incidentally, he does not
describe as if it had been a period of captivity, but rather one
of common danger and common need.[1]

The period between Patrick's return to Britain at the age of
twenty-two and his second arrival in Ireland, this time as a
bishop and not as a slave, is one of great obscurity. It was during
this period that he visited Gaul, if he ever visited Gaul, and it
was at this time that he acquired what education he had
beyond an elementary one. Patrick is acutely, perpetually,
embarrassingly conscious of his lack of education. It was
already something of a convention for a writer to protest at the
beginning of his work that he was insufficiently educated or
unsophisticated. Sulpicius Severus in the Introduction to his *Life
of St. Martin* expresses himself as apprehensive *ne (quod fore
arbitror) sermo incultior legentibus displiceret, omniumque reprehensione
dignissimus iudicarer, qui materiam disertis merito scriptoribus reser-
vandam impudens occupassem*.[2] The author of the *De Vita Christiana*,
whom some have thought to be Fastidius,[3] opens his work with
a vigorous protestation of his unworthiness, ignorance, and
sinfulness, calling himself *peccator et ultimus, insipientior ceteris et
imperitior universis*.[4] But Patrick's self-depreciation goes well
beyond the bounds of convention. He begins his *Confession* with
the words *Ego Patricius peccator rusticissimus et minimus omnium
fidelium et contemptibilissimus apud plurimos*. Later he speaks of his
inscientia et tardiori lingua (11), and shortly afterwards describes
himself as *rusticus, profuga, indoctus scilicet* (12). Later still he

---

[1] Bury (*LP*, p. 294) thinks that *Conf.* 21 refers to Patrick's whole period in
Ireland as bishop. Bieler (*Life and Legend*, p. 62) places this second captivity much
later in Patrick's life; McNeill, who already knows of the theory that the ship's
company travelled for fourteen days into the hinterland and for an equal period
returning, thinks that the shipmen were in their turn captured and held prisoners
with Patrick (*St. Patrick*, pp. 54–56). The author of the *Vita Tripartita* seems to
have taken a rather similar view.

[2] *PL* 20. 159; later (160) he refers to his *vitiosus sermo*. Later, in the *Dialogi* (i. 26
(200–1)), one of the interlocutors, Gallus, though he is a trained lawyer, apologizes
for his *sermo rusticior*.

[3] See above, pp. 40–41.

[4] Preface, *PL* 40. 1031; cf. *rudibus admonitionibus nostris* (1032). Constantius, *Vita
Germani*, in his Preface calls himself *peccator*. Gildas (*De Excid. Brit.* 62 (144)) refers
deprecatingly to *nostra mediocritas*; cf. 93.

speaks of God's indulgence towards *insipientiae meae neglegentiae meae* (46) and calls himself *imperitus in omnibus* (49). Again, he speaks of his *ignobilitas* and uses the expression *minimus minister* of himself (56). And he ends his *Confession* with the curious conjunction of epithets, *Patricius peccator indoctus scilicet* (62). This is precisely the expression with which he had earlier opened his *Epistle*, adding at the end of the chapter *et si contempnor aliquibus* (1).[1] His sense of the deficiency of his education obtrudes itself even in a letter where it was his duty and interest to make as much of his authority as possible.

The fullest information about Patrick's education, or lack of it, is given in a long passage early in the *Confession* which must be printed in full:

> *Quapropter olim cogitavi scribere, sed et usque nunc haesitavi: timui enim ne incederem in linguam hominum, quia non didici sicut ceteri, qui optime itaque iura et sacras litteras utraque pari modo combiberunt et sermones illorum ex infantia numquam mutarunt, sed magis ad perfectum semper addiderunt. Nam sermo et loquela nostra translata est in linguam alienam, sicut facile potest probari ex saliva scripturae meae, qualiter sum ego in sermonibus instructus atque eruditus. . . .[2] Sed quid prodest excusatio iuxta veritatem, praesertim cum praesumptione, quatenus modo ipse adpeto in senectute mea quod in iuventute non comparavi? Quod obstituerunt peccata mea ut confirmarem quod ante perlegeram. . . . Adolescens, immo paene puer imberbis,[3] capturam dedi, antequem scirem quid adpetere vel quid vitare debueram. Unde ergo hodie erubesco et vehementer pertimeo denudare imperitiam meam, quia desertis brevitate sermone explicare nequeo, sicut enim spiritus gestit et animus, et sensus monstrat adfectus.[4] Sed si itaque datum mihi fuisset sicut ceteris, verumtamen non silerem propter retributionem, et si forte videtur apud ali-*

---

[1] Cf. the *invidetur mihi* and *valde despicior* of *Ep.* 12.　　　　[2] *Conf.* 9.

[3] I here read *imberbis* ('beardless') for MSS. *inverbis* or *in verbis*. Bieler (*in loc.*) assumes that Patrick coined, or found somewhere, the word *inverbis* meaning 'speechless', 'not yet able to speak', of which he can produce no other example anywhere. Newport White (*Libri Sancti Patricii, in loc.*) took the desperate expedient of attaching *in verbis* to *capturam dedi*, and rendering 'I suffered captivity in speech'. The emendation, *imberbis*, originally made by Ware, was presumably adopted by McNeill, who quotes the passage as 'in my youth when I was still no more than a beardless boy' (*St. Patrick*, p. 48); but as McNeill never at any point in this book gives a single reference to Patrick's works, or to anything else, we cannot be sure whence he derived this reading. The emendation seems to me to be quite certain; *adolescens, immo paene puer imberbis* is an exact and precise description of a boy of not quite sixteen. Had Patrick described himself as 'a boy not yet capable of speech' (even supposing that there was such a word as *inverbis*) it would have been an absurd exaggeration.

[4] *Conf.* 10.

quantos me in hoc praeponere cum mea inscientia et tardiori lingua, sed etiam scriptum est enim: Linguae balbutientes velociter discunt loqui pacem. Quanto magis nos adpetere debemus, qui sumus, inquit, epistola Christi in salutem usque ad ultimum terrae, et si non deserta, sed ratum et fortissimum scripta in cordibus vestris non atramento sed spiritu Dei vivi. Et iterum Spiritus testatur, et rusticationem ab altissimo creatam.[1] Unde ego primus rusticus profuga, indoctus scilicet, qui nescio in posterum providere. . . .[2] Unde autem ammiramini itaque magni et pusilli qui timetis Deum et vos dominicati rhetorici audite et scrutamini. Quis me stultum excitavit de medio eorum qui videntur esse sapientes et legis periti et potentes in sermone et in omni re, et me quidem, detestabilis huius mundi, prae ceteris inspiravit si talis essem— dummodo autem. . . .[3]

The unmistakable impression created by this passage is that Patrick had had an opportunity of higher education, more particularly in rhetoric and law, before he was kidnapped by the Irish raiders, that he had not taken advantage of it, and that this opportunity had never occurred again. 'How I seek in my old age what I did not achieve in my youth; because my sins prevented me making secure what I had previously read superficially' (10). The 'sins' here can hardly be sins committed after he had returned to Britain from captivity, because he makes it clear time and time again that his period of sinfulness was past after his captivity. It was because he was no more than 'a beardless boy' when he was kidnapped that he now is ashamed to expose his lack of training (10); and this lack of training consists precisely in this that, as he says: 'I cannot discourse to well-educated people with conciseness of speech, as my spirit and soul desire and as my sentiments point the way' (10). He comforts himself that if he cannot speak in a well-educated way, 'rustic ways have been created by the Most High' (11). Behind this curious and pathetic misapplication of a text in Ecclesiasticus (vii. 16), referring to agricultural operations, lies long pondering by Patrick, alone with his Latin Bible, on God's will for those who suffer from lack of education (*rusticitas*). God's Word has an answer even for this difficulty! Even though Patrick is one of those who cannot 'provide for the future' (12), i.e. whose scanty education had not fitted him for his future career as a bishop, still the better educated people who ridicule his uncouthness, and who know all about rhetoric and law

---

[1] *Conf.* 11.   [2] *Conf.* 12.   [3] *Conf.* 13.

themselves, should be amazed at what God has done through him (13).

Whatever experiences we may imagine Patrick having, therefore, between his return to Britain after his escape from slavery in Ireland and his being chosen as bishop of the Irish, he certainly did not acquire a higher education during that period. He did during this time acquire a good knowledge of the Latin Bible, and he was at some point in it ordained deacon (*Conf.* 27). This is all that we can know for certain. Several scholars have been led by his words in *Confession* 23, *et iterum post paucos annos in Brittanniis eram cum parentibus meis*, to assume that these 'few years' elapsed between his reaching Gaul with the shipmen and his returning to his parents.[1] But we have seen[2] that it is very difficult to assume that Patrick landed anywhere else than in Britain, and the 'few years' could well be the six years that had passed since he had left his parents. Or they could simply mean that he was in Britain with his parents (to whom he had made his way after his adventures with the shipmen, and who had welcomed him warmly) a few years after the last related event, when he received the vision which called him to Ireland, and which he now proceeds to recount. In any event, his references to his education, or lack of it, leave us no firm ground for deciding that Patrick went to Gaul, or anywhere other than Britain. His words consist most with the suggestion that Patrick spent the period intervening between his return from captivity and his being elected bishop as a cleric (deacon or presbyter), and possibly as a monk,[3] in Britain. Christine Mohrmann is confident that in Patrick's Latin there are no signs at all of the sort of Latin which was spoken in Gallic or Continental monasteries generally.[4] This surely tells against any long residence of Patrick in Gaul. That higher education was available in Britain in Patrick's youth, had he taken advantage of it, cannot be doubted.[5]

[1] So Bury *LP*, p. 337, and Meissner, following him; but Bieler (*Life and Legend*, p. 63) appears to take the opposite view; and so does Binchy, *PB*, pp. 82–90.

[2] See above, pp. 119–23.

[3] The question of whether Patrick was a monk is discussed fully in the next chapter; see pp. 140–58.

[4] *Latin*, pp. 47–48.

[5] See Plinval, *Pélage*, p. 62; K. Jackson, *LHB*, pp. 156–7. I deliberately omit here the possible influences upon Patrick of various Christian fathers, such as Augustine and Cyprian, because no satisfactory case has yet been made out for

There are, however, two passages, one in the *Epistle* and one in the *Confession*, which must be considered seriously as possible evidence of Patrick's having visited Gaul. The first occurs in the *Epistle* (14): *consuetudo Romanorum Gallorum Christianorum*:[1] *mittunt viros sanctos idoneos ad Francos et ceteras gentes cum tot milia solidorum ad redimendos captivos baptizatos.* Where could Patrick have learnt this custom but in Gaul? The Franks were not neighbours of the British. The other passage comes in the *Confession* (43), where Patrick is protesting his determination to remain in Ireland for the rest of his life, in spite of inducements to leave the island. *Unde autem,* he writes, *etsi voluero amittere illas ancillas et ut pergens in Brittanniis—et libentissime paratus eram quasi ad patriam et parentes; non id solum sed etiam usque ad Gallias visitare fratres et ut viderem faciem sanctorum Domini mei; scit Deus quod ego valde optabam, sed alligatus Spiritu.* . . . . Grosjean makes the most of these two passages in advancing his theory that Patrick spent some time in Gaul before he became a bishop and returned to Ireland. In particular he insists that *fratres* in the second passage is virtually a technical term, used in ecclesiastical circles, meaning 'monks', and that this demonstrates that Patrick was a monk in Gaul for a period.[2] He thinks that we must place Patrick in Auxerre under Germanus. Christine Mohrmann directly traverses this conclusion. In Patrick, she says, *frater* means 'fellow-Christian' and not 'fellow-monk'; and

any such influence, and the general verdict still is that Patrick was *homo unius libri* — the Latin Bible. This does not, of course, exclude influences derived not directly through books, such as that of hymnody and liturgy. See Ryan, *St. Patrick,* p. 14; J. J. O'Mara, *Irish Ecclesiastical Review,* Mar. 1956, pp. 190–7; Christine Mohrmann, *Latin,* pp. 4–9. The strongest case that has been made out is perhaps the plea of P. Courcelle, who points out that, in addition to a number of slight and unimpressive resemblances between Augustine's *Confessions* and Patrick's *Confession,* Patrick uses the word *responsum* for the divine voice which addressed him, and that Augustine uses the same word for the same divine voice, *Confessions* iii. 11. 20. 4 (*Les Confessions de saint Augustin dans la tradition littéraire,* pp. 211–13). But this is apparently the only use (though it occurs twice in the same passage) of *responsum* in the whole of the work, and in these circumstances we cannot regard the resemblance as more than a coincidence or conclude that Patrick was here indebted to Augustine.

[1] The MS. P omits *Christianorum.* We cannot do better than quote Bieler's note (*LE, in loc.*): 'Whether P should be followed in the omission of *Christianorum* I dare not decide. It is not absolutely necessary because *Romanorum* alone can denote "Roman Christians", but Patrick's naïve rhetoric tends to accumulate long words for effect, and *Christianorum* is significant in view of the contrast: *tu vendis illos genti exterae ignoranti deum.*'

[2] 'Notes d'hagiographie celtique' (1957), pp. 158–74.

it certainly is true that a glance through both Patrick's works should convince anybody that he often uses this word in other senses than that of 'monk'. Similarly, *famuli Dei* (cf. *Ep.* 21) in Patrick are Christians and not monks. She is convinced that Patrick's language was not influenced by monasticism.[1] Grosjean can hardly be said to have made out his case for *frater* meaning 'fellow-monk'. It might still mean 'the monks', or, perhaps more probably, by the *faciem sanctorum Dei* Patrick meant 'monks' and by *fratres* 'fellow-Christians'. Even if this were admitted, however, we are not bound to assume that Patrick must have been in Gaul. The fact that he 'once was very anxious' (*optabam*) to pay a visit to the Christians and the monks of Gaul does not compel us to believe that he had ever paid this visit before. We cannot exclude the possibility that Patrick had once been in Gaul, though we can be sure that if he had he obtained there neither a higher education nor a monastic vocabulary. But we cannot be confident, either, that he had done so. There is no reason why in Britain he should not have heard about the Franks and the customary manner that prevailed on the Continent of ransoming Christian prisoners from them. After all, what other pagan nation could he have named from whose hands it was possible and customary to ransom prisoners? The Saxons? But till the second half of the fifth century they were either barbarian colonists settled in Britain, who would not take prisoners, or raiders by sea, from whom it would be very difficult, if not impossible, to ransom prisoners. If Patrick's parents made no attempt to ransom him from the relatively neighbouring Irish, it is not likely that facilities existed for ransoming prisoners from the Saxons. The Franks were the nearest example that he could think of, and of course it would be the Gallic Christians who would conduct negotiations with them for ransom. This passage in the *Epistle*, therefore, does not compel us to assume that Patrick had been in Gaul, though perhaps it is the more impressive of the two pieces of evidence.[2]

---

[1] *Latin*, pp. 26–27. Binchy (*PB*, p. 81) emphasizes this conclusion; he instances *Conf.* 14 as an example of *fratres* meaning 'fellow-Christian', but there are several more.

[2] Esposito ('The Patrician Problem', p. 151), Norah Chadwick (*SBH*, pp. 214–15, *SBC*, pp. 26–27), and Binchy (*PB*, pp. 82–90) all dismiss any theory that Patrick had visited Gaul.

We must now turn to what is probably the most obscure incident connected with Patrick's career, which is also, however, when properly understood, a very instructive one. This is the attack or accusation which was made against Patrick, to which he alludes several times in his *Confession*, and which, we may surmise, was the main cause of his writing this work. The fact that, in order to meet this attack, he has reason to recur to the circumstances under which he was sent as bishop has complicated the question and caused some scholars to assume, unnecessarily and against the evidence, that the attack came before he had been chosen as bishop, when the question of his being chosen was still in the balance.[1] It must be recalled, in attempting to unravel this intricate affair, first that Patrick's main intention is still not to give an autobiographical account of the events of his life, but to give thanks to God for the succour he has given him, and especially for reassurance given in dreams and similar spiritual experiences; and second that Patrick is capable of transferring his narrative without any warning from one event and period to a quite different one.

We must begin by paraphrasing or reproducing several chapters of the *Confession*. He has been recording various spiritual experiences he had after his return home to Britain from captivity, including the vision of the man Victoricus and the call from the *vox Hiberoniacum* and the people who were beside the wood of Foclut (23–25). Then he begins to record the period when he needed God's help most, and found it:

> *Et quando temptatus sum ab aliquantis senioribus meis, qui venerunt, et peccata mea, contra laboriosum episcopatum meum, utique illo die fortiter impulsus sum ut caderem hic et in aeternum; sed dominus pepercit proselito et peregrino propter nomen suum benigne et valde mihi subvenit in hac conculcatione. Quod in labe et in obprobrium non male deveni! Deum oro ut non illis in peccatum reputetur (26). Occasionem post annos triginta invenerunt me adversus verbum quod confessus fueram antequam essem diaconus. Propter anxietatem maesto animo insinuavi amicissimo meo quae in pueritia mea una die gesseram, immo in una hora, quia necdum praevalebam. Nescio, Deus scit, si habebam tunc annos quindecim et Deum verum non credebam, neque ex infantia mea, sed in morte et in incredulitate mansi donec valde castigatus sum et in veritate humiliatus sum a fame et nuditate, et cotidie (27).*

---

[1] Ryan, *Irish Monasticism*, pp. 70–74; Kenney *Sources*, p. 168; McNeill, *St. Patrick*, pp. 62–66; Bieler in *St. Patrick* (ed. Ryan), pp. 64 and 65, *Life and Legend*, pp. 67–68; Grosjean, 'Notes d'hagiographie celtique' (1957), pp. 163–5.

After referring again to his captivity in Ireland (28), he goes on to describe how on the night of the day when *reprobatus sum a memoratis supradictis* he was granted a vision of the divine displeasure manifested against this former friend who was attacking him (29). Patrick then thanks God *ut non me impedit a profectione quam statueram et de mea quoque opera quod a Christo meo didiceram* (30, 31). Then follows a particularly confused but particularly important passage:

> *Sed magis doleo pro amicissimo meo cur hoc meruimus audire tale responsum. Cui ego credidi etiam animam! Et comperi ab aliquantis fratribus ante ante defensionem illam (quod ego non interfui nec in Britannis eram nec a me oriebatur) ut et ille in mea absentia pulsaret pro me;*[1] *etiam mihi ipse ore suo dixerat: 'Ecce dandus es tu ad gradum episcopatus', quod non eram dignus. Sed unde venit illi postmodum ut coram cunctis, bonis et malis, et me publice dehonestaret quod ante sponte et laetus indulserat, et Dominus, qui maior omnibus est.* (32)

A number of observations must be made upon these eight chapters if their significance is to be perceived. It looks very much as if a deputation or group came to Patrick (*venerunt . . . illo die*) on one particular occasion to convey their accusation against him (26). It is almost impossible to construe the words *contra laboriosum episcopatum meum* in any other way than to mean that Patrick had been a bishop for some time before this accusation was made. The sentence *Quod in labe et opprobrium non male deveni* is particularly obscure. It could mean 'How great a mercy that I did not fall badly into disgrace and disrepute!' Or it could mean 'Indeed, I came deeply into disgrace and disrepute.' Patrick uses *quod* much as Sarah Gamp used the word 'which'. *Non male* could be a colloquial understatement, rather like the slovenly and widespread 'not too happy' of our day. On the whole, the context suggests that we should take the second interpretation: *Ut non me impediret a profectione, etc.* (30) is the only piece of solid evidence that can be adduced in favour of the view that the attack on Patrick came before he was made bishop and not after his going to Ireland as bishop, but it is far from compelling. Patrick is looking back on his period of greatest peril, when he had to face this undeserved

---

[1] Morris is mistaken in imagining ('Celtic Saints', p. 362, n. 3) that *pulsaret pro me* is translated 'put me to shame' by Newport White and 'let me down' by Bieler. These two writers are translating *dehonestaret*, a few lines later, by these words.

attack, and he declares that in spite of this unpleasant incident
he still thanks God that he did not prevent him from coming to
Ireland as bishop. The most involved but also most significant
passage for understanding this affair is Chapter 32. Careful
study of this passage will convince the reader that Patrick is
here referring to three separate occasions, in order the reverse
of chronological:

1. The attack, which he here calls *defensio*; cf. *conculcatio*
   (26). This apparently took place at some public gathering
   (*coram cunctis publice dehonestaret*), perhaps at a synod, in
   Britain.
2. When his close friend in his absence 'fought for him', an
   earlier occasion than the last mentioned.
3. When his friend said to him 'You are to be made bishop'
   (or 'you ought to be made bishop', for either rendering
   is possible). Patrick was, of course, present on this
   occasion, which was earlier than the occasion mentioned
   before it, when Patrick was not yet bishop.

It is absolutely clear that the second occasion, when his close
friend defended him, was in Britain, and that Patrick was not
then in Britain. The likelihood that Patrick was then in Ireland,
and a bishop, is overwhelming. The close friend is a Briton.
It is from Britain that Patrick was sent as a bishop to Ireland.
There it was that the friend said '*Ecce dandus es tu, etc.*', and we
cannot doubt that it was from there that the accusation against
Patrick, barbed by the treacherous betrayal of confidence on
the part of this friend, came, even though a deputation may
have travelled to Ireland to acquaint Patrick with the accusation. Only minds obsessed with the desire to reconcile Patrick's
writings with the later tradition about him could imagine that
Patrick was in Gaul on any of these three occasions. Even if we
ignore the logical inferences to be made from Patrick's words in
this chapter, we must ask how we can imagine a set of circumstances in which an accusation was levelled in Britain against
Patrick when he was in Gaul *before* he was made bishop, not
the accusation referred to in Chapters 26 and 29 (in which his
friend was arming the accusers with evidence), but one which
his friend, in Britain, repelled. To take this view would be to
multiply hypotheses quite unnecessarily. Involved and confused

though Chapter 32 is, it constitutes a very strong argument that Patrick's mission as a bishop came from Britain, that it was in Britain that both his friends and enemies were to be found, and that to look for the origins of his mission in Gaul is to follow a trail for which there is no evidence in his own writings.

That the attack upon Patrick came when he had been a bishop for some time, and not when the question of his consecration and dispatch as bishop was still in the balance, is made even clearer by two passages in the *Confession* where he refers to this period just before he went as bishop to Ireland in terms quite different from those in which he refers both to the accusation and the accusers. The first comes in Chapter 37:

> *Et munera multa mihi offerebantur cum fletu et lacrimis et offendi illos, nec non contra votum aliquantis de senioribus, sed gubernante Deo nullo modo consensi neque adquievi illis—non mea gratia sed Deus qui vincit in me et resistit illis omnibus.*

The other passage occurs in Chapter 46:

> *non cito adquievi secundum quod mihi ostensum fuerat et sicut Spiritus suggerebat . . . sed quod mihi pro his nesciebam de statu meo quid facerem, quia multi hunc legationem prohibebant, etiam inter se ipsos pos tergum meum narrabant et dicebant: 'Iste quare se mittit in periculo inter hostes qui Deum non noverunt?'—non ut causa malitiae, sed non sapiebat illis, sicut et ego ipse testor, intelligi propter rusticitatem meam—et non cito agnovi gratiam quae erat in me; nunc mihi sapit quod ante debueram.*

These two passages undoubtedly refer to the period when Patrick being sent as bishop to Ireland was being canvassed, and they breathe a different atmosphere from the passages which refer to the period of his being subject to accusation. Here it is a matter of friends attempting dissuasion; there of false friends, turned enemies, casting aspersions against his 'toilsome episcopate'. In the first instance gifts were offered and tears shed to restrain him. The dangers of the mission were vividly put before him. But all this was done in a friendly spirit. Patrick says so, as if to distinguish these approaches to him from the cruel accusations and imputations which were to be levelled at him later—*non ut causa malitiae, sed non sapiebat illis*—'there was no malicious motive, but they were not aware of the truth'. Patrick's Latin in Chapter 46 takes on a clumsiness and an unmanageableness unusual even with him. His words literally translated mean 'but what to me on behalf of those I did not know about my position', and they almost defy paraphrase. Perhaps they reflect the embarrassment he felt at the time. His friends were concerned about his safety and uneasy about his lack of education when they considered the prospect of his going to Ireland in this capacity. Patrick knew that God wanted him to go and was calling him to Ireland, but he lacked self-confidence and the ability to push himself forward. They did not realize that God would enable him for his task and overrule his deficiencies. But they were friends, not accusers; and this occasion is a quite different one from the other, later, occasion, when Patrick was to be faced, not by friends doubtful of his capacity and anxious for his welfare, but by open enemies whose mouths were filled with serious accusations against his conduct and his character. Patrick does not give us the slightest reason to doubt that both groups, friends and enemies, on both occasions came from Britain. In fact, everything combines to convince us of this. It is scarcely necessary to point out how incompatible all this is with the idea that Patrick was sent to Ireland by the Pope.[1]

One more point in this tangled affair remains to be decided.[2] We have noticed[3] how Patrick describes the betrayal of his confidence by his intimate friend which seems to have formed the gravamen of the accusation made against him: 'They found a pretext against me after thirty years, against a word which I had confessed before I was a deacon' (27). From what point are the thirty years to be measured? from the confession of the sin, or from the sin itself? If it is from the commission of the sin, then Patrick must have been forty-five years old when the accusation was made against him, for he tells us that it was when he was

---

[1] Even the theory of Bieler that though Patrick did not go to Rome 'the canonical character of St. Patrick's mission is sufficiently ensured by the fact that he was recognized as successor of Palladius, whose powers came directly from the Apostolic See' (*Life and Legend*, p. 89) receives no support whatever from Patrick's writings. Had he been approved by the Apostolic See, he would have had a magnificent weapon against his accusers; but it is a weapon which he leaves unused.

[2] In fact the great majority of those who have recently written on Patrick have taken the view here advocated that it was when Patrick had already been bishop that his friend's treachery and his enemies' accusations so greatly affected him. We may cite Todd, Bury, Gwynn, Newport White, O'Rahilly, Carney, Binchy, and Morris.

[3] See above, p. 131

fifteen that he committed the sin. In that case, the accusation must have taken place quite early in his episcopate, and the *Confession* must have been written early. This is a conclusion which would be difficult to reconcile with the reconstruction of Patrick's career which has begun to form itself in the course of this work. In particular, it would be virtually impossible to explain how Patrick could ever have taught from his childhood the presbyter whom he had sent to Coroticus and his soldiers a few days before he wrote his *Epistle* (cap. 3), for we cannot imagine either that Patrick was training young boys before he was made a bishop or that he was made bishop at the early age of twenty-five. It is altogether more satisfactory to assume that the thirty years are to be reckoned from the confession of this sin, and not from its commission. Perhaps Patrick means us to infer that he confessed this sin to his friend on the eve of his being made deacon, to clear his conscience before receiving holy orders. In that case we may deduce (what is in fact no very revolutionary conclusion) that his friend was a presbyter and an older man than he.[1]

Our survey, therefore, has established that there was no sustained and bitter opposition to Patrick's being chosen as Bishop of the Irish, only uneasiness inspired by motives of sympathy, even though it was mistaken sympathy. The elaborate reconstructions made in the past by scholars such as McNeill

[1] But not Germanus, as Grosjean romantically suggested ('Notes d'hagiographie celtique' (1957), pp. 163–5). But Grosjean believed that the thirty years were to be reckoned from the confession of the sin, as did Bury (*LP*, pp. 332–3), Esposito ('The Patrician Problem', p. 150), and Carney (*The Problem of Patrick*, pp. 163–7). Ryan dated them from the commission of the sin (*Irish Monasticism*, pp. 74–75). He asks how we can imagine bishops attacking a well-established bishop over so trivial a fault as this committed thirty years before. But if Patrick recalled this sin several years after its commission, before being made deacon, it may not have been a trivial one, and in fact Patrick never says that it was trivial, but only that it was done before he was converted. Some sins could be embarrassing later; was not the death of Adeodatus an advantage to Augustine's later career? Again, judging by the behaviour of Jerome over Pelagius and of Theophilus over Chrysostom, the magnifying of fairly trivial faults into major accusations was part of the stock-in-trade of ecclesiastical warfare in the fifth century. Bieler in the *Life and Legend* (p. 69) took the view that it was from the confession that the thirty years were to be calculated, surprisingly, for this was not consistent with his view that the attack came when Patrick was not yet a bishop. But later, in an article in the *Irish Ecclesiastical Review* (Mar. 1953, p. 174), he changed his opinion to favour the other view. I do not know that he has faced the chronological difficulty into which this brings him.

and Grosjean, involving Germanus's prohibition of Patrick's mission or Patrick's disappointment when Palladius was chosen and his dispatch on Palladius's death as a *pis aller*, are all beside the point. They have no support in the primary evidence and should be dismissed.

We cannot discern any more definite incidents in the rest of Patrick's career mirrored in his writings. We can only note a few of the circumstances which surrounded his ministry. In many ways he gives evidence of being a typical fifth-century bishop. He baptizes and confirms, he celebrates the eucharist, and ordains clergy.[1] He institutes monks and nuns.[2] He is capable of excommunicating[3] and regards the authority of the bishop (whom he calls either *episcopus* or *sacerdos*) as paramount.[4] He has a bishop's *familia*, where he brings up likely children for the priesthood.[5] It is worth noting that he gives no signs whatever of having at any stage in his career consecrated a bishop or bishops in Ireland. This statement is, in fact, too mild. A number of pieces of evidence suggest that Patrick not merely did not happen to mention having other bishops connected with his mission, but that we can be confident that there were none. He says of himself *Hiberione constitutus episcopum me esse fateor*, as if he were *the* bishop in Ireland and there was no other with him.[6] Had there been available a bishop to send to Coroticus instead of a presbyter, it is most probable that Patrick would have sent him.[7] In the *Confession* he declares that he is greatly in debt to God because *populi multi per me in Deum renascerentur et postmodum consummarentur et ut clerici ubique illis ordinarentur ad plebem nuper venientem ad credulitatem;*[8] and a little later, *unde autem valde oportebat retia nostra tendere, ita ut . . . ubique essent clerici qui baptizarent et exhortarent populum indigentem et desiderantem.*[9] Here, if anywhere, are the places to mention bishops, but no mention of them is made. When a little later

---

[1] *Conf.* 49 (eucharist) 38, 40, 50, 51; *Ep.* 3 (ordination); for baptism and confirmation see *Conf.* 38, 40, 51, *Ep.* 3, 17, 19.
[2] *Conf.* 41, 42, *Ep.* 12.　　　　[3] *Ep.* 7, 21.　　　　[4] *Ep.* 6.
[5] *Conf.* 52, *Ep.* 3.
[6] *Ep.* 1. For the evidence in *Conf.* 51 that he may have indirectly acknowledged the existence of another Christian mission in Ireland, see above, p. 56.
[7] *Ep.* 2.　　　　[8] *Conf.* 38.
[9] *Conf.* 40; there are similar references in 50 and 51.

he says that he will not leave Ireland because *timeo perdere laborem quem incohavi*,[1] it looks very much as if he did not have any episcopal colleague to carry on the work were he to leave.[2]

That Patrick never left Ireland once he had set foot in it as bishop seems certain. He declares that God gave him the privilege of evangelizing the Irish people at the cost of losing native land and kinsfolk;[3] and he resolves that in spite of all attractions beyond the shores of Ireland he will never leave the country. Christ had ordered him to remain with the Irish for the rest of his life.[4] He certainly had not succeeded in converting the whole of Ireland by the time he wrote his *Confession*, nor in entirely reconciling the secular authorities to Christianity, for on more than one occasion he alludes to persecution, he declares that he expects martyrdom, and he welcomes the prospect.[5]

On the other hand, Patrick did have friends in Ireland. He alludes to *necessarios amicos quos ante praevidimus*,[6] who engineered his release from a period of captivity while he was a bishop. There is an obscure passage in the *Confession* (42) in which Patrick is describing the large number of women who have been persuaded to embrace a celibate life *nihilominus plus augetur numerus (et de genere nostro qui ibi nati sunt nescimus numerum eorum) praeter viduas et continentes.* Who are the *de genere nostro qui ibi nati sunt*? Some[7] have thought that this is a reference to Christians, who are of the holy race and who have been reborn in baptism. But this is a

---

[1] *Conf.* 43; cf. 58.

[2] Muirchu represented Patrick as accompanied by a few episcopal colleagues, and Tirechan gave him a vast episcopal retinue and alleged that he consecrated hundreds of bishops. Todd (*Patrick, Apostle*, p. 503) and Bury (e.g. *LP*, p. 130) persuaded themselves that Patrick had carried out consecrations of bishops, and Grosjean subscribed to the old illusion that early Celtic consecrations such as (he believed) Patrick carried out were performed by a single bishop ('Notes sur les documents anciens concernent S. Patrice', p. 55). Owen Chadwick has disposed of this fallacy (in *SBH*, cap. vii, pp. 173–88). Bulloch (*Celtic Church*, p. 49) and Christine Mohrmann (*Latin*, p. 27) apparently also believe that Patrick consecrated bishops. But Tillemont had noticed long ago that Patrick had not mentioned any bishops (so Todd, *Patrick, Apostle*, pp. 385–6), and had made the unlikely suggestion that they should be included under the heading of *clerici*. Binchy (*PB*, pp. 147–8) and Morris ('Celtic Saints', pp. 367–8) doubt the existence of any bishops with Patrick.   [3] *Conf.* 36.

[4] *Conf.* 43; cf. 62, *haec est confessio mea antequam moriar*; and 58 *usque ad transitum meum*.

[5] *Conf.* 37, 42, 48, 51, 52, 55, 57, 59.   [6] *Conf.* 52.

[7] e.g. Ryan, *Irish Monasticism*, p. 92.

very much forced interpretation, and Patrick refers to baptism as *re*birth, not as birth without further qualification.[1] It is more likely that what he means is that he cannot reckon the number of daughters of people of British race living in Ireland who have taken the veil. No doubt there were a number of British residents in Ireland, and no doubt Patrick could count upon their support in his mission. Perhaps they were among the audience in Ireland to which in the second half of his *Confession* he seems, as we have seen,[2] to be particularly appealing.

Finally, there are several references to finance in Patrick's *Confession*. He refused gifts thrown on to the altar by pious women, in order to avoid calumny.[3] Again:

> *Forte autem quando baptizavi tot milia hominum speravi ab aliquo illorum vel dimidio scriptulae? Dicite mihi et reddam vobis. Aut quando ordinavit ubique Dominus clericos per modicitatem meam et ministerium gratis distribui illis, si poposci ab aliquo illorum vel pretium vel calciamenti mei, dicite adversus me et reddam vobis.*[4]

Far from acquiring money, Patrick had spent it freely for the sake of the Church. He gave gifts to local kings.[5] He distributed among the *brehons* (*iudices*, law-men) money amounting to a very large sum.[6] In fact, he was a poor man.[7] These protestations, which all come near the end of the *Confession*, suggest not only that Patrick was liable to be accused of feathering his own nest, but that he was constantly receiving financial support from somewhere. Everything points to Britain as the source for this.[8] It was the Church of Britain which had sent Patrick to Ireland, and it was that Church which continued to supply him with funds, even though at times it appears to have suffered from heart-searching as to whether Patrick should ever have been sent. The matter of finance is only one more proof that the key to Patrick's background is not in Auxerre or in Rome, but in Britain.

---

[1] Cf. *Conf.* 38 *populi multi per me in Deum renascerentur.*
[2] See above, p. 109.   [3] *Conf.* 49.   [4] *Conf.* 50.
[5] *Conf.* 52.   [6] *Conf.* 53; cf. 54.   [7] *Conf.* 55.
[8] Cf. the words of Binchy (*PB*, p. 145), 'So far as we can judge from his own words, he regarded himself as primarily responsible to the bishops in Britain who had organised and financed his mission.' See also Kathleen Hughes, *The Church in Early Irish Society*, pp. 3–9 and 34–35, for an interesting account of pagan Celtic society and for useful suggestions about the Celtic tribal system as a background to Patrick's account of his ministry.

V

ST. PATRICK'S BACKGROUND

SOMETHING has already been said in this work about St. Patrick's background. But two points remain to be discussed which cannot fail to affect our estimate of the influences that formed Patrick, and which demand treatment in a separate chapter. The first point is that of monasticism. Was St. Patrick a monk? Whence did he derive his acquaintance with monasticism? The second point is the nature of St. Patrick's Latin. Could he have acquired the peculiar kind of Latin he uses elsewhere than in Gaul? Only when some examination has been made of these two subjects can we turn to the question of the dates of St. Patrick's career, which will occupy the sixth chapter.

Monasticism in the Western Church was a plant of slower and later growth than monasticism in the East. While Augustine was encountering towards the end of the fourth century the early appearance of what might be called unorganized eremitic monasticism in the area round Milan, coenobitic monasticism in Egypt, in Cappadocia, and in Syria was already well-developed. Martin had, of course, by the year 370 founded a monastery at Ligugé, and from 372 onwards, when he was Bishop of Tours, had established another near his see. But though Martin's example was eventually to be very powerful, he encountered a great deal of opposition; perhaps it is significant that Augustine does not mention him as an example of monastic life in the *Confessions*. A little before this Jerome's experiments in ascetic life in Rome had aroused interest but also considerable antagonism. At the end of the fourth century Jovinian wrote a book against monasticism. By the second decade of the fifth century, however, the movement had become more widely known, partly as a result of the very popular writings of Sulpicius Severus about Martin. In 410 Honoratus founded his monastery at Lérins, on an island off the south coast of Gaul, and individual monks or small groups of monks were to be found in many other islands off the coasts of Italy and Gaul. In 415 Cassian had begun work at Marseilles and was to continue as a propagandist for monasticism in the West for the next twenty years. The author of the tract *De Divitiis*, if we are to date his work about 410,[1] was greatly attracted by monasticism. Germanus, who became Bishop of Auxerre in 418, was a strenuous promoter of monks and monasteries.[2] By about 430 Pope Celestine deemed it necessary to issue a letter condemning the practice prevalent in the provinces of *Gallia Narbonensis* and *Gallia Viennsis* of choosing monks as bishops. He objects to monks coming into churches from outside in order to preside over them, and to their dress and behaviour as bishops. He objects to their wearing the *pallium* and to their being *lumbos praecincti* (apparently signs of ascetic celibacy). Let monks who live away from others in remote places wear such garments, he says, but not bishops.[3] Celestine alludes with dislike, and indeed contempt, to monks of any sort, but it is clear that the monastic movement must have gained a considerable hold upon the life and imagination of the Western Church if a pope found it necessary to issue these strictures.

Had this monastic movement spread to Britain by the time that Celestine wrote? Several scholars have answered this question in the negative. H. Williams came to the conclusion that 'monachism' reached Britain 'in the form of the South Gallic discipline' not before 420, but not long after that date.[4] But then, Williams was relying for this verdict largely upon the account of Patrick's life given by Bury, so that we can hardly call this evidence independent of Patrick. Christine Mohrmann maintains that 'there is not a single indication or clue in [Patrick's] language that he personally had anything to do with monasticism', though she is, of course, aware that Patrick mentions both monks and nuns (*Conf.* 41, 42, *Ep.* 12).[5] His vocabulary, she says, is quite uninfluenced by monasticism. Any words which suggest this, such as *fratres, famulus, eremus, desertum*, and *vocatio*, have an apostolic and not a specifically

---

[1] See above, pp. 40–46, and Norah Chadwick, *SBH*, pp. 211–12.

[2] As Williams remarks (*CEB*, p. 233).

[3] *PL* 50. 430, 431 (*Epistola*, iv, Praef. 1 and 2). Bury refers to this letter (*LP*, p. 52, n. 1).

[4] *CEB*, p. 307; see also p. 78.   [5] *Latin*, p. 27.

monastic sense.[1] Patrick quotes the Psalms very rarely, in contrast to monastic writers; she points out that there are only five
literal quotations from the Psalms and ten allusions to texts of
the Psalms in his work.[2] And Grosjean, though he is quite sure
that Patrick was a monk, vigorously maintained that Patrick
could not possibly have learnt his monasticism in Britain, for
before 430 there were no monks in Britain.[3] Patrick's attitude
to monks is that of a bishop educated in Gaul in the first third
of the fifth century, who is addressing British colleagues several
years after his residence in Gaul; and these bishops were un-
acquainted with monasticism:

> Même si l'on y rencontrait parfois déjà quelques moines, les
> monastères épiscopaux organisés n'existaient sans doute pas en
> Grande-Bretagne vers 445, date vers laquelle nous plaçons l'Epistula
> et la Confessio. L'Église y était toujours épiscopale à l'ancienne
> mode, avec des prélats relativement riches et bien dotés, peu enclins
> à pratiquer l'ascèse, brefs, tels qu'on les rencontrait nombreux sur le
> continent. Le monachisme, pour ceux-ci, devait être quelque chose
> de bien neuf, en effet, comme dans tout l'ouest et le nord de l'Europe,
> exception faite de la Gaule seule.

Curiously enough, Norah Chadwick comes to precisely similar
conclusions about the absence of monasticism in the Britain of
Patrick's day, starting from diametrically opposite premises.
Because Patrick (as she thinks) never mentions monasticism in
his works and shows no sign of acquaintance with it, she dismisses the possibility of his having come from Gaul, and even
suggests that the missions of Palladius and of Patrick were part
of a concerted effort to combat monasticism, viewed as a new
subversive force, in the West.[4] When scholars can make such
totally different assumptions about Patrick's relationship to
monasticism, clearly the question of Patrick being a monk
and a monk who learnt his monasticism in Britain, is an

---

[1] *Latin*, pp. 26, 27; cf. pp. 47–48.   [2] Ibid., p.26
[3] 'Notes d'hagiographie celtique' (1957), pp. 172–3. We have seen above (pp.
129–30) that Grosjean interpreted the *fratres* of *Conf.* 43 as referring to the monks in
Gaul with whom Patrick had once lived.
[4] Ibid., p. 173.
[5] *ASCC*, pp. 23, 34, 35. The suggestion of Bulloch (though not perhaps first
made by him) that Germanus and Lupus during their visit of 429 first encouraged
monasticism in Britain (*Celtic Church*, p. 169) would leave Patrick (on the conventional chronology of his life) to gain his acquaintance with monasticism in Gaul.
This suggestion, of course, is pure conjecture.

entirely open one, and the subject lends itself to further exploration.

In fact, though it would be wrong to claim that it can be decisively proved that monasticism existed in Britain before the period 420–30, there is more evidence in favour of this view than could be gathered from the words of any of the writers just mentioned. In the first place, we may point to the visit to Britain at the very end of the fourth century of that champion of monasticism, Victricius of Rouen. Victricius became Bishop of Rouen about 380, and by 409 he must have been dead, for his friend Paulinus of Nola (in his 48th *Epistle*) mentions the chief bishops of Gaul in that year without naming him. Paulinus is known to have met him in the company of Martin at Vienne about 386. Gallus in Sulpicius Severus's *Dialogues* (iii.2) narrates a miracle performed by Martin in the presence of Victricius and Valentinus, Bishop of Chartres, about 395. In a sermon, called *De Laude Sanctorum*, preached about 396, Victricius refers to a journey he has recently made to Britain on ecclesiastical affairs. He tells us that he was sent among the Britons at the request of Continental bishops to bring to an end some dispute: *Nam quod ad Britannias profectus sum, quod ibi moratus sum, vestrorum fecit exsecutio praeceptorum. Pacis me faciendae consacerdotes mei salutares antistites evocarunt . . . Vobis intra Britannias obsequebar, et oceani circumfluo separatus vestro tamen detinebar officio.*[1] Morris suggests that in this visit of Victricius to Britain we should trace the origins of monasticism there. 'In 396 Victricius of Rouen, Martin's enthusiastic disciple, had visited Britain, advocating his overriding concerns, the worship of relics, the foundation of monasteries, and the conversion of country-folk and other barbarians. His visit is the most probable occasion for the foundation

[1] *PL* 20. 443 (*De Laude Sanctorum*, 1). For Victricius see Grosjean, 'Notes d'hagiographie celtique' (1945), pp. 94–100 (in the course of which he concludes that it is improbable that Patrick had any connexion with Victricius); Norah Chadwick, *SBH*, pp. 221–2; Simpson, *Ninian and Origins*, pp. 63–64; Kenney, *Sources*, pp. 159–60; Morris, 'The Dates of the Celtic Saints', pp. 352–3. The date of 396 for Victricius's visit to Britain is not quite certain. For the letter sent by Pope Innocent I to Victricius in the year 404 (which is curiously referred to in the *Anglo-Saxon Chronicle* under the year 403) see below, pp. 177–8. The conjecture made by (e.g.) Myres ('Pelagius and the End of Roman Rule in Britain', pp. 23–24) that this was the year of Victricius's visit to Britain, because the Pope was rebuking him for interfering in other dioceses, seems wholly improbable, for there is not a word of rebuke in the letter on this subject. On the contrary, it confirms the rights of metropolitans such as Victricius.

of Whithorn, St. Alban's, and doubtless other houses that perished without record.[1] It should be noticed that Victricius says of his visit to Britain *ibi moratus sum*, suggesting a long visit. The suggestion that British monasticism sprang from this visit can only be a conjecture, but it seems a likely conjecture. We can at least be sure that by about 400 the British Church had not only heard about monasticism from one of its most enthusiastic advocates, but had heard about the work and miracles of Martin too.

We may perhaps take a brief glance at the question of whether Pelagius, who certainly was a Briton, was a monk.[2] The only piece of serious evidence against the view that he was a monk is to be found in the tract *De Divina Lege*,[3] where the writer says: *Ego te Christianum esse nolo, non monachum dici, et virtutem propriae laudis possidere magis quam nomen alienum, quod frustra a Latinis in turba commorantibus imponitur cum a Graecis solitarie viventibus legitime deputetur*.[4] If this sentence was written by Pelagius, it means that he certainly could not have been a monk living in a community. But it is very doubtful if this work was written by Pelagius. Morris has given good reasons for thinking that it was not.[5] And if we abandon Pelagius's authorship here, we are left with nothing to set against the evidence that Pelagius was a monk. Marius Mercator calls him a monk.[6] Jerome, if we grant that in the Epistle in question he is referring to Pelagius, calls him a monk.[7] Plinval himself allots to Pelagius the authorship of the work *De Virginitate*, in praise of celibacy, and when Pelagius wrote to Demetrias, who was considering taking monastic vows, he certainly did not discourage her from this course.[8] Williams points out that the *Historia Lausiaca* (i, ii) tells us that men from Britain who were considering the adoption of an ascetic type of life were entertained by Melania in Jerusalem, and suggests that Pelagius originally came to Rome

---

[1] 'Pelagian Literature', p. 42.
[2] This apparently simple and insignificant question has sharply divided scholars. Bury (*LP*, p. 45), Simpson (*Ninian and Origins*, p. 38), Bulloch (*Celtic Church*, p. 105), and Norah Chadwick (*PLG*, pp. 173–4) assume that he was, and (as we shall see) so does Williams. But Plinval (*Pélage*, pp. 18, 102–3) and Grosjean ('Notes d'hagiographie celtique' (1957), p. 173) vigorously deny that he was more than a simple layman.   [3] For this work, see above, pp. 40–46.
[4] *PL* 30. 115 (*De Div Leg* 9).   [5] 'Pelagian Literature', pp. 36–37.
[6] *Pelagium gente Britannum monachum*; see above, p. 36.
[7] *Epistle* 50, *rumigerulum monachum*.   [8] So Williams, *CEB*, p. 208.

in order to see this sort of life as it was currently being practised.[1] It seems entirely probable that, while Pelagius joined no monastic community, he did adopt a monastic or ascetic kind of regimen in his own life, at a time when in the West the distinction between this kind of individual, unorganized, monasticism and fully developed coenbitic monasticism had not yet become clearly defined. But it must be admitted that there is no evidence that Pelagius, whose quitting of Britain for Rome must be dated before the arrival of Victricius in Britain, found this type of individual monasticism being practised in Britain. The most we can say is that he may have heard a rumour of it in Britain.

The next piece of evidence for monasticism in Britain is provided by the career of St. Ninian. We have already discussed Ninian's date and the extent of his activity, and have noted that Grosjean lent his eminent authority to the view that Ninian could not have dedicated a church at Whithorn to St. Martin as early as the opening years of the fifth century; and we have observed the tendency among scholars to dissociate Ninian from Martin altogether.[2] On the question of whether a church at Whithorn was ever formally dedicated to St. Martin in the traditional sense of church-dedication, no doubt Grosjean is right. The only piece of evidence which can be produced to suggest that dedication of churches to people other than martyrs or saints buried in the churches dedicated, or to a short list of primitive, scriptural, characters, before the sixth century or later, is to be found in a curious entry in the *Chronicles of the Picts and Scots* part of which runs thus: *Necton morbet filius Erip XXXIII regnavit. Tertio anno regno eius Darlugdach abbatissa Cilledara de Hibernia exulat pro Christo ad Britanniam. Secundo anno adventus sui immolavit Nectonius Aburnethige Deo et Sanctae Brigide presenti Dairlugdach que cantavit alleluia super istam hostiam.* The entry goes on to detail the extent of the land at Abernethy given to the church dedicated to God and to St. Bridget, and to explain that while he was in exile in Ireland earlier in his career Nechtan Morbet had asked for the prayers of St. Bridget for his return to his kingdom, and had dedicated his church as a thanksgiving for obtaining his request.[3] This is the only mention of the dedication of a church

---

[1] *CEB*, pp. 199–200; on page 200 he calls Pelagius both layman and monk.
[2] See above, pp. 56–62.
[3] W. F. Skene, *Chronicles of the Picts and Scots*, pp. 6 and 7.

in the *Chronicles of the Picts and Scots*, a rare addition in an otherwise bare list of kings. This part of the *Chronicles* is a translation into Latin from an original Irish document, and was probably composed in some monastery in Brechin between the years 977 and 995.[1] Presumably the date of this dedication would be shortly after 525, the year of the death of St. Bridget, who was directly succeeded as Abbess of Kildare by Darlugdach.[2] On the face of it, this looks like quite a likely incident, but the historical value of the *Pictish Chronicle* is very dubious. Wainwright can say that 'the Abernethy notice, being common to all manuscripts in one form or another, is comparatively early';[3] but his general verdict is far from encouraging: 'The plain fact is that historians at present cannot place any trust in or draw any conclusions from that part of the *Pictish Chronicle* which claims to cover the period before about A.D. 550.'[4]

It is highly likely, however, that both Grosjean in denying church-dedications to Martin, outside Tours, in the fifth or early sixth centuries, and Duke in affirming them[5] are reading into the practice of this period a precision and definiteness which did not exist.[6] To have shown that Ninian could not have formally dedicated a church at Whithorn to St. Martin, that Ninian never went to Rome and never visited Martin in Tours is not necessarily to dissolve all connexion between Ninian and

---

[1] W. F. Skene, *Chronicles of the Picts and Scots*, Preface, pp. xviii–xxiii.

[2] But if we are to place the career of Nechtan Morbet in the fifth century, as Duke (*The Columban Church*, pp. 159–62) does, the chronology becomes impossible.

[3] F. T. Wainwright (ed.), *The Problem of the Picts*, p. 19.

[4] Ibid., p. 18; cf. his whole discussion, pp. 16–19.

[5] *The Columban Church*, pp. 159–62.

[6] The question of church dedications is a thorny one. Williams (*CEB*, p. 268) represents the older view that names of churches in British and Old Welsh very rarely represent the name of the saint to whom the church was dedicated, but rather the name of the saint who founded the church. Owen Chadwick (cap. vii, pp. 173–88, 'The Evidence of Dedications in the Early History of the Welsh Church' in *SBH*) strongly contested this viewpoint, and produced evidence to suggest that early Celtic churches were called after the saint whose remains or whose relics were enclosed in the church (not after the founder), and to show that during the fifth and later centuries original names of churches (either those of Scriptural saints or of founder saints) were often abandoned in favour of the names of those whose bones or relics had been later transferred to the church. But MacQueen, a more recent authority than Chadwick, thinks that the older view (as presented by Simpson) is in substance correct (*St. Nynia*, pp. 65–66), though he doubts whether Simpson is justified in identifying all traditional Ninianic sites as genuine foundations by Ninian.

Martin.[1] But what if Ninian did not dedicate a church formally to Martin but brought a relic of Martin to Whithorn? The cult of relics and the search for them was well begun by the end of the fourth century. We are told that Sulpicius Severus had placed a portrait of Martin in the church at Primuliacum, where Sulpicius lived, even during Martin's lifetime.[2] There were, of course, *martyria* dotted all over the Roman Empire, where the bones of martyrs were venerated on or near the spot where they had been martyred, or were supposed to have been martyred.[3] There is clear evidence that some of these were to be found in Britain. Gildas mentions the Martyria of St. Alban at Verulamium and of Aaron and Julius at Caerleon, and speaks of *clarrisimos lampades sanctorum matryrum . . . quorum nunc corporum sepulturae et passionum loca, si non lugubri divortio barbarorum quam plurima ob scelera nostra civibus adimerentur.*[4] Williams, the editor of Gildas, at this point adduces many place-names in Wales beginning with the prefix 'Merthyr' (martyr), including a Merthir Iun (Iulius) et Aaron mentioned in the Index of the *Book of Llandaff.* But there is definite evidence from Augustine that in the first decades of the fourth century the practice was growing of founding churches, not where the martyr had suffered, but to house a relic of the martyr, or of bringing a relic of a martyr to a church which had not hitherto possessed it. Augustine is careful to explain that though we have *memoriae* (memorial shrines) to the saints, we do not dedicate churches to them: *non eis templa, non eis altaria, non sacrificia exhibemus. Non eis sacerdotes offerunt: absit, Deo praestantur.*[5] In a later sermon Augustine recounts to his congregation the story of a certain Leporius, a pious presbyter who among other good works *etiam basilicam ad octo martyres fabricavit de his quae per vos Deus donavit.* There is nothing here to suggest that Leporius's church was built on the spot where the eight martyrs had suffered; it no

---

[1] It is for these reasons that Norah Chadwick (*SBH*, pp. 199–200; *Proceedings of the Dumfriesshire and Galloway Natural History and Antiquarian Society*, xxvii (1950), 46 ff.) and Owen Chadwick (*SBH*, p. 182) dismiss all connexion between these two saints.

[2] Norah Chadwick, *PLG*, p. 98.

[3] Cf. W. H. C. Frend, *Martyrdom and Persecution in the Early Church*, p. 455: 'Swarms of churches dedicated to the saints were to spring up in the Numidian villages during the fourth century.'

[4] *De Excid. Brit.* 10 (24, 26).

[5] *PL* 38. 1251 (*Sermones*, 273. 7).

doubt held a *memoria* with relics of the martyrs.[1] At one point in the *De Civitate Dei* Augustine is giving a list of miracles for whose authenticity he personally can vouch: *Victoriana dicitur villa, ab Hippone Regio minus triginta milibus abest. Memoria martyrum ibi est Mediolanensium Protasii et Gervasii. Portatus est eo quidam adulescens,* etc.[2] The bones of Protasius and Gervasius cannot possibly have been in this place; they were jealously guarded in Milan. But some small relic, perhaps a piece of cloth which had been in contact with their shrine, may have been there. In the next chapter he refers to *ad viginti martyres quorum memoria est aput nos celeberrima,*[3] and to a Lucillus, Bishop of Castellum Sinitense, who carried round a *memoria* of St. Stephen in his hands, which clearly was a relic,[4] to a farm called Audurus where there was a church, *et in ea memoria martyris Stephani,*[5] and to a *memoriam martyrum* in the suburb of a town.[6] Two of Augustine's sermons (325 and 326) were preached on the occasion of the anniversary of martyrs, probably in churches which held relics of them,[7] and another sermon (or at least a section of it) was given when a church was being newly dedicated, in which Augustine declares that though the church is being dedicated in God's name, yet God *fecit etiam sanctorum martyrum reliquis amplius honorari.*[8] We may well conjecture, then, that many of the *martyria* in Britain were not buildings erected on or near the site of actual martyrdoms (of which the British Church must by the nature of the case have suffered an acute shortage), but buildings which constituted or enclosed the *memoriae* of martyrs, containing their relics.

We must now draw the reader's attention to a curious piece of evidence at Whithorn itself. An upright inscribed stone, known as 'the stone of St. Peter', from its inscription,[9] dated to the seventh century, used to stand half a mile away from the Cathedral, in the direction of the Isle of Whithorn. The authors

---

[1] *PL* 39. 1578 (*Serm.* 356. 10).
[2] *De Civ. Dei* (ed J. E. C. Weldon) xxii. viii. Y.
[3] Ibid. viii. CC.   [4] Ibid. viii. FF.   [5] Ibid. viii. LL.
[6] Ibid. viii. OO.   [7] *PL* 38, 1447–50.   [8] *PL* 38. 1475 (*Serm.* 336).
[9] The inscription, as far as it can be made out, runs LOCI TI PETRI APOSTOLI. See Duke, *The Columban Church*, p. 141, and Simpson, *Ninian and Origins*, fig. 14. J. Wall, in an unpublished dissertation, following Macalister, confidently restores the true reading as LOGI T PETRI APOSTOLI, i.e. *logium tau Petri Apostoli*, 'the lodging-place of the seal of the Apostle Peter'. He argues from the shape of the Chi Rho to date the inscription about 670.

of the Official Guide to Whithorn conjecture that it may have marked the site of a relic brought back from Rome by some pilgrim: 'it may even replace an earlier stone marking the place of a relic brought by St. Ninian himself.'[1] Is it not likely that here we have a clue to what really happened over the 'dedication' to Martin at Whithorn? The theory of Norah and Owen Chadwick, of Levison and of Grosjean,[2] that Bishop Picthelm and Bede between them invented or imagined the association of Whithorn and of Ninian with Martin is, coolly considered, decidedly implausible. Why Martin rather than Peter? St. Peter was the patron saint of the party in the English Church of the seventh century who were anxious to introduce Roman observances and the Roman method of calculating Easter. It was St. Peter's authority that King Oswy chose in his fateful decision at the Synod of Whitby in 664. If Picthelm and Bede had wanted to imagine an original dedication of Ninian's church at Whithorn which would favour their romanizing policy, they would have been far more likely to choose Peter than to choose Martin. In fact, the 'Peter stone' at Whithorn may mark precisely the period when Peter's policy, the romanizing one, was adopted at that ecclesiastical centre; its date, the seventh century, would fit this well. Françoise Henry (*Irish Art in the Early Christian Period to A.D. 800*, pp. 119–20) calls attention to an interesting parallel with this 'St. Peter Stone' in Kilsaggart, Co. Armagh, where there is a stone with an inscription in Irish, 'this place has been given by Ternoc, son of Ciaran-the-Little, under the protection of Peter the Apostle', which has been dated to about 700 and connected with the aftermath of the Synod of Whitby.

We may add a little more evidence to this stock. At Brampton, not very far from Whithorn, there is the site of an ancient church inside the walls of the Roman fort dedicated to St. Martin, with Ninian's well hard by. According to Simpson and I. A. Richmond, this church became the church of the Saxon settlement, and this suggests continuous use of the site up to Saxon times.[3] Salway accepts that this church was dedicated to St. Martin in sub-Roman times and points out that there is

---

[1] C. Ralegh Radford and G. Donaldson, *Official Guide to Whithorn and Kirkmadrine*, p. 8.

[2] See above, pp. 58–59.　　　[3] Simpson, *Ninian and Origins*, pp. 81, 85–86.

evidence for the existence of 'Dark-Age princelings' in nearby
Netherby and Old Carlisle.[1] It can hardly be contended that
Picthelm invented the original dedication of this church also.[2]
The name of the site of Martin's monastery, Logo-tigiae
(Ligugé) may have the same meaning as *Candida Casa*, the
latter being a translation into Latin of the former.[3] Kenney[4]
suggested that Irish monasticism began under the influence of
the work of St. Martin. He pointed out that St. Martin was
peculiarly venerated in the early Irish Church. We may observe
that the only other documents in the *Book of Armagh*, compiled
in the seventh and eighth centuries in Armagh, besides documents connected with St. Patrick and the text of the New
Testament, are the works of Sulpicius Severus about St. Martin,
and that it looks very much as if Sulpicius Severus's *Life of
Martin* lies behind the peculiar jumble that appears in Nennius's *Historia Brittonum* 26 (166). It is not unreasonable to
conjecture[5] that the cult of Martin was first introduced into
Britain by Victricius, Bishop of Rouen, when he visited Britain
about 395, for Victricius was a great admirer of Martin and a
great champion of monasticism and of the veneration of relics.

We conclude, then, that Ninian's association with St. Martin
can stand, and that he probably brought a relic of Martin to
Whithorn and set up some *memoria*, perhaps quite separate from
the church, to enshrine it. We need not assume either that
Ninian visited Rome or that he visited Martin in Tours. It is
enough to hold that he undertook his work under the influence
of Martin's example and form of monasticism, perhaps inspired
by Sulpicius Severus's writings, that he was a monk in the
tradition of Martin, perhaps one of the first British monks, and

[1] *The Frontier People*, p. 16.

[2] And the existence of this church, and of a Ninianic dedication at Nynekirks,
near Brougham, sorts ill with the statement of Norah Chadwick that 'no early
dedications to either St. Martin or St. Ninian have survived in the neighbourhood
of Whithorn in Galloway' (*SBH*, p. 200).

[3] So several scholars have suggested; most recently J. Wall, in an unpublished
dissertation.

[4] *Sources*, pp. 159–60. Kenney was not, of course, the first to make this conjecture. The first appearance of this theory may be attributed to the seventeenth-century
Bollandist editor of the *Confession* of Patrick for the *Acta Sanctorum*, Papebroch, who
at Confession 23 read *Victricius* for *Victoricus*.

[5] This conjecture has been made several times, most recently, perhaps, by
W. D. Simpson, *Ninian and Origins*, pp. 1–22, 63–64, and J. Morris, 'Celtic Saints',
pp. 353, 354.

that he brought with him fellow monks to work at Whithorn,[1] in the very early years of the fifth century, well before Patrick reached Ireland as a bishop (according to the conventional date), and well before Germanus visited Britain.[2]

There is one small but striking piece of evidence that monasticism already existed in Britain at this early period, which has not received the notice it deserves. Orosius describes the elevation of two of the three emperors in Britain in the year 407, in reaction to the great barbarian invasion across the Rhine, in these terms:

apud Britannias Gratianus, municeps eiusdem insulae, tyrannus creatur et occiditur. Huius loco Constantinus, ex infima militia, propter solam spem nominis, sine merito virtutis eligitur, qui continuo ut invasit imperium in Gallias transiit. Ibi saepe a barbaris incertis foederibus illusus, detrimento magis reipublicae fuit.

Then he relates the opposition in Spain to Constantine's representatives, shown by Didymus and Verinianus, Honorius's relations.

Adversus hos Constantinus Constantem filium suum, proh dolor!, ex monacho Caesarem factum, cum barbaris quibusdam qui, quondam in foedus recepti atque in militiam allecti, Honoriaci vocabantur, in Hispanias misit.[3]

C. E. Stevens points out that an edict from Honorius, dated 27 November 408, against men who abandoned clerical orders, is probably directed against this move of Constans from religious to secular life, and identifies the Honoriaci who were put in Constans's charge as 'men, as it seems, from the wilder parts of Britain, taken into treaty relationship by Stilicho during his campaign of 396, who bore—strangely for the immediate circumstances—the name of Honorius but with a Celtic suffix'.[4]

---

[1] Bulloch (*Celtic Church*, pp. 38–39, 169) allows Ninian's association with Martin and thinks that he was a monk. MacQueen sees no reason to doubt that the dedication of *Candida Casa* to Martin was older than the eighth century (*St. Nynia*, p. 86).

[2] We must, however, allow the verdict of Norah Chadwick and others to stand, that the church dedicated to St. Martin, which Augustine found in Canterbury when he reached it whose origin Bede (*HE* 1. 26) attributed to the British Church of the Roman period, was in fact no older than the period of King Ethelbert's wife, Bertha.

[3] Orosius, *Hist. adv. Pag.* vii. 40 (1166).

[4] C. E. Stevens, 'Marcus, Gratian, Constantine', pp. 325–6, 327 (from which the quotation is taken).

If we had no presuppositions about British monasticism we should have to assume that Constantine III's son Constans was a monk *in Britain* before his elevation as Caesar. Constantine, according to Orosius, was a very humble soldier indeed before he was made emperor (*ex infima militia*), whom we should not normally expect to have a son in a Gallic monastery. Besides, the first action which Constans as Caesar is called to perform is to bring a body of barbarian *foederati* troops to Spain from Britain; where else in that area could *foederati* barbarians be found? This suggests that Constans was in Britain when his father called him from the cloister. It is true that Orosius is the only historian to mention that Constans was a monk. Sozomenus (*HE* ix. 11. 4) merely calls him the eldest of Constantine's sons, and Zosimus makes no mention of his monastic status either. But Sozomenus is not very well informed on western affairs anyway, and Zosimus was strongly prejudiced against monks; elsewhere he emphasizes their celibacy, which he views with disfavour, their social uselessness, and the amount of land they have acquired: 'On the pretext of distributing everything to the poor they reduce almost everybody to poverty.'[1] The fact that Constans had been a monk he would not have thought worth recording. But Orosius, who was shocked by Constans's desertion of his monastic life, is well informed about both this period and this part of the world, for he is writing not long after 417, and he came from Spain, the scene of much of Constans's later career. We must accept the fact that Constans had been a monk, and unless we have already made up our minds that there could not have been monks in Britain at that date, we must conclude that he was a monk in Britain.[2]

We have already noted[3] that at some point during the third

---

[1] *Historia* v. 5. 23 (244): προφάσει τοῦ μεταδιδόναι πάντων πτωχοῖς πάντας ὡς εἰπεῖν πτωχοὺς καταστήσαντες.

[2] Williams (*CEB*, pp. 177–8) discusses the possibility of Constans having been a British monk, but decides that, because his father after his elevation associated with some bishops who had been disciples of Martin, his son must have been a monk at Tours previously. But this is a very tenuous foundation upon which to place a theory of Constans's residence in Gaul as a monk, and Williams does not face the evidence that Constans's first act as Caesar was to bring troops from Britain. Morris ('Celtic Saints', p. 353) refers to Constans *en passant* as a British monk, in a rather mixed list which includes Caelestius and the author of the *De Virginitate*.

[3] See above, pp. 63–65.

decade of the fifth century Faustus left Britain to join the monastery of Lérins. We may conjecture that he was of wealthy and
perhaps aristocratic parents, and would not find such obscure
monastic communities as existed in Britain so attractive in his
search for an ascetic life as the monastery founded by St.
Honoratus, which was beginning to gather fame. We have also
observed[1] the appearance in Gaul in 476 of Riochatus, monk
and bishop from Britain, probably ministering to the Britons
who had emigrated to Armorica, and concluded that his existence allows us to assume with confidence that monasticism
must have been established in Britain at least twenty years
before that date, and we thereby approach perilously near to
the date at which Grosjean stoutly maintained that monasticism
could not have existed in any force in Britain![2] We have only to
add two faint indications which may slightly strengthen the case
we have put forward for the existence of British monasticism
early in the fifth century. The first is the existence in Old Irish
of a very early list of Latin loan-words, which Binchy dates with
some confidence before the arrival of Patrick, or even of Palladius, in Ireland, and which can only have reached Ireland from
Britain; among them is the word for 'nun', *caillech*, and, probably but not certainly, the word for 'monk', *manach*.[3] The other
faint indication is the possibility that in the fifth century there
was a Celtic monastery at Glastonbury. Excavation there has
established the existence of a very early wattled chapel 13 feet
wide and at least 17 feet long, without a paved floor. The fragments of pottery trodden into the clay included pieces ranging
in date from the first to the sixth centuries. A broad ditch, 8
to 9 feet in depth, discovered on the same site was no doubt
part of the enclosing boundary of the original Celtic monastery.
The site had clearly been occupied from very early times. The

[1] See above, pp. 64–66.   [2] See above, p. 142.
[3] Binchy mentions this list in *PB*, pp. 166–73, but he speaks of these two words, *caillech* and *manach*, only in a private communication to me. O'Rahilly (*The Two Patricks*, pp. 142–4) mentions this list of words also, ascribing the original identifica-tion of them to a Danish scholar, Sarauw, about 1900. But, according to Bury, Zimmer first called attention to this list. Binchy at least would place the period during which these words reached Old Irish as occurring during the first half of the fifth century, but other scholars (such as K. Jackson) would place the period later than this. For an earlier discussion of this point, see above, pp. 55–56. These facts, or at least the conclusions drawn from them, have been challenged. See Carney, *The Problem of Patrick*, p. 156. See also Morris, 'Celtic Saints', p. 363.

existence there of a monastery in the fifth century is not impossible but no more than this can be said.[1]

Having established that the existence of monasticism in
Britain in the early years of the fifth century cannot be ruled out
with the doctrinaire brusqueness with which Grosjean treats the
subject, we are now in a position to examine the question of
whether Patrick himself was a monk. Opinions on this subject
have differed, as on all subjects connected with Patrick. Bury[2]
thought that he was, so did McNeill,[3] so did Grosjean,[4] and so
does Bulloch.[5] But, as we have seen,[6] Norah Chadwick thinks
that he was positively anti-monastic, and Binchy thinks that he
never took monastic vows, and describes this as 'the opinion of
most of the orthodox Patriciologists'.[7] Christine Mohrmann, as
we have also seen,[8] can find no specifically monastic vocabulary
in his language, and declares that his biblical quotations show
no such preponderance of citations from the Psalms as might be
expected from a monk.

In fact, Patrick does quote from the Psalms more than from
any other book of the Old Testament, and Bieler in his very
valuable study of Patrick's text of the Bible specially notes this.[9]
As for monastic vocabulary, the first half of the fifth century
was still a period of only incipient monasticism in the West, and
we need not be surprised at the absence of a fully formed
monastic technical language at this period, especially if we are
to assume that Patrick's monastic background, if it existed, was
British and not Gallic. Let us first examine Patrick's own references to those who have adopted a monastic way of life. In
Epistle 12 (which we take to be the earlier work) he writes, of
Coroticus's soldiers, *Lupi rapaces deglutierunt gregem Domini, qui
utique Hiberione cum summa diligentia optime crescebant, et filii Scottorum et filiae regulorum monachi et virgines Christi enumerare nequeo.*
In the *Confession* there are two passages whose language echoes
that of the *Epistle*, so much so that they constitute a good argument (along with other verbal similarities between the two

---

[1] See Joan and Harold Taylor in *CS*, pp. 253, 256–7, and Norah Chadwick,
CB, p. 146.

[2] *LP*, p. 41.   [3] *St. Patrick*, p. 46.

[4] 'Notes d'hagiographie celtique' (1945), pp. 93–94.

[5] *Celtic Church*, p. 49.   [6] See above, p. 142.

[7] *PB*, p. 118.   [8] See above, pp. 141–2.

[9] 'Der Bibeltext des Heiligen Patrick', p. 239.

works) that the *Confession* cannot have been composed very long after the *Epistle*:

Unde autem Hiberione qui numquam notitiam Dei habuerunt nisi idola et inmunda usque nunc semper coluerunt quomodo nuper facta est plebs Domini et filii Dei nuncupantur, filii Scottorum et filii regulorum monachi et virgines Christi esse videntur? (41). Et etiam una benedicta Scotta genetiva nobilis pulcherrima adulta erat, quam ego baptizavi; et post paucos dies una causa venit ad nos, insinuavit nobis responsum accepisse a nuntio Dei et monuit eam ut esset virgo Christi et ipsa Deo proximaret: Deo gratias, sexta ab hac die et avidissime arripuit illud quod etiam omnes virgines Dei ita hoc faciunt—non sponte patrum earum, sed et persecutiones patiuntur et improperia falsa a parentibus suis et nihilominus plus augetur numerus (et de genere nostro qui ibi nati sunt nescimus numerum eorum) praeter viduas et continentes. Sed ex illis maxime laborant quae servitio detinentur: usque ad terrores et minas assidue perferunt; sed Dominus gratiam dedit multis ex ancillis suis, nam etsi vetantur tamen fortiter imitantur (42).

It is clear that Patrick is not anti-monastic; on the contrary, he encourages actively some form of ascetic life among those of his converts who feel drawn to it, even against opposition and difficulties. But, at least as far as women are concerned, these passages make it unlikely that he is referring to women living a religious life in community. The words are much more easily reconcilable with a picture of individual Christian women taking vows to live a celibate life in their own homes, among their parents and kinsfolk, or, if they were slaves, with their owners.[1] The pride with which Patrick singles out the young and beautiful woman of the aristocracy who took this vow suggests that he had not made many converts to this way of life among her class. *Viduas* must mean widows who, once having lost their husbands, resolve not to remarry; and *continentes* married people who live together but refrain from sexual intercourse, either wholly or according to determined rules. Patrick tells us more about the women who live specially ascetic lives than about the men. We cannot determine from his words whether he means men who take individual vows of celibacy in their homes or those who live in communities of celibates.

There are a few passages in the *Confession* where Patrick uses language which might be regarded as suggesting that he had

---

[1] Meissner gives some useful parallels in the fourth century for this way of life among Christians (*History of the Church of Ireland*, vol. i, pp. 155–7).

embraced a monastic manner of life. He is excusing himself at one point concerning the sin which he had committed as an adolescent of barely fifteen, and he says that he committed it *in pueritia mea una die . . . immo in una hora, quia necdum praevalebam* (27). What does *praevalebam* mean here? Newport White translates 'I had not yet overcome', and Bieler 'I was not yet strong'. White's is more literal, Bieler's makes better sense in the context. But when did Patrick overcome or gain strength, and over what? The word does not precisely suggest 'I was not yet mature', but rather that Patrick had not yet gained control of himself. The conjecture that this sin was a sexual one and that what he means is that he had not reached the stage (as he did later) when he could take a vow of celibacy is one that readily suggests itself. That deacons and presbyters in Patrick's day did not have to take vows of celibacy (though abstinence from sexual intercourse with their wives was being encouraged among clergy) is sufficiently evidenced from contemporary Church history, and perhaps from the fact that Patrick was the son of a deacon and the grandson of a presbyter.[1] Next, in *Confession* 30 Patrick gives thanks to God *ut non me impediret a profectione quam statueram et de mea quoque opera quod a Christo Domino meo didiceram.* His *opera* is his evangelizing work in Ireland. What is his *profectio*—his resolve or enterprise in determining to go to Ireland? Or is it his resolve to live as a monk? In Chapter 44 his language becomes even more suggestive. He writes:

sed memet ipsum non credo quamdiu fuero in hoc corpore mortis, quia fortis est qui cotidie nititur subvertere me a fide et praeposita castitate religionis non fictae usque in finem vitae meae Christo Domino meo, sed caro inimica semper trahit ad mortem, id est ad inlecebras inlicitate perficiendas; et scio ex parte quare vitam perfectam ego non egi sicut et ceteri credentes, sed confiteor Domino meo, et non erubesco in conspectu ipsius, quia non mentior, ex quo cognovi eum a iuventute mea crevit in me amor Dei et timor ipsius et usque nunc favente Deo fidem servavi.

Do not the expressions *praeposita castitas religionis non fictae* and *vitam perfectam agere* suggest a monastic life? Patrick does indeed say that he did not live a perfect life *sicut et ceteri credentes*, but this could mean 'as much as some other believers'. He is here

---

[1] For further information on this subject, see below, p. 176–9.

essaying the difficult task of justifying his moral character without appearing to be vain and self-righteous, but these words do
suggest that he was trying to live a special sort of life, to do what
he calls in the case of the noble lady who became a consecrated
virgin, *Deo proximare* (42). Finally, there is the statement in *Confession* 55: *mihi melius convenit paupertas et calamitas quam divitiae et
diliciae (sed et Christus Dominus pauper fuit pro nobis, ego vero miser et
infelix etsi opes voluero iam non habeo, neque me ipsum iudico).* This
could be interpreted as an allusion to his state of monastic
poverty, undertaken in imitation of Christ. It should be remembered that he has earlier, at *Confession* 42, said of those who
maintain their vow of virginity in spite of opposition and difficulties, *tamen fortiter imitantur.*

To these points we might add the occurrence twice in his
Confession of a phrase which has puzzled commentators,
seniores mei. In *Confession* 26 he tells us that he was attacked *ab
aliquantis senioribus mei,* who impugned his toilsome episcopate
by bringing up his long-past sins. And in Chapter 37 he says
that in allowing himself to be put forward as one who might be
sent as Bishop of the Irish people, he did so *nec non contra votum
aliquantis de senioribus meis,* and these *seniores* seem here to be a
group distinct from his kinsfolk. Grosjean said that they were his
superiors in the monastery from which he came, and if we grant
that the monastery was in Britain and not in Gaul, this seems
the most likely interpretation of the phrase. It could hardly
mean 'senior bishops', because in the second passage Patrick is
not yet a bishop, and he has no hesitation in using the word
sacerdos for bishop when he wants to name bishops. We have
already suggested[1] that the expression in Chapter 43 *usque ad
Gallias . . . ut viderem faciem sanctorum Domini mei* implies a desire
to visit the monasteries in Gaul, which might well have been a
source of inspiration for Patrick's life as a monk without his ever
having seen them. Add to this the fact that Sulpicius Severus'
works about Martin were circulating widely at a period when
Patrick's ecclesiastical formation was taking place, and we
may well conclude, without wishing to be dogmatically certain
upon the subject, that the facts decisively incline to the view
that Patrick was a monk, perhaps in the tradition of Martin,
and that he had lived in a monastery in Britain and had there

[1] See above, pp. 129–30.

learnt his knowledge of the Latin Bible, before he arrived in Ireland as a bishop.[1]

We now turn to a further source of illumination of St. Patrick's background, his use of Latin. On this subject the reader will find three main authorities: K. Jackson's book, *Language and History in Early Britain*; the commentary upon Patrick's works printed by L. Bieler in *Classica et Mediaevalia*, vol. xii (1951), entitled *Libri Epistolarum Sancti Patricii Episcopi*, Part II; and Christine Mohrmann's monograph, *The Latin of St. Patrick*. None of these authorities finds it easy to discover parallels of any sort for Patrick's Latin, though Bieler is the most successful in doing so. Clearly Patrick's Latin is Vulgar Latin, not literary Latin; very few extended texts of Vulgar Latin of the fifth century survive. The most useful parallel is the *Peregrinatio* of Etheria, which is thought to date from about 400.[2] But it is possible to make too much of this parallel. Etheria's Latin flows easily and simply; clearly this Vulgar Latin is her native language; the reader feels as he progresses that she could go on in her chatty, loquacious style indefinitely, and that if he could have met her in the flesh she would have been an intolerable bore. The impression she creates is that she finds the writing of her kind of Latin all too easy. Patrick produces an entirely opposite impression. The reader feels that Patrick is struggling to express himself, and often struggling unsuccessfully, and the reader suffers with him. Indeed, Patrick admits this himself: *Nam sermo et loquela nostra translata est in linguam alienam, sicut facile potest probari ex saliva scripturae meae*[3] . . . *Unde ergo hodie erubesco et vehementer pertimeo denudare imperitiam meam, quia desertis brevitate sermone explicare nequeo, sicut enim spiritus gestit et animus, et sensus monstrat affectus.*[4] He often gives the effect of using blunt tools, of being forced to use words and periphrases which do not express his meaning accurately, because he knows no others. He indulges in clumsy repetitions, his syntax breaks down helplessly

---

[1] Where his monastery was we can only guess; if we are to guess, I should fix on Glastonbury. But too much speculation of this kind has already bedevilled the reconstruction of Patrick's origins and career, and I refrain from elaborating upon this guess.

[2] Another parallel which might well be considered is provided by the latest part of the *Excerpta Valesiana Anonyma*, written apparently in the first half of the sixth century, probably at Rome and perhaps by a monk.

[3] *Conf.* 9.   [4] *Conf.* 10.

in the middle of a complicated sentence, grammar is thrown to the winds as another thought occurs to him and is awkwardly stuck on to the existing construction. But in spite of these grave handicaps, sometimes because of them, he achieves effects which the deadly, even, flow of Etheria's conventionally pious travelogue could never achieve. He enables us to realize his agonies and triumphs, to sympathize with his friendless exile, to feel the keen humiliation of his lack of education, to share the pride of his final achievement, to respect and admire his immense trust in God. This is why there is really no satisfactory parallel for Patrick's Latin, for there is no parallel for Patrick's experience. As we enter the debate about the origins of his Latin, therefore, we must beware of trusting too readily the comparisons to it which may be brought forward. In one sense Patrick's Latin is incomparable.

K. Jackson, in his classic book, has given us a description of what, as far as it can be reconstructed in the imagination, Latin spoken in fifth-century Britain must have been like.[1] After a description of the various kinds of people in Roman Britain who used Latin, he summarizes:

Latin was the language of the governing classes, of civil administration and of the army, of trade, of the Christian religion, and very largely (but perhaps not entirely) of the people of the towns. The rural upper classes were bilingual; the peasantry of the Lowland Zone, who constituted the great bulk of the population, spoke British and probably knew little Latin; and the language of the Highland Zone (apart from the army and its native camp-followers) was to all intents and purposes exclusively British. . . . 'There can be no doubt that the people of Roman Britain generally spoke not Latin but British. They did not write it down, however. In Britain the speaking of Latin, among the officials and perhaps as a second language—a polite tongue of the upper classes—coincided roughly with the ability to read and write.'[2]

Jackson goes on to suggest that while the army, the merchants, and the middle and lower classes in the towns spoke ordinary standard Vulgar Latin, the Latin words which were taken into

[1] *LHB*, pp. 90–121.
[2] *LHB*, pp. 105, 106 (the last quotation from Whatmough). Contrast the extraordinary statements of Meissner to the effect that in certain parts of Britain Latin had *displaced* the native language (*History of the Church of Ireland*, vol. i, pp. 59, 60–61). He has been misled by Haverfield's generalizations.

British and Old Welsh suggest a Latin which is still Vulgar Latin but which has a certain archaic purity about its pronunciation, and that this is the Latin spoken by the rural aristocracy in Britain, formed by schoolmasters and consciously a little different from the ordinary Vulgar Latin of the middle and lower classes. This, he suggests, is precisely *not* the Latin spoken by Patrick; it is the Latin of the 'skilled master-rhetoricians', whom Patrick challenges and envies.[1] To the decay of town life Jackson attributes the rarity of words from ordinary Vulgar Latin which survive in British or Welsh.[2] And he conjectures that, while in its earliest period the Church on the Continent used the low-class Vulgar Latin of the low-class people who were its members (and this, we may conjecture, accounts for the presence of so many Vulgar Latin words in the Latin Bible), the Latin spoken by the clergy in Roman Britain in the fifth century must have been the same rather archaically pronounced Latin as was spoken by the upper-class people whom we have just been considering.[3] Elsewhere he concludes that the absence of Latin words taken into Anglo-Saxon makes it unlikely that any significant body of people survived at the time of the Saxon Conquest 'who used the ordinary Continental Vulgar Latin as distinct from the more archaic language of the Romano-British upper classes'.[4] Jackson relies for his evidence, of course, much more upon the phonology of Latin loan-words in ancient Celtic languages than upon literature.

Christine Mohrmann, in her very interesting and useful monograph, *The Latin of St. Patrick*, notes that there is about Patrick's Latin 'a lack of culture and school education', and that he often has to have recourse to a biblical quotation, not because he desires to quote the Bible, but because the words of the Bible come more readily to him than the words of ordinary speech. Patrick is what experts in phonetics called a 'bilingual',

---

[1] *LHB*, pp. 107–10. For the 'skilled master-rhetoricians' see above, pp. 109–12.
[2] *LHB*, p. 112. [3] *LHB*, p. 119.
[4] *LHB*, p. 261. Cf. the same writer, in *SBH*, p. 61 : 'The rural landowners of the villa economy seem to have talked Latin as a polite language among themselves, but to have known British and to have employed it with their servants and labourers; but there is strong evidence that the upper classes, and specifically the rural aristocracy, spoke Vulgar Latin with a much more refined and literary, almost archaising, pronunciation than the normal speech of the masses which became the ancestor of the Romance languages on the Continent.'

i.e. while he uses Vulgar Latin, he uses it as a foreign language in which he does not find it easy to express his thoughts.[1] Patrick, she says, writes as if he were dictating orally and almost thinking aloud, adding unsyntactically clauses embodying ideas which have just struck him.[2] She summarizes her conclusions about the colloquial elements in Patrick's Latin thus:

All the elements I have mentioned here—and I could add many others—are so unbookish, they belong so evidently to the stream of living Latin—that they can go back only to a personal contact with living—and that means continental—Latin. This living Latin does not show the features of very late Latin in which the whole structure of the language had already changed. . . . Given the fact that popular Latin in Gaul was developing very quickly in the course of the fifth and sixth century, I think that the popular elements of the Patrician Latin point more to the first than to the second half of the century.[3]

Next she says that the 'essential stock' of Patrick's vocabulary goes back to 'normal Christian Latin with a certain archaic flavour'. She thinks that the archaism is due to Patrick's being in an 'apostolic situation' like that of the early Christians.[4] The eschatological vocabulary, for instance, 'is decidedly archaic and partly at least technical'.[5] Later she says that Latin does not appear to have been the language of Patrick's daily intercourse.[6] 'In Britain', she declares, 'Latin had never been, as it was in Gaul or Spain, the mother tongue of the British population, but it was the second language of higher culture and education, as well as that of the Church.' Patrick was no doubt brought up to speak Latin only as a second language.[7] She is quite convinced that the elements of living, colloquial Latin in Patrick's speech could not possibly have come to him from his early British Latin, but must have been picked up by him on the Continent.[8] She concludes by stating that the two outstanding elements in Patrick's Latin are its contact with living colloquial Latin and its archaic flavour. The first she attributes to Patrick having

---

[1] *Latin*, pp. 9–12; for his employment of biblical language see also p. 34. Bieler gives some striking examples of this, 'Der Bibeltext', pp. 56–58.
[2] *Latin*, pp. 12–15; her examples come from *Conf.* 9. 32, 18, and 41.
[3] *Latin*, p. 21.   [4] Ibid., p. 22.   [5] Ibid., p. 25.
[6] Ibid., p. 33.   [7] Ibid., pp. 45–46.   [8] Ibid., pp. 47, 50.

lived for a period on the Continent and the second to his working in an 'apostolic' situation.[1]

The work of Bieler upon Patrick's Latin is confined very
largely to comments upon individual words. We have had
occasion to profit from his wide and discerning scholarship
more than once already. He does not on the whole make judge-
ments about the quality or provenance of Patrick's Latin,
though it is virtually certain that he would agree with Christine
Mohrmann's verdict about its largely Continental origin. He
does once say that the evidence of Patrick's vocabulary as a
whole suggests that this vocabulary was more advanced (i.e.
more like later Latin) than the average Latin of the fifth century;[2] and this fits in with his inclination to date Patrick's
career rather more in the second half of the century than Bury
did. But he puts forward this opinion tentatively and with no
great confidence.[3]

To differ from three eminent authorities on fifth-century
Latin is a serious undertaking, but careful consideration of the
subject suggests that though we are indebted to these scholars
for discovering many important facts in connexion with Patrick's Latin their interpretation of these facts is at many points
open to question. In the first place, it is quite misleading to say,
as Jackson does, that Patrick in challenging the 'skilled master
rhetoricians' is referring to the rural British aristocracy who
speak Vulgar Latin with an archaic and perhaps, in Patrick's
view, refined pronunciation. We know virtually nothing about
how Patrick *pronounced* Latin, and he never suggests that the
difference between him and the class whom he challenges is one
of pronunciation. One of the difficulties in this case is that Jackson has of necessity to speak mainly about phonology, while we

---

[1] *Latin*, pp. 52–53. It is difficult to understand how Norah Chadwick can write
that Patrick's 'simple (!) and direct (!) prose . . . perhaps represents the more
conservative style of classical Latin prose taught in the Roman schools of Britain'
(*SBH*, p. 249), and that his Latin, 'despite its poor quality, is the ordinary Latin
of the schools, such as we would expect from a provincial Roman of a remote
western province' (*ASCC*, p. 23).

[2] *LE*, Part II, p. 81.

[3] Bieler's opinion here certainly does not justify Carney in his attempt (*The
Problem of Patrick*, p. 180) to reject Esposito's theory of Patrick's period as bishop in
Ireland covering the years 395–430. What really wrecks Esposito's theory is not
Patrick's *Latinity* (which in the nature of the case cannot be dated to any one or two
decades), but his acquaintance with the Vulgate N.T., which Carney does not
mention.

know Patrick's Latin only by literature. We can easily understand what Patrick means by the rhetoric which he lacks. It is the final stage in higher education, the capacity to use words persuasively, to write elegant, well-ordered, and flowing Latin. Patrick calls it *desertis brevitate sermone explicare*,[1] and tells us that it necessitates a continuous acquaintance with literary Latin from an early age and an unbroken practice in using it.[2] He obviously means the capacity to write Latin as, for instance, Pelagius and Faustus write Latin, or as any of the hundreds of Latin Fathers of the fifth century write it. They were all trained in rhetoric to a greater or lesser extent; they had all learnt how to dress their statements in effective, interesting, and carefully ordered, though often artificial, literary form; how to conduct an argument, how to make a telling point, how to sustain a narrative; how to win the reader's assent and admiration by appeals to his sense of justice, his compassion, or by elegant writing simply to his literary sense. This is as true for those who protest their *rusticitas*, like Sulpicius Severus and the author of *De VC* as it is for masters of eloquent writing like Augustine and Jerome. Patrick had none of these powers. He could not conduct a sustained argument in Latin. He could not carry through a narrative in a well-ordered way. He had no literary devices, no store of syntactical variations, no reserves of vocabulary, no art at all, in using Latin. He had just to struggle on as best he could with his very much limited resources. No doubt the Latin he learnt before he was kidnapped was the archaic Vulgar Latin of the British rural aristocracy; he did come from the aristocracy; he speaks of his *ingenuitas* and *nobilitas*.[3] What Patrick lacked and envied in others was not the Latin of this rural aristocracy; the basis of his Latin was the same as theirs. What he lacked was the higher education which could develop this Latin into a passable literary medium. Instead of undergoing this development, Patrick's Latin had been arrested when he was sixteen years old, and had only thereafter been completed by something else, which was not the Latin of well-educated men.

It is wholly likely that the archaism which Christine Mohrmann detects in Patrick's Latin is not the archaism of an 'apostolic' situation, but precisely the archaism which Jackson attributes to British Latin of the upper classes. Christine

---

[1] *Conf.* 10.   [2] Ibid.. 9.   [3] *Ep.* 10; *Conf.* 37.

Mohrmann is, of course, speaking of an archaism of vocabulary and expression and Jackson of an archaism of pronunciation, but the two would almost certainly go together. It is a surprising fact, but Christine Mohrmann had apparently not read Jackson's work when she wrote *The Latin of St. Patrick*. It is all the more striking that both authors should in this case detect an archaism, and it can hardly be a coincidence. We need not take very seriously the argument about Patrick being in an 'apostolic' situation. It is doubtful if this concept has any recognizable meaning; St. Paul was in an 'apostolic' situation, but he does not use archaic Greek; Irenaeus was in an 'apostolic' situation, but neither his Greek nor the translation of it into Latin gives an impression of archaism. The same may be said for Tertullian. We may, in short, confidently claim for Patrick's Latin that its basis was the Latin of the British rural aristocracy, like that, presumably, of Faustus and of Pelagius. What it lacked was development through higher education.

If we next ask what ingredients Patrick's Latin received instead of an education in rhetoric, which would have developed it into a proper medium of literary communication, we can see the main outlines of an answer without difficulty: an element of living colloquial ordinary Vulgar Latin like the Vulgar Latin of the Continent, and an element of ecclesiastical and biblical Latin. But where can Patrick have acquired these? Christine Mohrmann answers decisively, only on the Continent, and Morris has recently supported her.[1] But this argument, based as it is partly on the fallacious assumption that we can rely on the later tradition about Patrick to locate his ecclesiastical education on the Continent, has to face at least one fatal objection.

If we agree with Christine Mohrmann, as we may with entire confidence, that Patrick's Latin was not for him the medium of ordinary intercourse, we may ask the following question: if Patrick spent some years on the Continent in some ecclesiastical institution, what language did he *speak* during that period? Not, we may be sure, Gallic or Gothic or German, and not, of course, his native language, British. The only possible answer is, Latin. But if this was so, why does he not exhibit a greater fluency in Latin, for fluency is just what he lacks, and what he admits that he lacks? The question of what particular type of Latin was used

[1] 'Celtic Saints', p. 366.

in what particular type of monastery in Gaul in the fifth century, Auxerre or Lérins, which has been raised by some scholars,[1] is really irrelevant. We do not know enough to argue on either side of the case about what the spoken Latin in monasteries was then. We know the sort of Latin that Etheria and her fellow nuns spoke in their convent in Aquitaine or Spain, but nobody has ever seriously suggested that Patrick spent any period in those regions. The fact has to be explained that, even in his execrable Latin, Patrick is not fluent. How could he have failed to become a fluent speaker of Latin (some sort of Latin) if he had spent years in a monastery or a bishop's *familia* in Gaul? But if his years of ecclesiastical formation had been spent in a monastery or a bishop's household *in Britain*, then his lack of fluency is explained. There he would have used for the most part his native language, British, while acquiring enough Latin to study the Latin Bible carefully and to write and speak Latin, if need arose, according to the low standard of Latin that prevailed there. There he certainly could have found the ecclesiastical elements which are present in his Latin. Nobody could deny that. But could he there have picked up the elements of living colloquial Vulgar Latin which are also to be discerned in his stock of Latin?

Here we encounter one of the most extraordinary features of this whole debate concerning Patrick's Latin, the assumption of Christine Mohrmann that no Vulgar Latin was spoken in Britain at the end of the fourth and the beginning of the fifth century.[2] In fact this assumption can quite easily be proved false. It is possible that what has misled Christine Mohrmann on this occasion is the fact that Vulgar Latin did not in Britain develop into the vernacular of the British nation, as it did in France and Spain. But the example of Egypt should warn us against relying upon this argument. There can be no doubt whatever that Vulgar Latin was spoken in Egypt under the late Roman Empire. Finds of papyri have put this fact beyond dispute. Yet no vernacular developed in Egypt from Vulgar Latin. In the case of Britain, we are not, unfortunately, able to draw on any literature to help us in our investigation.[3] We have almost

[1] Binchy, *PB*, pp. 34, 88–90; Morris, 'Celtic Saints', p. 366.
[2] Bulloch (*Celtic Church*, p. 28) makes the same curious assumption.
[3] The statement of Morris that 'we possess ample texts of early fifth century

no sources from Britain with which we can compare Patrick's Latin and determine its provenance and its milieu. But that is no reason for concluding that these sources never existed. Because today we cannot summon abundant examples of British Vulgar Latin, it would be illogical to assume that there never were any. We have seen[1] that Jackson in his investigation of the Latin spoken in Roman Britain is quite sure that Vulgar Latin was spoken by some elements in the population.[2] And, though the vestiges of this British Vulgar Latin are scanty and fragmentary, vestiges do exist, and they are worth reviewing here.

We can bring forward in evidence a few inscriptions and a few *graffiti*. That some of the lower classes and some Celtic-speaking traders in Roman Britain in the course of their business spoke Latin is quite clear. There is a wooden writing-tablet from Walbrook, London, on which is a business letter from a *peregrinus*, no doubt engaged in trade, to a responsible servant and his fellow slaves about an inventory and about the selling of a slave-girl. The writer is called Rufus, son of Callisumus (a Celtic name) and he writes, in perfectly good Latin, to Epillicus (another Celtic name).[3] This example dates from somewhere between the end of the first and the middle of the second century. But Haverfield has illustrated the use of Latin by the lower classes in a period much nearer that of Patrick from *graffiti* found at Silchester. These are all in normal Latin, though most are so brief that we cannot really determine the quality of their language; they are mostly scratched on bricks and walls; one reproduces a Virgilian tag, *conticuere omnes*. There is no sign of Celtic influence in them, and they derive from the third and fourth centuries.[4] Most of these *graffiti* were made by people whom Haverfield called 'Callevan workmen' (after the Roman

British Latin' ('Celtic Saints', p. 366, n. 2) depends upon his assumption that these texts are British. But even if these texts were proved to be British, they would be irrelevant to this case, for they are all written in good literary Latin.

[1] See above, pp. 159–60.

[2] Binchey (*PB*, pp. 23–25) rightly assails this illegitimate *argumentum e silentio* on the part of Christine Mohrmann.

[3] I. A. Richmond contributed a note about this to *The Antiquaries Journal* for 1953 (xxxiii), pp. 206–8, and Plate xxvii.

[4] See 'Romano-British Hampshire', by F. Haverfield, in *Victoria History of Hampshire*, vol. i, pp. 265–349, especially pp. 282–4; *Corpus Inscriptionum Latinarum*, ed. A. Hübner, vol. vii, p. 229, no. 1259; F. Haverfield, *The Romanization of Roman Britain*, pp. 24–29.

name for Silchester, *Calleva Silurum*). Even if they do not justify Haverfield's claim that all workmen in the towns of Roman Britain spoke and wrote Latin,[1] they certainly show that some people of these classes spoke and wrote Latin. It is really impossible to maintain that all these are likely to have spoken good Latin, Ciceronian, or, at any rate, Silver Age Latin. The likelihood that Vulgar Latin was the sort they spoke is overwhelming. In fact we have a little evidence to support this. There is an inscription at Camulodunum, of the reign of Alexander Severus (222–34), put up by a barbarian, Celt or Pict, who spells *campestrium* as *campestum* and *nostri* as *nosi*.[2] There are a number of curses called *defixiones*, consisting of leaden plates inscribed with a curse invoked upon some person or persons, which brings us nearer the world of Patrick's Latin, e.g.:

> *Tretia(m) Maria(m) defico et illeus vita(m) et me(n)tem et memoriam [e]t iocinera pulmones interm ⟨x⟩ ix⟨i⟩ta fata cogitata memoriam sci [= sic] no(n) possitt loqui (quae) secreta si(n)t, neque . . .* (unintelligible thereafter).

Not only does this exhibit bad writing and bad spelling but also positively ungrammatical expression—*Tritia Mario defico* and *no possitt loqui secreta sint*.[3] Another leaden curse at Bath, written backwards, when deciphered runs:

> *Qui mihi Vilbiam involavit sic liquat comodo aqua. Ella muta qui eam voravit si* (there follows a list of eight names).[4]

Comodo for *quomodo* looks like Vulgar Latin, and is paralleled elsewhere; *ella muta qui* for *illa muta sit quae* is certainly not good Latin. A tombstone found at Maryport in Cumberland has the inscription *D(is) M(anibus) Mori Regis filii et heredes eius substituerunt; vix(it) a(nnos) LXX*, where *substituerunt* appears to be colloquial Latin for *instituerunt*.[5] Another from the same area

---

[1] See Jackson, *LHB*, pp. 99–101, and cf. the craftsman who carved the inscription on the signal-tower at Ravenscar in Yorkshire, who knew Celtic but knew no Latin (C. E. Stevens, 'The British Sections of the *Notitia Dignitatum*', pp. 151–4).

[2] *Ephemeris Epigraphica* ix (ed. F. Haverfield), p. 522, no. 1005.

[3] R. G. Collingwood and R. P. Wright, *The Roman Inscriptions of Britain*, pp. 3–4, no. 7. Letters in round brackets are omitted in the original and supplied in the text; those in square brackets are letters originally there in the inscription but lost through damage; letters in brackets, thus ⟨ ⟩, were wrongly put in by the original writer.

[4] Ibid., pp. 49–50, no. 154. In a private letter, Mr. R. P. Wright tells me that these curses are of fourth-century date.

[5] Salway, *The Frontier People*, p. 241, no. 74.

has the inscription [. . .*f*] *ilia Serquina, nat*(*a*) *Galatia, dec*(*u*)*buit*
(*?*) *Galat*(*ia, vi*)*xit ann*[*os*] . . ., where *decubuit*, which can be used
of the fall of a defeated gladiator, is probably a colloquial word
for 'died'.[1] And there is the tombstone of a freedman at South
Shields, to be dated to the latter half of the second or first half
of the third century, which reads *D*(*is*) *M*(*anibus*) *Victoris, natione
Maurum,* (*a*)*nnorum xx, libertus Numeriani* [*e*]*q*(*u*)*itis ala*(*e*) *I Asturum
qui piantissime pr*[*ose*]*qutus est,* where both grammar and spelling
have gone astray.[2]

Two inscriptions are of peculiar interest, and bring us
nearer, both in their dates and the quality of their Latin, to
Patrick than any others. One of them is scratched on a leaden
plate found in or before 1817 at Lydney Park, Gloucestershire.
It is a dedication or promise to the Celtic god Nodens, whose
imposing shrine was at Lydney. It runs:

> *Devo Nodenti Silvianus anilum perdedit demediam partem donavit
> Nodenti inter quibus nomen Seniciani nollis petmittas sanitatem donec
> perfera*(*t*) *usque templum* [*No*]*dentis.*

To the god Nodens, Silvianus has lost a ring. He has given half
(the value) to Nodens. Among those who have the name Senicianus,
do not (Nodens) allow them health until he brings (it) to the temple
of Nodens.

There is plenty of Vulgar Latin here: *devo* for *deo, anilum* for
anulum, perdedit for *perdidit, inter quibus* for *inter eos quibus* or for the
more correct attraction *inter quos.* This temple of Nodens at
Lydney is of the late fourth century; it was elaborately rebuilt
some time between the barbarian ravages of 367 and the year
400.[3] The other inscription is an epitaph from Carlisle. It is
certainly of the fourth century and very probably Christian.
It reads thus:

[1] Salway, *The Frontier People*, p. 240, no. 72.

[2] Ibid., pp. 257–8, no. 108. For further misspellings see p. 245, no. 83; Collingwood and Wright, p. 302, no. 908 (*vigsit* and *segsaginta* for *vixit* and *sexaginta*, which
suggests to Salway a dialect form of a comparatively late date), and p. 255, no. 105
(*mesibus* for *mensibus*, which reflects a change of pronunciation that occurred under
the Middle Empire); and Collingwood and Wright, pp. 381–2, no. 1154 (early
third century, *vixillus* for *vexillum*) from Corbridge. Cf. also the *graffiti* on wall-
plaster in Leicester, recovered from the courtyard-house in Blue Boar Lane, *equa
g ella culo fidis fidis*, which is Vulgar Latin in more senses than one, and which may
in the word *fidis* exhibit a Celtic -*is* ending applied to the Latin *fides* (R. P. Wright,
Journal of Roman Studies, liv (1944), 1. 182).

[3] The inscription is to be found in Collingwood and Wright, p. 104, no. 306; the
date of the temple is given by Norah Chadwick, *SBH*, p. 197 and *CB*, p. 35.

D(is) M(anibus) Fla(viu)s Antigon(u)s Papias civis Grecus vixit annos plus minus LX quem ad modum accomodatam fatis animam revocavit. Septima Do. . . .

To the spirits of the departed. Flavius Antigonus Papias, a citizen of Greece, lived sixty years, more or less, and gave back to the Fates his soul lent for that extent of time. Septimia Do . . . (set this up).[1]

D M can be paralleled on Christian tombstones, according to both Haverfield and Jocelyn Toynbee. What is striking about this inscription is the unusual senses of both *accommodo* and *revoco* in the clumsy and difficult sentence *quem ad modum accommodatam animam revocavit*. *Revoco* is found on name-plates of collars of slaves and dogs, meaning 'return (to owner)', and *accommodo* can mean 'lend' in commercial Latin. This is Vulgar Latin, used, probably by a Christian, in fourth-century Britain, and it has very much the same ring of clumsiness and periphrastic inefficiency as we hear in Patrick's Latin. Both authors were attempting to express large thoughts with a slender store of language. If we allow that Flavius Antigonus may have composed his own epitaph (which is not improbable), both are bilingual.

Finally, we may tentatively regard the name attached to Ninian's establishment at Whithorn as an example of fifth-century Vulgar Latin. *Ad Candidam Casam* did not mean, as it would in good Latin, 'To the White Hut', but 'At the White House'.[2]

It is surely significant that Patrick writes his two works in Vulgar Latin and expects them to be read and appreciated. He apologizes for the quality of his Latin in the *Confession*, it is true, but there must have been some (perhaps many) of his friends in Britain whose Latin was no better. He does not apologize for his Latin in the *Epistle*, beyond calling himself *indoctus scilicet* in the first chapter. He expected Coroticus, or his clerical staff, to

---

[1] This inscription can be found in both Collingwood and Wright, p. 318, no. 955, and Salway, *The Frontier People*, p. 216, no. 20. It is also described by Wall, *Christian Evidences*, pp. 203–5.

[2] I must withdraw the suggestion made in *St. Patrick, a British Missionary Bishop* (p. 15), that two sentences attributed by Patrick to companions or associates of his in Britain represent their original words—*Ecce dandus es tu in gradum episcopatus* (*Conf.* 32) and *Iste quare se mittit in periculo inter hostes qui deum non noverunt* (*Conf.* 46). These are certainly in Vulgar Latin, but they no doubt represent Patrick's account in Latin of sentiments originally expressed in British. For a parallel to this usage with *ad*, describing a site, see above, p. 61.

accept Vulgar Latin as a normal medium of communication. We must, in short, rid ourselves of the misleading results of assuming that Patrick was educated on the Continent, that somehow his writings do not count as British literature, are somehow not representative. We do not have 'ample texts' of British fifth-century ecclesiastical literature, but we do have Patrick's works. His is the kind of Latin that was written and, when necessary, spoken by most British churchmen, in British monasteries and by the staff of British bishops. He makes it quite clear that he had no other opportunity of improving his education, once it had been cut short by his captivity at the age of sixteen. He does not speak or write Latin fluently, as he certainly would have done had he lived in a Continental monastery. The necessary conclusion is that he spent the years between his escape from captivity and his return as a bishop to Ireland in some British milieu, where he received a thorough grounding in the Latin Bible, where his unfinished progress in Latin was completed by learning some ecclesiastical terms and picking up the Vulgar Latin which was spoken and written in these circles whenever Latin had to be spoken and written. Jackson's demonstration that the Latin which was taken into British and Old Welsh was the archaic, upper-class Vulgar Latin of the rural aristocracy applies largely to phonology, to the pronunciation of Latin. There is not enough evidence to determine anything definite about the syntax and vocabulary of the Latin which found its way into these ancient Celtic languages. The striking absence of Latin words (Vulgar or other) in Anglo-Saxon is accounted for by the gulf between these two cultures, the Christian Celtic and the pagan Saxon. The situation in Arthur's day, says Morris, 'ended with half the island in the power of the Germans, almost entirely free of native Roman influence, the other half a run-down limb of the Roman Empire, almost uninfluenced by German custom'.[1] This is the situation Augustine found when he reached Britain at the end of the sixth century. The linguistic evidence, therefore, is inadequate to disprove what appears to be the plain verdict of Patrick's own writings, unobscured by later tradition, that Patrick came from fifth-century Christian Britain, and that all his formation and education came from there too.

[1] 'Dark Age Dates', p. 175.

VI

ST. PATRICK'S DATE

LACK of confidence has not hitherto been a characteristic of those who have attempted to supply dates for Patrick's career; on the contrary, many of them have evinced so ready a trust in what they regarded as evidence that they have dated many of Patrick's movements to the very year (and sometimes to the very month and day) in which they happened, or were thought to have happened.[1] The most influential of these was Bury, who relied for his dates on a selection from the Irish Annals (for it is, of course, impossible to harmonize all the dates allotted to Patrick in all the Annals), aided by various means of external dating which he regarded as reliable. But it has already been shown how uncertain and unreliable are the dates for any events in Patrick's career given in the Annals,[2] and all the external dates upon which Bury relied have proved deceptive. Bury was inclined to connect Patrick's kidnapping with a raid of Niall of the Nine Hostages, whose death he placed about 405, and in consequence of this he estimated the date of Patrick's birth as about 389.[3] He connected Patrick's escape with the great barbarian invasion of 407, as we have seen.[4] Collingwood and Myres, under the influence of Bury's theories, reckoned that the Irish raids on Britain had ended by about 429.[5] But O'Rahilly believed that Nath I', King of Connacht, was still carrying out raiding expeditions up to his death in 445, and that Patrick was the victim of one of these;[6] and Carney places the death of Niall in the second half of the fifth

---

[1] For an account of three quite different attempts to date the main events in Patrick's career, all of them almost equally fallacious, see *St. Patrick, a British Missionary Bishop*, pp. 7–10.

[2] See above, pp. 96–105.   [3] *LP*, pp. 25–26, 334.

[4] *LP* 40; see above, p. 122, n. 3.   [5] *RBES*, p. 312.

[6] *The Two Patricks*, pp. 34–35. The careers of Niall and of Nath I' are dealt with at length in cap. xii of O'Rahilly's *Early Irish History and Mythology*, an account which quite supersedes Bury's.

century.[1] McNeill dates Patrick's capture to 401, in order to synchronize Patrick's escape with the great barbarian invasion of 407, but, curiously, describes the year 401 as 'six years later than the Emperor Gratian' (who was murdered in 383!).[2] It ought to be clear that to attempt to date Patrick by events whose dates are themselves subject to such a wide range of conjecture is to make ropes of sand.

J. E. L. Oulton in 1940 made an attempt to prove that Patrick had used Jerome's revision of the *Commentary on the Apocalypse* by Victorinus of Pettau. Victorinus had been martyred in the persecution of Diocletian in 304, and Jerome had published his revision of Victorinus's commentary in 406. The words of Patrick's profession of faith (*Conf.* 4) seemed to Oulton so similar to a passage in Jerome's revision as to necessitate a dependence on Patrick's part. And Patrick uses (*Conf.* 14) the expression *in mensura itaque fidei trinitatis oportet distinguere*; the words *mensura fidei* are used by Victorinus as a description of the creed-like statement which he gives in his commentary.[3] It is usually assumed that in the phrase *mensura fidei* Victorinus and Jerome and Patrick are simply reproducing the Latin version of St. Paul's phrase at Romans xii. 3,[4] even though the context in which Victorinus produces the phrase is that of the measuring of Jerusalem in Revelation xi. 1 ff. Some commentators have observed that neither Victorinus nor Patrick uses the term *mensura fidei* in the same sense as Paul did.[5] In fact the formula

---

[1] *The Problem of Patrick*, pp. 8–9.

[2] *St. Patrick*, pp. 50–51, 53–54. On p. 70 of the same work McNeill has an even more curious statement, 'The Roman imperial power had made a kind of rally under great commanders like Stilicho and Aetius', as part of an explanation why Irish raids on Britain had ceased by about 430. But Stilicho's intervention in Britain is dated 395 or 397, just before the time when Niall was able to make a vast raid, according to McNeill, and Aetius flourished *c.* 430–50, and expressly refused an appeal for aid by the British in 446!

[3] J. E. L. Oulton, *The Credal Statements of St. Patrick*. Esposito had already, in 1918, pointed out that early scholars, Kattenbusch and Hausleiter, had noticed the resemblance between Patrick's confessional statement and Victorinus's (M. Esposito, 'Notes on the Latin Writings of St. Patrick', p. 343), and Oulton acknowledges Kattenbusch's interest at the beginning of his work (op. cit., p. 1). Newport White (*History of the Church of Ireland*, vol. i, pp. 107–8) connects Victorinus with the formula, and in a note at the end of cap. iv mentions Haussleiter's theory that Patrick knew Jerome's recension of Victorinus.

[4] ἑκάστῳ ὡς ὁ Θεὸς ἐμέρισεν μέτρον πίστεως; *et unicuique sicut Deus divisit mensuram fidei*.

[5] e.g. Christine Mohrmann, *Latin*, p. 10. Bieler in his article 'Der Bibeltext'

is not a creed, but precisely what Victorinus and Patrick describe it as being, 'the rule of faith', an exact translation of the Greek expression κανὼν τῆς πίστεως. The fact that Victorinus as late as about 300 can still use this expression shows how conservative a theologian he was,[1] and the fact that Patrick can reproduce it also shows in what conservative circles he moved. But, if we could be sure that Patrick had read and used Jerome's revision of Victorinus's *Commentary on the Apocalypse*, which appeared in 406, we should indeed have a valuable clue to the period when Patrick was undergoing his theological education.[2] Bieler has examined this theory carefully, however, and has found that the evidence does not support the conclusions. Patrick's rule of faith in *Confession* 4 is more likely to have come from some other symbol, which itself was based on or influenced by that of Victorinus, than to represent a direct borrowing from Victorinus. The coincidences with the rule of faith of Jerome's revision of Victorinus are not as striking as Oulton suggested, and may be the result of mere chance or even some common Gallican formula.[3] This attempt, then, to find an absolute date for Patrick's education must be held to have failed.

An attempt has also been made to date the contents of Patrick's works by detecting in them a deliberately anti-Pelagian note. If this could be established, it would be very likely that we could place Patrick's education and career during the years of the Pelagian controversy in Britain, roughly between 420 and 450. D. S. Nerney has endeavoured to do this,

(pp. 48, 49, 52, 53) consistently calls it a 'credo' and also all through his article 'The "Creeds" of St. Victorinus and St. Patrick'. But Todd earlier had noted that Patrick's 'creed' omitted much that we should expect in a creed (*Patrick, Apostle*, p. 390). Newport White (*History of the Church of Ireland*, vol. i, pp. 107–8) realizes that this is a rule of faith and not a creed.

[1] For the history of the use of this and similar expressions, see R. P. C. Hanson, *Tradition in the Early Church*, pp. 75–84.

[2] This was a serious and able attempt to date Patrick, of which not enough notice has been taken. Bulloch (*Celtic Church*, pp. 90–91) is one of the few writers about Patrick who appears to have read it.

[3] Bieler, 'The "Creeds" of St. Victorinus and St. Patrick'. In this article Bieler assumes throughout that Patrick found his rule in Gaul. There is, of course, no reason to assume this. We know nothing of doctrinal formulae current in Britain, but we must assume that they existed, and that they would be in all probability originally derived from the Gallic Church. There is no reason to doubt that Patrick found this rule of faith of his in the British Church.

in an article in which he takes the formal Augustinian doctrine of grace as it was developed during the Pelagian controversy and reads these theological propositions into the devotional and pious phrases of Patrick.[1] But the desired conclusion is likely to evade the reader, simply because Patrick is not writing formal theology and Nerney insists upon treating him as if he was. To quote from various parts of the *Confession* and *Epistle* such words as *beneficium, donum, gratia, virtus, pia misericordia, emendatio, correptio, castigatio, humiliatio*, and *inspiratio*,[2] proves nothing, if only because many of these words come from Scripture. It is absurd to make such a claim as 'It is not difficult to show that St. Patrick professes the Catholic doctrine that grace operates interiorly, in intellect and will',[3] for if we allow the sort of evidence for this doctrine offered by Patrick we shall have to read the same doctrine into almost any other author we may choose—St. Paul, Origen, the Psalmists. It is not enough to show that Patrick mentions baptism in order to prove that he explicitly disavowed the Pelagian rejection of the doctrine of original sin.[4] Patrick never mentions the eucharist. Does this mean that he regarded it as inefficacious? The attempt to read into Patrick's pious acknowledgement of God's initiative and assistance in every part of his life, his conversion, vocation, etc., an explicit denial of the error of the Massilienses (followers of John Cassian), that in man's power lies the *initium salutis*, is simply perverse.[5] It is an easy but futile exercise for the theologian trained in all the intricacies of the Pelagian controversy to read anti-Pelagian formulae into Patrick's record of his spiritual life, full of ardent prayers and biblical phrases. It would probably be just as possible, and just as futile, to read Pelagian doctrines into his works. Does he not aspire to live a sinless life—*Christus Dominus, qui me imperavit ut venirem esse cum illis residuum aetatis meae, si Dominus voluerit et custodierit me ab omni via mali, ut non peccem coram illo (Conf.* 43)? Does he not consciously aim at *vitam perfectam (Conf.* 44)? Does he not say that he is given as an assistant to God—*qui adiutor datus sum (Conf.* 46)? Does he not regard, as the Pelagians did, both Old Testament and New Testament as law, *totam legem (Ep.* 10)? This is not to say that Patrick was a Pelagian, but only that he

---

[1] D. S. Nerney, 'A Study of St. Patrick's Sources III'.   [2] Ibid., p. 97.
[3] Ibid., p. 98.   [4] Ibid., pp. 106–7.   [5] Ibid., pp. 108–9.

was not an anti-Pelagian. He did not move in circles intellectu-
ally advanced enough to become embroiled in this controversy,
and we cannot therefore date him by it.[1]

There are in fact two pieces of evidence which enable us to
date Patrick's *floruit* within very broad limits. One is that he
refers to the Franks as still pagan when he writes to Coroticus
(*Ep.* 14).[2] It is known that the Franks became Christians in the
year 496. This letter must therefore have been written before
that date. The other is that we can with reasonable confidence
place Coroticus, identifying him as the ancestor of Riderch Hen,
son of Tutwal, as existing between approximately 420 and 470.[3]
We can therefore be sure that Patrick lived in the fifth century,
and neither so early in the fifth century as to have died before
Coroticus came on the scene, before, say 420, nor so late as to
have missed Coroticus altogether, and to have lived after the
period when the Franks became Christian, say 480 or 490 or
500. But this still leaves us a very large field of conjecture.

If we look carefully, however, we shall find that more evidence
exists which can help us to fix the dates of Patrick within
narrower limits than these. The evidence is not such as to
enable us to date Patrick's movements to a precise year.
Previous students of Patrick, misled by the deceptive appearance
of accuracy in the later tradition about Patrick, have constantly
been tempted to do this. Our method of dating Patrick will be
by arguing from a series of indications to be found in his works,
or from a consideration of the secular and ecclesiastical history
of the fifth century which we have already reviewed. These
indications all converge independently of each other to fix the
dates of Patrick's life and career within limits which can hardly
vary more than a decade in either direction, and their cumulative effect is such as to make this conclusion virtually certain.
They rely neither upon Later lives nor on the Irish Annals, nor
even upon the assumption that we can fix Patrick's dates by
those of Palladius.

[1] Newport White agrees that there is no sign of the Pelagian controversy in
Patrick's writings, even though White thought that Patrick was Germanus's
protegé and disciple (*History of the Church of Ireland*, vol. i, p. 109). And so does
Morris, 'Celtic Saints', p. 356, n. 2.

[2] Grosjean has noted this, 'Notes d'hagiographie celtique' (1957), pp. 161–3;
but so have many others.

[3] See above, p. 23.

We begin by observing the significance of the fact that Patrick's father, Calpornius, was both a *decurio* and a deacon, and that his grandfather, Potitus (presumably, but not certainly, Calpornius's father), was a presbyter (*Conf.* 1, *Ep.* 10). The likelihood that Calpornius was both deacon and *decurio* at the same time is very strong indeed; he certainly was in possession of his *villula* when Patrick was kidnapped. It is impossible to believe that Calpornius, abandoning his possessions, took holy orders late in life, out of motives of sheer piety and desire to serve God, because the picture that Patrick gives of his home is, as we have seen, that of one where religion and piety meant virtually nothing and were practised only out of convention, if they were practised at all.[1] We may therefore conclude that Calpornius became a deacon simply in order to evade the burden of taxation which, as a *curialis*, would have befallen him. As a deacon, he could escape this burden. The history of this matter in the fifth century can be summarized as follows. In 313 Constantine I, in the first flush of his decision to favour Christianity, exempted all clergy from curial duties. By 323 or 328 it had become evident that this measure was opening too large a loophole for tax evaders, and, swinging to the other extreme, Constantine enacted that men of curial rank were not to be ordained. Later, however, it was laid down that men of curial rank could be ordained, but that if they were they must surrender all their property to their next-of-kin, or to some relation, upon ordination. By 365, however, these rules had become so slackly observed that Valentinian and Valens re-enacted them, again insisting that decurions must always surrender their property on ordination. Theodosius I at some point after 388 again re-enacted this legislation, which by then appears again to have become largely a dead letter, making it retrospective to the year 388. In 398 Arcadius (the Eastern Emperor) reimposed an absolute ban on the ordination of curials, but not so Honorius (the Western Emperor). The absolute ban on curials' being ordained was not enforced in the West until much later, by Valentinian III, in 439 or 452. As a general rule, however, the higher clergy (bishops, priests, deacons, and subdeacons) who were curials were allowed to retain their orders, but had to surrender two-thirds of their

[1] See above, p. 178.

property. The lower clergy did not gain exemption from the
burden of tax-raising at all.[1] The pronouncements of two Popes
whose reigns are likely to have covered the period of Calpornius's later life cast considerable light on this problem. Siricius
384–99) in a decretal letter addressed to the Bishop of Tarragon
in 454 made regulations about the wives of clergy, and forbade
the clergy to have sexual intercourse with their wives; we can
conclude from his language that many clergy used to have
intercourse without any sense of impropriety.[2] He also, in a
later decretal letter, addressed to the Gallic bishops, forbade the
ordination, even for financial inducements, of people holding
important public offices, and rejected the choice of the people
(*populus*) as a sufficient motive for this practice.[3] The words of
his next successor but one, Innocent I (402–17), are even more
pertinent. They are addressed to Victricius, Bishop of Rouen in
the north of Gaul, in the province of Lugdunensis Secunda, and
we are entitled to assume that the conditions revealed in this
area are very likely to have obtained in the neighbouring sees
of Britain. The letter is dated 15 February 404. Victricius is
treated as a metropolitan.[4] Innocent repeats Siricius's regulations about the wives of the clergy, and the ban on their having
sexual intercourse, applying to Gaul the rules which his
predecessor had applied to Spain.[5] At the end of his letter he
has a most interesting section disapproving of the ordination
of *curiales*, which is clearly based on his own experience, and
not merely borrowed from Siricius:

Further, some of our fellow-bishops often attempt to make clergy
of *curiales* or of people who are employed in any sort of public office.
But they experience much greater trouble when the Emperor makes

---

[1] For this information see A. H. M. Jones, *The Later Roman Empire*, pp. 745–6;
the position is summarized also on pp. 925–6. Bury (*LP*, pp. 19–20) refers to Calpornius's double status as *decurio* and deacon, but does not draw any conclusions
from it.

[2] Siricius, *Ep.* i. 8–11. vi (*PL* 13. 1138–41). Kathleen Hughes gives some further
information about the marriage of clergy in the fourth and fifth centuries (*The
Church in Early Irish Society*, pp. 41–42).

[3] Siricius, *Ep.* x. 13. v (1190–1).

[4] Incidentally, there is no evidence whatever in this letter that the Pope intended
to rebuke Victricius. Victricius had, however, not long before been staying in
Rome with Innocent, and a letter of Paulinus of Nola suggests that he had there
cleared himself of some accusation.

[5] Innocent I, *Ep.* ii (7. iv (473); 8. v (474); 9. vi (474–5); 12. ix (475–7)).

some rule about their being brought back to public office than satisfaction at acquiring them [as clergy]. The usual result is that while fulfilling these functions they put on entertainments which have, without doubt, been invented by the Devil and either preside over or are present at exhibitions of games or public shows. Surely the anxiety and dismay of the brethren which we have often experienced in the presence of the Emperor when we were often making requests for people of this sort, which you yourself [Victricius] when you were staying with us witnessed, should be a warning. Very grave penalties were threatened against these people to secure their return [into the imperial service] not only of lower clergy who had been *curiales* but also of those who had been consecrated bishops.[1]

If we ask ourselves how this history of legislation can apply to Calpornius, who managed to retain his orders and his property too, we can assume that there were certain periods when he is likely to have achieved this happy position with impunity and others when he is not likely to have done so. The year 365 and the next few after it would be unpropitious for doing so, because imperial legislation tightened up the regulations in that year. Anyway, if Patrick is to be placed in the fifth century, between *c.* 420 and *c.* 470, it is inconceivable that his father could have been old enough to be a deacon in 361. But if Potitus was the father of Calpornius, we may perhaps conjecture that in 365, or shortly after it, Potitus sought ordination and handed his property, or most of it, over to his son Calpornius. From 383 to 388 Magnus Maximus was in control of Britain; he was famous for his financial exactions,[2] and he took a great interest in ecclesiastical affairs. It is unlikely that under his control Calpornius would have found the atmosphere favourable for his clerical tax-evasion. Maximus was deposed by Theodosius in 388, and it is generally agreed that imperial authority was not effectively reimposed upon the distant

---

[1] Innocent I, *Ep.* ii. 14. xii (1477–8). *Praeterea frequenter quidam ex fratribus curiales vel quibuslibet publicis functionibus occupatos clericos facere contendunt; quibus postea magna tristitia, cum de revocandis eis aliquid de imperatore praecipitur quam gratia de ascito nascitur. Constat enim eos in ipsis muniis etiam voluptates exhibere quas a diabolo inventas esse non dubium est, et ludorum vel munerum apparatibus aut praeesse aut interesse. Sit certe in exemplum sollicitudo et tristitia fratrum quam saepe pertulimus imperatore praesente cum pro his saepe rogaremus quam ipse nobiscum positus agnovisti quibus non solum inferiores clerici ex curialibus verum etiam iam in sacerdotio constituti ingens molestia ut redderentur imminebat.*

[2] e.g. Sulpicius Severus, *Dialogues* iii. 11 (217–18), remarks that Maximus was notorious for *avaritia* in finance.

province of Britain until some time between 395 and 399. Stilicho did not reach Britain and chase the barbarians away from its confines until late in the last decade of the fourth century.[1] From about 398 to about 400, or a little after, it might have been unwise to attempt the tax-evasion we have been considering. We may assume that after 408 nobody would have had any particular motive for becoming both *decurio* and deacon. Indeed, there is no evidence that the decurionate continued after that date, though *decurio* as a title of honour would have been known and remembered well into the fifth century in Britain.

Putting ourselves for a moment in the position of Calpornius, then, we may well conclude that the years immediately following the collapse of Maximus were the most propitious for a rural aristocrat in Britain to evade the tax-burden of his curial status by taking holy orders and at the same time to retain his property. It is reasonable to conclude that between 388 and 395 was the period when Calpornius succeeded in becoming deacon without ceasing to be *decurio*, and it is equally reasonable to conclude that it was within these years that Patrick was born. The fulminations of Siricius against clergy having intercourse with their wives might have reached Britain by then, or they might not. But even if they had, it is more likely that Calpornius provided occasion for the fulminations of Siricius's successor than that he took any notice of this rule.[2] What St. Patrick says of his home encourages us to believe that Calpornius was not likely to have taken much notice of conventions of this sort.

We may therefore conclude that Patrick was born not before 388 and not after 408. This approximate date for his birth can be controlled by 'another piece of evidence, namely that provided by an examination of the type of biblical text he used. This is a subject which has interested scholars for some time, but it is only comparatively recently that it has been thoroughly explored. Jerome completed his Vulgate version of the New Testament in 383 and published his Vulgate Old Testament 391–404. Bury came to the tentative conclusion that Patrick knew the Old Latin (i.e. pre-Hieronymian) Old Testament as a

[1] So Collingwood and Myres, *RBES*, p. 288.
[2] See above, pp. 118 and 177. A. H. M. Jones, op. cit., pp. 927–9.

result of his early training, but that he had with him in Ireland a Vulgate New Testament, and that he sometimes looked up his New Testament references in the Vulgate version.[1] Newport White examined the subject more fully than anybody had done before him.[2] He could not discover for certain that Patrick had before him any of Jerome's translations of the Psalter (i.e. his Roman Psalter of 383 or the Gallican Psalter of 387, or his new translation from the Hebrew, which was later still), and he was confident that for the rest of the Old Testament Patrick used an Old Latin version. But he found some New Testament readings in Patrick which appeared to be of an unmistakably Vulgate kind. In 1947, however, Bieler published two articles in *Biblica*, entitled 'Der Bibeltext des Heiligen Patrick', which took into account a greater range of manuscripts than Newport White had had access to; it represents the fullest and most thorough examination of the subject to date, and must be accepted as authoritative. Bieler summarizes his findings as follows:[3]

1. Patrick's text of the Psalter is clearly Gallic (i.e. the type which was known in Gaul, but not necessarily Jerome's 'Gallican' version), later than that of the time of Hilary of Poictiers (mid-fourth century). It contains some certain traces of Jerome's readings.

2. His text of the rest of the Old Testament and of Revelation is clearly pre-Hieronymian.

3. His text of Acts is pure Vulgate, with two exceptions characteristic of the *Book of Armagh*.

4. No certain decision can be made about his text of the other books of the New Testament. It can be said that his text here was essentially pre-Hieronymian, corrected by the Vulgate. A special connexion with 'Celtic' texts of the Gospels (particularly with the *Book of Armagh*) cannot be established, and in the letters of St. Paul opposition to the text of the *Book of Armagh* prevails (except in Romans).

---

[1] *LP*, p. 319. Bury thought that he could find proof or this rather complicated theory. But Bieler ('Der Bibeltext des Heiligen Patrick', pp. 255–6) has disposed effectively of this theory.

[2] In his study *Libri Sancti Patricii* (1905). I am here relying on the later Summary of his findings given in *St. Patrick, His Writings and Life*, pp. 1–4 (1920). Williams (*CEB*, p. 185) merely repeats Newport White's findings.

[3] 'Der Bibeltext', p. 257.

5. A list of variants (about twelve in all) which reflect Greek readings probably indicates a new addition to our knowledge of the Latin text of the Bible.

6. Occasional variants (all in allusions rather than in direct quotations) indicate readings from the Fathers. There seems to be a special agreement with Cyprian.[1]

Bieler goes on to compare Patrick's text of the Bible with those of 'Fastidius'[2] and of Faustus of Riez, with negative results. He has no doubt that Patrick's text of the Psalter came from Gaul, but deprecates attempts to locate it more narrowly than this.[3] He next discusses the relation of Patrick's text to that of the 'Celtic' texts which have been preserved. He can find no special relation to these, except in the quotation of Matthew xxviii. 19–20. This quotation takes so isolated a position in the whole Bible-text of Patrick that it merits special attention. It was one of Patrick's great quotations, and Bieler thinks that it probably entered the 'Celtic' texts in the form in which Patrick quoted it from Patrick's works. Generally Patrick's Gospels are at least basically Old Latin, but the 'Celtic' Gospels basically Vulgate.[4] There are no certain traces of the Vulgate text in use in the Celtic Church before the sixth century, except in the case of the Acts of the Apostles. Patrick's text of Acts is almost pure Vulgate, except for two readings reminiscent of two in the *Book of Armagh*. Therefore the Acts in the *Book of Armagh* is probably the text as Patrick left it, and we can probably assume the same for Romans, because of the unusual relation of Patrick's text of Romans to that of the *Book of Armagh*.[5]

Bieler is anxious to use the fact that Patrick certainly knew a Psalter like that which was current in Gaul in the fourth century as a proof that Patrick had received his ecclesiastical education in Gaul. But of course we are not bound to draw this conclusion, simply because we do not know what type of Psalter

---

[1] Bieler summarizes these results briefly in his later *Life and Legend* (p. 38) by saying that Patrick's biblical quotations were 'from a text at the point of transition from Old Latin to Vulgate'.

[2] Bulloch (*Celtic Church*, p. 143) essayed the same rather futile task.

[3] 'Der Bibeltext', pp. 258–9. Newport White had tried to allocate it to South Gaul, and so to Lérins.

[4] Ibid., pp. 259–60.   [5] Ibid., pp. 260–1.

was current in the British Church. Both Bieler and Christine Mohrmann, who writes of the Continental elements of St. Patrick's Bible-text, and deliberates whether he could have encountered them in Ireland,[1] seem to make the extraordinary assumption that the Psalter was not used in Britain in the first half of the fifth century, though it may have been used in Ireland! But the fact that we have no documents—apart from Patrick's works—which could give us any clue to the British Church's Psalter is no proof that it never existed. A moment's reflection should, of course, assure us that a British Psalter must have existed, that it is wholly likely to have been derived from the Psalter of the Gallic Church, and that this would account for Patrick's Psalter being so like the fourth-century Gallic one.[2] Bieler himself gives us one faint clue that Patrick was using a British text of the Old Latin Old Testament when he tells us that Patrick cites Job xx. 15, 16, and 26 in direct succession, suggesting that in his version these verses followed each other directly, and adds that Jerome informs us that in the Old Latin version of Job between 700 and 800 verses had throughout the book fallen out, and that Gildas evidences further examples of such lacunae in Job.[3] Does this not suggest that both Patrick and Gildas were citing the type of Old Latin version which was current in Britain?[4]

The important point to emerge from Bieler's magisterial study of Patrick's Bible-text, as far as the determination of Patrick's date is concerned, is that Patrick undoubtedly does reproduce some of the readings of the Vulgate version of the New Testament which was made by Jerome in the year 383. We must therefore place the period of Patrick's ecclesiastical education some considerable time after the year 383. How long

---

[1] *Latin*, p. 51.

[2] Bieler's attempt (in *St. Patrick*, ed. Ryan, p. 65) to use the phrase *ex saliva scripturae meae* (which also occurs in Jerome's Letter to Pope Damasus, prefixed to his version of the Gospels) as a proof that Patrick studied in Gaul must be held to be unconvincing because, not only might the word have been used metaphorically in some writing not known to us but known to Patrick, but Patrick might have picked it up second- (or third- or fifth-) hand from somebody who had read Jerome's Preface, or the Preface might have reached the British Church by Patrick's day.

[3] 'Der Bibeltext', p. 36.

[4] A thorough comparison of the Bible-text of Gildas with that of Patrick is much needed.

that time should be it is hard to estimate. We can perhaps take
the practice of Patrick's compatriot Pelagius as a comparison.
Souter, after an exhaustive examination of Pelagius's text of the
New Testament, came to the conclusion that Pelagius made no
use at all of Jerome's Vulgate New Testament, but that 'in
Pelagius we find the textual form of the Epistles used in Britain
in the pre-Vulgate period, and for long afterwards, and that
here we have the oldest form in which the Pauline Epistles were
used in the British Isles, the missing British form of the Old-
Latin',[1] and he went on to conjecture that 'Britain got its Pauline
text from the Rhine country, via its oldest colony Camulodunum (Colchester)'.[2] It certainly would be astonishing if
Pelagius, who spent the early part of his life, when he was
writing his *Expositions*, in the very city where Jerome had
published his Vulgate New Testament, showed no influence of
this version at all. Souter himself admits that Augustine after
about the year 400 uses the Vulgate of the Gospels when he
wishes to quote learnedly, though he uses the Old Latin text for
the rest of the New Testament, and even for the Gospels, when
he is quoting from memory.[3] Plinval, who conducted his
investigation later than Souter, came to the conclusion that
Pelagius's text of the Epistles of St. Paul, though mostly dependent on the Old Latin, does show some undoubted signs of
knowing and using Jerome's Vulgate translation of these.
He scouts Souter's theory of the British text arriving from the
Rhine country via Colchester, and points out that Pelagius's
Expositions are much more likely to reflect the text as it was
known in Rome when he wrote than as it had been in Britain,
which he had left perhaps twenty years before.[4] It certainly
seems easier to believe Plinval than to follow Souter on this
point. The debate does, however, suggest that we must allow
quite a long time for Jerome's Vulgate version of the New
Testament to have reached Britain and Patrick. Gildas, writing
in the British Church a century later than Patrick, still uses the
old Latin text of the Bible when he is quoting from memory,
though he does show acquaintance with the Vulgate of both

---

[1] A. Souter, *Pelagius' Expositions of the Thirteen Epistles of St. Paul*, vol. i, p. 146.
But see the whole discussion, pp. 119 ff.
[2] Ibid., p. 147, and see also pp. 46–147.   [3] Ibid., pp. 119–20.
[4] Plinval, *Pélage*, pp. 140–3.

Old and New Testaments.[1] On the whole it would be reasonable to conclude that we must allow at least thirty years to elapse between Jerome's publication of the Vulgate New Testament and Patrick's encountering its readings during his ecclesiastical training, and that it would not be surprising if it was forty years before the British Church assimilated this new translation. This would mean that Patrick can hardly have undergone this training before about 415; it might even be preferable to make the earliest possible date for this training 420 or 425. We do not know how long Patrick spent as a cleric or a monk between his escape from captivity at the age of twenty-two and his going to Ireland as bishop at the age of at least thirty, and probably more. But it would not be unreasonable to conclude that most of that period must have been occupied with his preparation for the ministry and his life as a cleric (certainly as a deacon, probably as a presbyter). In short, the limits between which we must place his birth are 388 and 406, and the date before which he cannot have encountered the Vulgate New Testament is *c.* 420. These two reasonably reliable conclusions give us a firm, though not precise, framework for the dates of Patrick's career.[2]

There are other evidences for Patrick's dates that, though resulting in figures less precise even than these, contribute their weight to, and converge to confirm, their implications. One of them is Patrick's references to the end of the world, which he thinks to be approaching. In the year 410 Alaric and his Goths captured and sacked the city of Rome. The shock of this calamity was so great that many people thought that it portended the end of the world. The catch-phrase *totus mundus*

---

[1] So Williams, *CEB*, pp. 366 ff. Bulloch (*Celtic Church*, p. 143) gives a rather different, but not necessarily irreconcilable account of Gildas, saying that he used the Vulgate for Isaiah, Jeremiah, Lamentations, and Malachi, but for the New Testament used a text largely dominated by the Old Latin.

[2] Perhaps it should here be remarked that this last fact completely disables Esposito's theory that the years of Patrick's ministry in Ireland were 395–430, and that his childhood, captivity, escape, and training must all be put before that period. It equally disposes of Olden's view, based upon that of Whitley Stokes, that Patrick was born *c.* 373, taken captive *c.* 389, escaped *c.* 395, and then went to Gaul and studied with Martin; that he then went to Auxerre, was ordained and consecrated by Bishop Amator, and (a restless young man of twenty-four!) then went to Ireland; alternatively, Olden thought, following Nennius, that Patrick reached Ireland in 405 (*The Church of Ireland*, pp. 19, 23, 405–19). But all this must disappear *pulveris exigui iactu*.

perit came readily to the lips for many years afterwards and is
found in the literature of the first half of the fifth century. We
find this thought echoed in Patrick's writings. He has been sent
by God to the last people in the world in the last age of the
world as a prelude to the end. He speaks of the law of God which
He has in His generosity planted *in supremis temporibus*,[1] and He
has designated Patrick to preach the gospel *usque ad extremum
terrae*;[2] this is evidently no merely conventional phrase to
Patrick. Many parts of the west coast of Ireland do give an
impression of being 'Finisterre'. The last country in Europe
ends in barren hill and rocky cliff; beyond is nothing but the
endless unexplored waste of waters. He describes himself as one
of God's hunters and fishers *quos olim Deus in novissimis diebus ante
praenuntiavit*.[3] Patrick's fullest expression of this thought occurs
in the *Confession*. He thanks God that He has heard Patrick

*ut ego inscius et in novissimis diebus hoc opus tam pium et tam mirificum
auderem adgredere, ita ut imitarem quippiam illos quos ante Dominus iam
olim praedixerat praenuntiaturos evangelium suum in testimonium omnibus
gentibus ante finem mundi, quod ita ergo vidimus itaque suppletum est: ecce
testes sumus quia evangelium praedicatum est usque ubi nemo ultra est.*[4]

It is difficult to resist the conclusion that Patrick connects the
fall of Rome with the end of the world, which he expects to
arrive soon. The later we place his activity in the fifth century
the less likely is it that he would have entertained this idea. This
is another indication that Patrick's main activity must have lain
in the first half of the fifth century, and it fits in well with the
chronological data we have already reconstructed around him.

We may perhaps see another indication of date in the sense
of Roman citizenship which Patrick so obviously fostered and
valued, in his boast that his father had been a *decurio* and he
himself an aristocrat, in his expression *consuetudo Romanorum,
Gallorum, Christianorum*,[5] in the pride with which he uses the
word *cives*.[6] By the fourth century the Celtic peoples under
Roman rule felt no sense of oppression or yearning to be free.

[1] *Ep.* 5.
[2] *Ep.* 6; cf. *Conf.* 11: *epistola Christi in salutem usque ad ultimum terrae*; 38: *plebem
. . . quam sumpsit Deus ab extremis terrae*; 58: *plebem suam quam adquisivit in ultimis
terrae*; and *Ep.* 9: *filiorum Dei quos nuper adquisivit in ultimis terrae*.
[3] *Ep.* 11.
[4] *Conf.* 34; cf. *usque ad exteras partes ubi nemo ultra erat*, 51.
[5] *Ep.* 2, 10.   [6] *Ep.* 2.

On the contrary, they appear to have wanted romanization. 'There is in fact', says Salway, 'absolutely no evidence for anything but the most wholehearted desire on the part of the heterogeneous population of the *vici* to be considered Roman, at least in public.'[1] The further the fifth century advanced the more this sense of Roman citizenship, this identification of Christians with Roman citizens, would tend to fade. Again in *Confession* 46 Patrick represents those who deprecated his going as bishop to Ireland as asking why he should expose himself to danger *inter hostes qui Deum non noverunt*. It is doubtful if in the second half of the fifth century the people of Britain would have regarded the Irish as enemies. Certainly this phrase accords better with the first half of that century, when the Irish were frequently encountered as raiders, along with the Picts, and the most serious enemies, the Saxons, though already on the scene had not yet begun large-scale land annexation and settlement.

Generally speaking, what we have been able to discover in the course of this work about conditions in Britain during the fifth century, and about the British Church, suggests very strongly that the greater part of Patrick's career must be placed in the first half of the fifth century.[2] After the departure of the Roman field-army and the emancipation of Britain from direct Roman government there followed a period on the whole characterized by tranquillity and even a modest prosperity. The British Church increased in numbers and sent out at least one mission to a neighbouring territory, that led by Ninian. Strathclyde was evangelized, and probably Rheged also. The Church was able to afford the luxury of fostering a heresy, Pelagianism. It continued its close relations with the Church of Gaul. Monasticism established itself. Martyrs' shrines began to draw visitors. But in the second half of the fifth century strife and disaster overtook Britain. However obscure and difficult to interpret the evidence may be, we cannot fail to see that both civil war and aggression from a foreign power marked the second part of the century in Britain. It is very unlikely that in the circumstances the British Church should have found the opportunity, the resources, or the energy to send Patrick to Ireland as its bishop, to finance him, and even to inquire

---

[1] *The Frontier People*, p 18.   [2] See above, pp. 27–28, 70–71.

narrowly into his administration of his charge. It is clear that in fact Patrick was sent from Britain, supplied with money from there, and held to account by some persons in Britain. Everything we know about Britain in the fifth century suggests that this must have taken place in the first half of that century, certainly before 460. Patrick tells us that he would have liked to travel *usque ad Gallias visitare fratres et ut viderem faciem sanctorum Domini mei.*[1] What prevented him was his sense of duty towards his flock in Ireland, not civil disturbances in Britain and movements of barbarian armies in Gaul. In fact it is likely that, had he attempted to travel on some pious pilgrimage in Gaul after about the year 460, he would have found himself gravely incommoded not only by the presence of Visigoths but by the movements of large numbers of immigrants from Britain. Far less can we imagine Patrick (or, for that matter, Auxilius or Iserninus or anybody else) being sent during the second half of the century to Ireland from Gaul, for the same reason: that during that time the Christians of Gaul had much more pressing and immediately urgent matters to deal with than sending evangelizing missions to Ireland, even on the supposition that the Gallic Church, or any part of it, would at any time have felt itself free to consecrate a bishop for a mission field which was so clearly within the area of influence of the British Church.

We can therefore confidently identify Patrick as a product of Britain in the late fourth century, and confine his activity wholly, or almost wholly, within the first half of the fifth century. Everything that we know of him from his writings must have happened before 460, and may have happened considerably before that date. The statements of annals which place his death in the last decade of the fifth century, and the conjectures of recent scholars such as O'Rahilly and Carney, which have placed Patrick's career between 450 and 500, must be categorically described as impossible, if, that is, they refer to the Patrick who wrote the *Epistle to Coroticus* and the *Confession.*[2] We cannot give exact dates for Patrick. All that we can say is that he must have been

---

[1] *Conf.* 43.
[2] These conclusions are, of course, equally fatal to the earlier theory of Todd (*Patrick, Apostle*, p. 392) that Patrick's mission to Ireland was inaugurated between 440 and 460 and ended between 480 and 490.

born some time between 388 and 408, and that he cannot have received his ecclesiastical education much before 420. It would be legitimate to conjecture that he was born about 390, was kidnapped about 406, escaped in 412, and went to Ireland as bishop at some point between 425 and 435, and that he died about 460. But it must be emphasized that these detailed dates are only conjectural. They have been reached, it should be noted, without any reference at all to later tradition about Patrick or to the Irish Annals.

VII

ST. PATRICK

THE investigation of Patrick's origins and career which has been conducted in the previous six chapters of this work has resulted in certain conclusions, stated in the last two. In the course of this last chapter these conclusions will be compared with some recent theories advanced about Patrick, some details of the later tradition will be examined again, and finally an estimate of Patrick himself will be attempted.

Recent writers on the subject have tended to suggest that there were in effect two Patricks, one earlier and one later. They have been encouraged to do this by the occurrence in the later tradition of references to 'Old Patrick' (Irish *Sen-Pátric*) as a distinct figure from the original or authentic Patrick. The first allusion to this *Sen-Pátric* is usually reckoned to be that in the *Martyrology of Oengus* (ninth century), against the date 14 August; but the Hymn of Fiacc (*Génair Patraic*) has the couplet

> 'When Patrick went to the other Patrick,
> Together they ascended to the Son of Mary',

and if we ascribe this hymn to Aedh of Sletty, this is the earliest mention of a second Patrick.[1] The *Chronicum Scottorum* has against the date 457 the sentence *Dormitatio sancti senis Patricii episcopi* and an allusion to the church at Glastonbury; the *Annals of the Four Masters* record against the date 451 '*Sen-Pátric* breathed out his spirit'; and at the end of the mention of Patrick in the *Book of Lecan* (*c.* 1400) is found the sentence *Secundinus et senex Patricius in pace dormierunt.*[2] The other fact which has encouraged such theories is that in three sources Palladius and Patrick appear to be identified, or at least the name Patricius appears to be attributed to Palladius. The earlier of these sources is in Tirechan's

---

[1] But for the solid reasons for not attributing so early a date to this document, see above, p. 77.
[2] The evidence is usefully summarized in Olden, *The Church of Ireland*, pp. 414–15.

work in the *Book of Armagh*. A separate note towards the end of the second part of his work states *Paladius episcopus primo mittitur, qui Patricius alio nomine appellabatur.*[1] An entry in the *Annals of Innisfallen* also identifies the two. The third source is the *Anglo-Saxon Chronicle*; the Parker Chronicle in this records under the year 430 'In this year Palladius (*vel Patricius*) was sent by Pope Celestine to the Scots to strengthen their faith.'[2] Esposito goes as far as to believe that Tirechan himself held a theory of two Patricks.[3] Grosjean attempted to show that the confusion of Palladius with Patrick arose originally from a misreading of Bede's account (*HE* i. 13) of Palladius's mission, followed by a mention a line or so later of *Aetius vir illustris qui et patricius* (i.e. a patrician) *fuit*. He suggested that this mistake was first made in the *Book of Armagh* and later copied in the *Annals of Innisfallen*.[4] But he has been followed in this conjecture by no other scholar. It is not certain that Tirechan wrote the note in the *Book of Armagh*. Bieler describes it as 'a corrupt source known to us from an interpolation in the *Annals of Innisfallen*'.[5] The reader will realize from these facts how slender are the foundations in the later tradition for any theory of two Patricks. This has not prevented several being put forward. Todd a century ago had conjectured that much of Palladius's activity had been ascribed to Patrick.[6] But the classic formulation of this theory came from O'Rahilly, in his little work, *The Two Patricks*, which was published in 1942. Briefly, his conclusions were that Palladius was also called Patricius, that his mission in Ireland lasted from 431 to 461, and that his successor (who by a surprising coincidence was also called Patricius) reached Ireland about 462 and died in 492; this second Patrick was the author of the *Confession* and *Epistle to Coroticus*.[7] Auxilius and Iserninus accompanied Palla-

---

[1] Stokes, *TL*, ii. 332, 16 a 1 (Gwynn 31). The passage has already been quoted above, p. 80.

[2] The Parker Chronicle (known as **Ⱥ**) originally belonged to the Old Minster at Winchester, and up to the eleventh century was still there; later, probably after the Conquest, it went to Christ Church, Canterbury. The first scribe copied up to the end of the annal for 891, and then stopped writing. The entry about Palladius is in Anglo-Saxon, the entry identifying him with Patrick is in Latin and added by a later hand.

[3] 'The Patrician Problem', pp. 133–4.

[4] 'S. Patrice d'Irlande et quelques homonymes dans les anciens martyrologes', pp. 169–71.

[5] *Life and Legend*, p. 85.   [6] *Patrick, Apostle*, pp. 335, 338–9, 393–9.

[7] *The Two Patricks*, p. 8 and n. 5 (p. 48).

dius, and not Patrick II, to Ireland.[1] It was Palladius who paid
a visit to Rome as Bishop of the Irish and not Patrick.[2] The
circular letter of Patrick, Auxilius, and Iserninus emanates from
Palladius-Patrick and the other two.[3] This Palladius-Patrick
died in 457 or 461 (for *Sen-Pátric* is, of course, Palladius).[4]
Secundinus's *Hymn* was written about Palladius-Patrick during
his lifetime.[5] Patrick II had (unlike Palladius-Patrick) a special
connexion with Armagh.[6] He was sent from Britain to succeed
Palladius-Patrick (Iserninus and Benignus, though bishops,
being apparently unsuitable to succeed him).[7] Carney, nearly
twenty years after the appearance of O'Rahilly's theory, has
produced another version of the two Patricks theory. He
believes that Secundinus reached Ireland before Patrick and
that much of his activity has been attributed to Patrick. Secundinus landed in 432, from the Continent. Carney's chief piece
of evidence for this is that in the earliest list of the bishops of
Armagh Secundinus's name appears first. He believes that
Patrick was born in 422, taken captive in 438, escaped in 444,
returned to Ireland in 456, and died in 493.[8] Binchy, though
he has subjected Carney's arguments to searching, and indeed
fatal, criticism, does nevertheless incline to the view that there
were two Patricks. Though he does not agree with every detail
of O'Rahilly's theory, he is in sympathy with his general
approach.[9]

The conclusions to which the investigation conducted in this
book has led suggest that all strictly dichotomous two-Patricks
theories must be abandoned. If we define—as we must—the
true, authentic Patrick as the Patrick who wrote the *Confession*
and *Epistle to Coroticus*, then we cannot either place the true
Patrick's career in Ireland at the beginning of the fifth century,
well before Palladius came on the scene, with Whitley Stokes
and Olden and Esposito; nor can we move the true Patrick to
the second half of the century, so as to place his death in 493 or

[1] Ibid., p. 17.   [2] Ibid., p. 22.   [3] Ibid., pp. 22–23.
[4] Ibid., p. 24.   [5] Ibid., p. 27.   [6] Ibid., pp. 29–30.
[7] Ibid., pp. 36, 40–41. O'Rahilly finds his two Patricks not only in the note in
Tirechan's work, but also in the *Stowe Missal*, the *Martyrology of Oengus*, Fiacc's
Hymn, the Law of Adomnan (? sixth century), and the references to *Sen-Pátric*
in the Annals; see *The Two Patricks*, p. 10.
[8] *The Problem of St. Patrick*, pp. 1–16, 26 ff., 114–22.
[9] *PB*, pp. 114, 129–56.

thereabouts, with O'Rahilly, Carney, and perhaps Binchy. The Patrick who wrote the *Confession* and *Epistle* must have had his career as a bishop in Ireland between 425 and 460 In fact, we can limit this period rather more exactly. If the British Church was cut off from contact with the Roman Church by 457, so that it could not adopt as its custom the Easter Cycle of Victorius,[1] it is unlikely that Patrick's opponents, who caused him to write his *Confession* in self-defence and protest, would have been free from civil disturbance and Saxon aggression after that date, and therefore able to pursue their case against him. If the *Epistle* was written before the *Confession*, and if when it was written Patrick had been at least twenty years in Ireland, long enough to bring up a man of at least thirty from childhood (*ex infantia, Ep.* 3), then he must have been in Ireland since a date no later than 437, and probably earlier than that. But if we allow that his words in *Confession* 51[2] imply that, though Patrick had penetrated to quite unevangelized parts, another bishop had functioned in Ireland before him or even simultaneously with him, we must place his advent in Ireland as bishop no earlier than 431, and therefore can determine his career within quite narrow limits: from 431 or a year or so later to 457 or a few years later. It is easy to see that this chronology is fatal to all consistent theories of the existence of the two Patricks.

This conclusion raises unavoidably the question of Patrick's relation to Palladius. We do not know what happened to Palladius after he reached Ireland. Muirchu says that, deterred by the hostility of the Irish and suffering from homesickness, he started on his journey home but died *in Britonum finibus*;[3] Tirechan (if it be he) that he was martyred by the Irish;[4] the *Vita Tripartita* that after founding three churches he was frightened off by Nathi, son of Garrchu, and died in the land of the Picts;[5] in the *Historia Brittonum* Palladius apparently does not even reach Ireland but is prevented by a storm and goes to Britain and dies in the land of the Picts.[6] The variety of these stories

---

[1] See above, pp. 66–69.

[2] *ubique pergebam causa vestra in multis periculis etiam usque ad exteras partes, ubi nemo ultra erat et ubi numquam aliquis pervenerat qui baptizaret aut clericos ordinaret aut populum consummaret.*

[3] Stokes, *TL* ii. 273, 2 a 2 (Gwynn 3).

[4] Stokes, *TL* ii. 332, 16 a 1 (Gwynn 31).

[5] Stokes, *TL* i. 30–31.

[6] 50 (194).

shows the ignorance of their authors.[1] Palladius left very little impression on folk-memory in Ireland.[2] He can hardly have carried out a long and memorable ministry there. On the other hand, if he had met any of the forms of an early end attributed to him by later tradition, it is difficult to explain why neither Prosper nor Bede knew of it. The most likely explanation of the relationship between Palladius and Patrick, seems to be that suggested by both Norah Chadwick[3] and Binchy[4] that the careers of Palladius and of Patrick in Ireland overlapped. Palladius arrived first, and began his mission somewhere in the south of Ireland. Patrick arrived later, sent by different people, by the British Church instead of by the Pope, under different auspices, as an Irish-speaking Briton with previous experience of Ireland, to spread the Christianity of the British Church, instead of as the representative of a Roman mission to spread Roman or Gallic Christianity, and to the north of Ireland (perhaps to the north-east).[5] Palladius must have died quite early, so that by the time Patrick wrote to Coroticus he could call himself *Hiberione constitutum episcopum* (*Ep.* 1) with an easy mind. Even if Palladius had left some bishops behind him, Patrick had been in charge of a mission to Ireland before them.

If we allow conjecture to range thus far, we can perhaps envisage two different forms of Christianity as existing in Ireland for some considerable time during the fifth century, the Palladian and the Patrician. This is not a theory of the existence of two Patricks, certainly not of two *consecutive* Patricks, but it does open the lively possibility, which has, of course, often been canvassed by scholars, of the Palladian and the Patrician traditions having become confused, and of the existence of a tension between them. It is possible that the opposition to Patrick, which his *Confession* was designed to challenge, was partly inspired by a Palladian party, or a party of the Palladian tradition, which had its supporters in England. It could easily represent itself, we may guess, as that of men of education and

---

[1] O'Rahilly (*The Two Patricks*, pp. 14–15) has little difficulty in showing that the accounts of the later career of Palladius are worthless and must be rejected *in toto*, and that even Bury's attempt to make sense of them failed. Binchy (*PB*, pp. 134–48) has a useful discussion of Palladius, including a summary of all the evidence about him. Morris discusses Palladius's activity, 'Celtic Saints', pp. 357–8.

[2] So Binchy observes, *PB*, p. 143.   [3] *CB*, p. 143.

[4] *PB*, p. 146.   [5] So Binchy suggests, *PB*, p. 144–8, 168–9.

learning in justified protest against the episcopal policy of the unlearned and provincial Patrick. This double tradition within Irish Christianity could account for one phenomenon also which has at once puzzled and impressed Binchy, what he calls 'the cumulative effect of the list of sixth-century obits'.[1] According to the annals, a large number of those who had been friends and disciples of Patrick died between 480 and 530. Binchy maintains[2] that 'the saint with whom these men were in contact cannot have died as early as 461'. According to the facts which this book has been concerned to bring to light, Patrick's contemporaries are not likely to have survived till 480, and certainly could not possibly have died as late as 530. But it is quite possible that prominent men who stood in the Patrician, in contrast to the Palladian, tradition, having inherited it from the generation before, survived to the period 480–530.

If the results arrived at in this investigation of Patrick's origins and career are correct, it must be acknowledged that in one point the later tradition, both of lives and of annals, was right. The later tradition is almost unanimous in its testimony to the fact that Patrick's date of arrival as bishop in Ireland was very close to that of Palladius. There is great variation about the dates of Patrick's birth and his death, but about this there is no variation. The result of the work of O'Rahilly, of Carney, and of Binchy was in effect to destroy the causal connexion between Palladius's arrival in Ireland as Bishop and Patrick's. The research embodied in this book has restored to Patrick a career contemporary with that of Palladius, but it has not restored a causal connexion between the two careers. This is just the kind of point which later traditions would invent, and we may reasonably conclude that it has been invented. But if we accept this conclusion, the accuracy of the later tradition in dating Patrick's arrival as bishop in Ireland is all the more impressive. This is one point in which later tradition has proved itself reliable. But it could not be proved reliable until evidence from Patrick's own writings and from contemporary history had shown its authenticity.

It is not difficult to account for the other dates allotted to Patrick in the Lives and Annals, and for their inconsistency; they result from attempts to reconcile diverse sources about

---

[1] *PB*, p. 32; see also pp. 111–12.   [2] *PB*, p. 113.

alleged activities in Ireland, a desire to assimilate Patrick's life
to that of Moses, or to make the important moments in his
career coincide with those of some eminent and memorable man
like Pope Leo, and guesswork, intelligent and unintelligent.
The list of Patrick's companions assigned by later tradition—
Auxilius, Iserninus, Secundinus, and later in his career Benignus
—is a more puzzling problem.[1] Two facts which seem reasonably certain from our previous inquiry militate against an easy
acceptance of the theory that these men originally accompanied
Patrick as bishops. It is virtually certain that Pope Celestine did
not send Patrick to Ireland; if Patrick was a monk (and the
weight of evidence appears to be in favour of this), it is absolutely certain that Celestine did not send him; Pope Celestine
did not like monks as bishops.[2] It is inconceivable that he should
have sent one as a bishop to Ireland. Even if Patrick was not a
monk, he did encourage monks, people whom he calls *monachi*
(*Conf.* 41, *Ep.* 12). It is hard to believe that Celestine should
have singled out as bishop someone who favoured monasticism.
And, as we have already indicated,[3] had Patrick been originally
sent by Celestine he had every reason to state this in his *Confession*, yet he does not do so. We must therefore abandon the
picture of Patrick arriving for his Irish mission surrounded with
bishops consecrated by the Pope's hands. This is the fantasy of
Tirechan, not sober history. But we must also take into account
Patrick's entire silence about any fellow bishop labouring alongside him. The evidence suggests strongly that he had no such
fellow bishops, and never contemplated having any.[4] If Auxilius
and the rest were bishops, then they were not companions of
Patrick, and the evidence is just as strong against their being
bishops consecrated by Patrick during his ministry, even if we
could accept the theory that the early Irish Church tolerated
consecration of a bishop by only one consecrator.[5] In fact it is
far more likely that Patrick's mission to Ireland was what might
be called a one-bishop mission. The people of Ireland—the *vox
Hiberionacum*—who were Christians, asked for a bishop. They

---

[1] Bury accepted most of them as companions of Patrick; so did Meissner,
McNeill, and Ryan. Binchy (*PB*, pp. 144–8) gives some convincing reasons for
being sceptical about their attachment to Patrick.

[2] See above, p. 141.   [3] See above, pp. 100, 135.

[4] See above, pp. 137–8.   [5] See above, p. 138, n. 2.

were given one. When he dies, they will go to the same source, or an equivalent one, and ask for another bishop. At this very early, rudimentary stage, when Christianity is only just establishing itself in Ireland against considerable opposition,[1] this is all that is needed, or contemplated, in the way of episcopal provision. There are parallels for this in the Early Church. We may cite the example of the Gothic Christians, both Catholic and Arian.[2] That may, indeed, have been the normal missionary policy of the Early Church, in as far as it had one. But this does not account for Auxilius and the others. We may perhaps ask, how much historicity is left to these names if we reject the *Hymn* of Secundinus, the canons, the circular letter, and the fragment of the *Letter to the Bishops of Mag Ai*? They were certainly not busy bishops administering dioceses under Patrick's metropolitan care. They might, presumably, have been presbyters who accompanied Patrick on his mission. But none of them have Celtic names and the only presbyter mentioned individually by Patrick is one whom he certainly did not bring with him as a presbyter to Ireland. It is possible that we have in the list of names an example of the transfer of tradition from Palladius to Patrick. Auxilius, Secundinus, Iserninus, and the others may have been companions of Palladius, not necessarily bishops but presbyters, at least presbyters when they accompanied Palladius originally, who carried on the Palladian tradition after his death, and whose memory has been detached from the misty and relatively ephemeral Palladius and attached to the figure of Patrick, who worked for a longer period in Ireland and impressed himself more strongly on the folk-memory.

We may confidently dismiss the possibility of Patrick's having made a journey (or more than one journey) to Rome, in spite of Bury's belief that he did so. Even Bieler does not think this story probable.[3] And we may with equal assurance dismiss the legend of his having wandered on the Continent, whether we place his sojourn in the islands of the Tyrrhenian sea, with the

---

[1] Binchy, indeed, believes not only that King Loeghaire was never converted to Christianity, but that 'his five immediate successors were also pagans, or at least adopted an ambivalent attitude to the new religion' ('The Fair of Tailtu and the Feast of Tara', p. 136).

[2] See E. A. Thompson, *The Visigoths in the time of Ulfilas*, chaps. 4 and 5 and App. 3.

[3] *Life and Legend*, p. 89.

first of the *Dicta Patricii*, or in Lérins, or in Auxerre,[1] if only because he would then have become a fluent speaker of Latin, which he clearly was not.

It is impossible to reconstruct Patrick's movements in Ireland. That is why we cannot today write a *Life* of Patrick, as has been done too confidently and too often in the past. We can only come to one positive and several negative conclusions. Patrick probably did make his headquarters at Armagh. He educated sons of local chieftains and others for the priesthood or for the monastic life (*Conf.* 41, 52, *Ep.* 3, 12), and even though some of them may have on occasion travelled round with him, it is highly probable that he had one fixed spot where this education could regularly be carried out, the place of residence of the bishop's *familia*. Binchy suggests that Patrick founded his church at Armagh at a time when the dynasty in power in that area was the Ulidian dynasty, holding an hegemony in the north of Ireland with its centre at Emain Macha, two miles from Armagh. This would be before the rath or fort at Emain Macha was sacked, and the hegemony taken from the Ulidian dynasty by the three sons of Niall of the Nine Hostages, 'who carved out for themselves three kingdoms in the north-west, and whose descendants were known as the Northern Uí Níall'. Patrick would have fixed his headquarters at Armagh because it was so near the administrative centre of the most powerful kingdom in the territory with which he was concerned. There is evidence that a cult of Patrick was already well established in Armagh by the time Tirechan wrote, and the existence of a local cult is good evidence for the historical reality of the saint commemorated there. But unfortunately the date of the sacking of Emain Macha is uncertain. It might have occurred in the last quarter of the

---

[1] Bury, of course, and Newport White and Meissner, placed him in Lérins; McNeill and Ryan brought him to some Tyrrhenian island and then to Auxerre; Grosjean allowed him a period of travel on the Continent and then stationed him in Auxerre ('Notes d'hagiographie celtique' (1945), pp. 93–94). But Lérins has its more recent supporters too. O'Rahilly stationed his (late fifth-century) Patrick there (*The Two Patricks*, pp. 29–30), and Bulloch not only places him in Lérins, but allows him a tour round the Tyrrhenian islands first (*Celtic Church*, pp. 45 and 168). He does not improve his case by stating, quite inaccurately, in the last passage referred to, 'Patrick explicitly tells us in his *Confession* that he had spent some time during his continental wanderings "in the islands of the Tyrrhenian sea".' Norah Chadwick and Binchy rule out any likelihood of such a period on the Continent for Patrick.

fifth century; but it could have happened as early as 450, or even earlier. It is even possible that the event happened in Patrick's lifetime, that he accompanied the vanquished to their reduced kingdom across the river Bann, and that this accounts for the story of Patrick's death not taking place in Armagh but (possibly) in Ulidian territory, in Downpatrick.[1] That Patrick did not die at Armagh and was not buried there is quite certain; the later tradition about him is unanimous on this point.[2] Whether he was buried at Saul instead (as Tirechan says, and the *Vita Tripartita* at one point suggests) or at Downpatrick (which the *Vita Tripartita* elsewhere favours) cannot be determined. Patrick did not visit Slemish, for this had not been the scene of his captivity, and he did not climb Croagh Patrick, however much later tradition and custom may have hallowed these places. This is not, of course, to say that all authentic memory of Patrick died out soon after his death. We have the preservation of his two works, the *Confession* and the *Epistle to Coroticus*, to warn us against this assumption, and the manner in which the sixth-century tradition used the *Confession*, adding to it and embroidering upon it rather than ignoring and suppressing it, and also the influence which Patrick's biblical text appears to have had upon that of the *Book of Armagh*.[3] But the exploration of Patrick's movements in Ireland is a task for the future, a delicate and difficult one, in which careful and open-minded study of comparable literature and traditions, and a much greater attention to archaeological investigation, will have to take the place of the dogmatic assumptions and confident but speculative guesses of the past.

We turn, finally, to attempt an estimate of Patrick as an historical figure, relying only on the facts of which we can be reasonably sure and putting out of our minds distracting speculations based on later tradition about him. A preoccupation with his

---

[1] Binchy, *PB*, pp. 148–54; the quotation is from p. 150. McNeill believed that the kings of Connacht had captured Emain Macha about a century before Patrick's mission began (*St. Patrick*, p. 72). For a useful account of this question see also O'Rahilly, *Early Irish History and Mythology*, cap. xii, and especially the Summary on p. 234.

[2] Muirchu (Stokes, *TL* ii, 290, 6 b 2 (Gwynn 12); and 295–6, 7 a 2 (Gwynn 15); Tirechan (Stokes, *TL* ii. 332, 15 b 2 (Gwynn 30–31); *Vita Tripartita* (Stokes, *TL* i. 114–15, 252–3).

[3] See above, pp. 180–2.

alleged formation in Lérins or Auxerre has hitherto prevented a proper appreciation of Patrick as a figure genuinely representative of the British Church of the first half of the fifth century. Hugh Williams, for instance, in his otherwise admirable book, *Christianity in Early Britain*, was blinded by the dazzle of Bury's *Life of St. Patrick*, so that he quite failed to do justice to Patrick as one of the most important sources of information about the very subject upon which he was writing his book. But Patrick was a product of the British Church. He is more completely representative of it than any other historical figure about whom we have any information, more so than Pelagius and Faustus of Riez, who spent their careers outside Britain, more so even than Gildas, who wrote at a time when the power of the British Church had been crippled and the current of its life choked and reduced by the Saxon conquests. It is no injustice to Gildas, indeed, to say that Patrick gives us a more favourable picture of the British Church than he does. Patrick, for instance, does not hesitate to excommunicate a British tyrant who has conducted a cruel massacre, and it seems clear that he expects his instructions for both boycott and excommunication to be obeyed. One gathers from Gildas that, though the Church of his day has plenty of atrocities to witness, it cannot do more than deplore and denounce their perpetrators. The British Church of Patrick's day converts savage barbarians; the British Church of Gildas's day merely abuses them. Gildas shows quite a wide acquaintance with theology, rhetoric, and learning, but in his day they appear to be in danger of degenerating into verbosity and pedantry. Patrick certainly has very little learning and no rhetoric whatever, but he is aware of his deficiency and honest about it, and succeeds in a surprising way in compensating for his lack of these things. Gildas writes much about God's wrath and punishment, Patrick constantly harps upon God's loving care.

Patrick's writings in fact are the first literature of the British Church about whose identification we can be certain. Conjectures can be made about Fastidius's work, and about some other Pelagian documents, but they are no more than conjectures. We can recover some of the works of Pelagius and of Faustus, but only works written long after these authors had left their native land and had been exposed to many other influences. Patrick's

works were, of course, written on Irish soil, but they are
characteristic of the British Church in a way in which no previous or contemporary literature that has survived is, nor any
for the next century after his day. In Patrick we have the first
witness for the text of the Bible used by the British Church, the
first evidence of the kind of Latin which that Church used, the
first source of information about its doctrines, its worship, its
discipline, its customs.[1] One could almost go further than this
and say that Patrick is the first British personality in history
whom the historian can know; he makes himself transparent to
us to a very unusual extent, in a manner comparable to that in
which Augustine makes himself transparent to us. This can be said
of very few personalities in the ancient world, and of absolutely no other British persons in the whole of ancient history. We can
know him as a bishop. He has a high sense of the authority of
his office: *sacerdotes ipsius*, he can write, *quos elegit et indulsit illis
summam divinam sublimem potestatem, quos ligaverit super terram
ligatos esse et in caelis* (*Ep.* 6). He has an intense pastoral care for
his flock. He travels round baptizing, confirming, ordaining,
instituting monks and nuns. He educates boys for the ministry,
he celebrates the eucharist and is immersed in the financial
responsibilities which seem inseparable from the work of a
bishop in any age. He is a missionary too. He sees himself as a
fisher of men: *idcirco itaque oportet quidem bene et diligenter piscare
. . . unde autem valde oportet retia nostra tendere ita ut multitudo copiosa
et turba Deo caperetur et ubique essent clerici qui baptizarent et exhortarent populum indigentem et desiderantem* (*Conf.* 40). He has a peculiar
concern for the abolition of paganism (*Conf.* 18, 19), of idolatry
(*Conf.* 41), and of sun-worship (*Conf.* 60). He shields his people
from persecution and unpopularity as far as he can. He makes
no distinction of classes in his evangelism, for though he is naïvely
pleased at the accession to the ranks of the consecrated virgins
of an Irish aristocrat, and does not fail to remind his hearers
of his own *ingenuitas* and *nobilitas*, he encourages even the
slave-girls to take vows of virginity and to persevere in spite of ill-
treatment and threats. He is ready himself to undergo imprisonment for the sake of the Gospel, and he is not afraid of death in
the cause of Christ either. In St. Patrick we have a full-length
picture of a British bishop, and it is a most attractive one.

[1] See *St. Patrick, a British Missionary Bishop*, p. 20.

It is inaccurate, strictly speaking, to say that we can give an account of St. Patrick's doctrine, and certainly the essay upon this subject by Newport White is an utterly unsatisfactory one.[1] Patrick gives us, indeed, early in his *Confession*, a passage containing his rule of faith (4). It is a very conservative one, deriving originally from a very conservative writer, Victorinus of Pettau. Though it is entirely orthodox, it does not show much sign of influence from the doctrinal controversies of the fourth century, and no consciousness whatever of fifth-century controversies, such as Pelagianism and Nestorianism. Patrick was not an academic theologian, even in an age when academic theologians were much commoner than they are now and theology was much less of an academic subject than it is now. His educational equipment was not adequate to allow him to take part in theological discussions and controversies, and he knew this. But there are three points concerning his convictions which are worth noting. We have already had occasion to note his expectation of the end of the world.[2] Though he is an enthusiastic missionary he has no vision of the vistas of Christian history ahead of him. He thinks that he is living *in novissimis diebus*, and bringing the Gospel in the latest period of the world's history to the furthest people, who live on the very edge of the world. This is part of his incentive and dynamic. In this he is characteristic both of Christianity at all times and of fifth-century Christianity in particular. Eschatology has time and time again been the dynamic that moved and fired the Christian Gospel, eschatology partly realized but never completely realized. Eschatology is an ingredient in Christianity which, however bizarre and uncongenial it may seem to us, appears to be indispensable. It is typical of the fifth-century Church that it should be laying the foundations for the vigorous and intense spread and development of Christianity over the whole of Europe during the next thousand years while the men who were doing the work of foundation-laying imagined that civilization, the very fabric of society and the course of history itself, were about to collapse, perhaps before their work was completed. Patrick's eschatology makes him a figure characteristic of the Church of the first half of the fifth century.

Another interesting feature of Patrick's doctrine is its scriptural

[1] See above, pp. 33, n. 2; 51, n. 1.   [2] See above, pp. 184–5.

quality. As we have had occasion to remark frequently during
this work, the one book which we can be absolutely certain that
Patrick has read is his Latin Bible. There are very few chapters
in all the eighty-three into which his work is divided in which
he does not quote the Bible. Biblical words and phrases come
more naturally to him in Latin than do those of ordinary
speech. He uses his Bible not only in season but out of season,
for instance to console himself for his lack of education by a
misunderstood sentence from Ecclesiasticus (*Conf.* 11; cf. 8). He
uses the Bible as a kind of magic volume with which to threaten
the soldiers of Coroticus: *Non mea verba sed Dei et apostolorum
atque prophetarum quod ego Latinum exposui, qui numquam enim mentiti
sunt. Qui crediderit salvus erit, qui vero non crediderit condempnabitur,
Deus locutus est* (*Ep.* 20). But for the most part his biblical quotations, which often are no more than little snatches or half
sentences, are appropriate enough. Occasionally he can plunge
into a long series of quotations, as when he produces a great list
of texts exhorting men to spread Christianity (*Conf.* 40) or piles
tag on tag in an attempt to reach his opponents in Britain
through his letter to the soldiers of Coroticus (*Ep.* 11). It is a
remarkable fact that the book which this unlearned bishop, who
had had no opportunity to study theology among the highly
educated, quotes more than any other book in the Bible is St.
Paul's Epistle to the Romans. There are at least twelve but perhaps as many as fifteen quotations from this book in St. Patrick's
two works. This suggests that his interest in the Bible and his use
of it were genuinely theological. He did not merely use it as a
source of suitable vocabulary on all occasions. He had genuinely
assimilated its profoundest doctrines. In fact, as we have already
hinted, the most prominent doctrines in Patrick's writing are a
conviction of God's goodness, love, care, and providence towards
those who know Him and seek Him, and a boundless sense of
gratitude for this goodness. This is indeed the motive and the
keynote of his *Confession*, not primarily to hit back at his opponents, not even to justify himself, but to declare his gratitude to
God:

    *Unde autem tacere non possum tanta beneficia et tantam gratiam quam
mihi Dominus praestare dignatus est* (3); *Unde ergo indefessam gratiam ago
Deo meo* (34); *Quia valde debitor sum Deo qui mihi tantam gratiam donavit*
(38); *Unde autem debueram sine cessatione Deo gratias agere* (46); *Hoc*

erit gloria mea, quia filius sapiens gloria patris est (47); *Unde autem retribuam illi pro omnibus quae retribuit mihi* (57).

Again and again he returns to this theme. But he is no mere pietist obsessed with his own religious experience. He knows that behind all God's mercies to him there lies His greater mercy to the whole human race; Patrick has one or two moving and effective references to the Atonement: he speaks of the Christians enslaved by Coroticus as *servos Dei et ancillas Christi baptizatos, pro quibus mortuus est et crucifixus* (*Ep.* 7); and in the *Confession* he records this message which he received: *Qui dedit animam suam pro te, ipse est qui loquitur in te.*[1]

We may, indeed, say that Patrick has a truly evangelical understanding of the Christian faith. This is said in no sectarian spirit. Patrick has occasionally in the past provided a happy hunting-ground for those who wanted to enrol him in their party, from Tirechan to Todd. But such treatment of Patrick is patently absurd. He was not a Roman Catholic bishop, controlled by the Curia, solemnly issuing Lenten pastorals full of correct doctrine for the edification of his flock. He was not a Protestant evangelist preaching justification by faith and believers' baptism in defiant independence of the papacy. As far as most modern points of controversy go, he was a fifth-century bishop. He does not have occasion to mention the eucharist and the papacy, but we can be sure that if he had he would have voiced some such 'realistic' doctrine of the consecrated elements as was widely current in the fifth century, and he would certainly have acknowledged the primacy of the pope in some form. It seems not unlikely that he brought Sulpicius Severus's books about Martin with him to Ireland, and it is therefore probable that he would not have been averse to the veneration of relics. He certainly was a favourer of the monastic life. When we describe Patrick's doctrine as evangelical, we mean that he put first in his thought and teaching the great central message of God's love, God's act of redemption in Christ, the call to men to respond to this in faith and love, and the presence of the Spirit in the Church now making that love and redemption a reality for those who believe and obey.[2]

---

[1] *Conf.* 24, cf. 55, *sed et Christus Dominus pauper fuit pro nobis.*
[2] For his mention of the Spirit see *Conf.* 4, 20, 25, 33, 40, 43, 46.

When we think of the Western Church in the fifth century we tend perhaps to dwell on these features of its life which most Christians today find repulsive, and even sub-Christian. We think of the dreary thaumaturgy that fills the pages of the saints' lives, the lifeless narratives filled with miracle after improbable miracle, which begin by being uncongenial and end by being utterly wearisome. We think of the crude piety and creaking rhetoric that fills Constantius's *Vita Germani* and that occasionally offends us even in Sulpicius's *Life of St. Martin*. We are inclined to regard the Christianity of the fifth century as a religion which was deplorably vulgarizing itself. But though Patrick's Latin was Vulgar Latin, there was nothing vulgar about his piety. Indeed, it has a surprisingly modern ring about it. He does not relate a single miracle in the whole account of his spiritual pilgrimage. His *Confession* would have profoundly disappointed most fifth-century readers of hagiography. In this respect the authentic Patrick is as far as possible from the menacing, ever-successful, omniscient, bloodless, superman of the later Lives of Patrick. Patrick is a man of like passions with ourselves, a man of flesh and blood, and his piety is not a piety nourished with miracles, but rather it is fed on faith in God's love. Patrick believes, of course, in God's providential ordering of events; God caused Patrick and his shipmen companions to encounter a herd of swine at a critical moment; God delivered Patrick from his original captivity and from later imprisonments more than once. But Patrick realizes perfectly well that God's providence is quite compatible with his meeting disaster and death. He is prepared for the worst to happen (*Conf.* 50 and 55). His faith in God is not a faith that God will always work a miracle to save him, but a conviction that he can entirely trust God to bring about a good result whatever may happen, the faith of a man who has cast himself on God: *cotidie spero aut internicionem aut circumveniri aut redigi in servitutem sive occasio cuiuslibet; sed nihil horum vereor propter promissa caelorum, quia iactavi meipsum in manus Dei omnipotentis qui ubique dominatur.*[1]

Patrick's religious experience was clearly most intense. From the period when, in his captivity in the west of Ireland by the

---

[1] *Conf.* 55; cf. 54: *sufficit honor qui nondum videtur sed corde creditur; fidelis autem qui promisit numquam mentitur*; 56: *ecce nunc commendo animam meam fidelissimo Deo meo pro quo legatione fungor in ignobilitate mea.*

remote shore of the Atlantic Ocean, he turned to God for help, his consciousness of God's presence and succour continually increased. It is perhaps futile to ask whether Patrick had mystical experiences; the word 'mystical' is too often used very loosely or abused. But he certainly had unusual experiences in prayer. He saw visions and heard voices; it is hard to judge from his description, because, as is natural, his inadequate Latin tends to fail more sadly than usual when he describes these experiences; but it is very likely that they were interior rather than exterior sights and sounds.[1] Clearly Patrick was a great man of prayer, and his prayer was nourished on biblical imagery and biblical language. This perhaps is why his piety has so surprisingly modern a ring about it. It was a piety in the tradition of St. Paul and reminds one more of that of St. Augustine than of any other of his contemporaries. There is nothing whatever artificial or forced or extravagant about it. His piety is warm, deep, living, and never insincere.

One of the reasons why we can say this about his piety is that his manner of writing, for all his clumsiness, is transparently honest and, as we have already noted, unexpectedly effective. There are moments, of course, when we cannot know exactly what Patrick means because he is incapable of expressing his meaning at these points in Latin.[2] But on the whole Patrick manages to convey through his very imperfect Latin not only his meaning but his feelings; indeed, we are conscious of having glimpses into his very soul as he speaks to us in his artless, ill-ordered, repetitive, paratactic Latin sentences. The Latin language lends itself peculiarly to rhetoric, almost as much as the Greek language does, and ever since the time of Sallust, of Cicero, and of Livy educated writers of Latin had been using rhetorical expression in order to enhance what they had to say. A hundred supple and varied syntactical devices adorn and enrich their prose, the rhetorical question, the inverted constructions, chiasmus, deliberate breaking off of a sentence, careful subordination of clause to clause; and so on. And, in the realm of meaning, dozens of different tricks are effectively employed, irony, satire, generalization, apostrophe, alliteration,

---

[1] *Conf.* 17, 20, 21, 23 (the most famous of all), 24, 25, 29; Patrick mentions no less than eight such visions.

[2] See, for instance, *Conf.* 29, 32, 46 (the obscurest of all), *Ep.* 2.

epigram, and many more. The tradition of rhetoric was well maintained by the Christian writers of Latin. We can journey in our mind from Minucius Felix, through Tertullian, in some ways the greatest of writers of Christian Latin, Cyprian, Novatian, Lactantius, Hilary, Ambrose, and innumerable others till we reach the supremely subtle and supremely effective rhetorical prose of Augustine. They had all been well educated in the writing of Latin. They had all learnt rhetoric. Their Latin was always carefully constructed and deliberately designed for effect, even when they were writing letters, like Jerome or Ambrose, or literature deliberately composed for a wide, popular audience, like Sulpicius Severus. And this applies to the historians, such as Rufinus and Orosius, as much as to the theologians or commentators. History in the ancient world was to a large extent rhetorical literature. The discipline of the study of rhetoric has left its mark on almost every sort of literature in the ancient world, and not least on Christian literature. But Patrick had missed a higher education, and so he had missed a training in rhetoric. He lacks all these accomplishments. He suffers from the disadvantages of lacking them. He cannot express himself freely, fluently, accurately, or elegantly, and often not even clearly. But he also benefits from the advantages of missing these sophisticated arts. Whatever he says, it is quite clear that he means it. He does not write a line simply for effect. He never exaggerates, never distorts. No rhetoric enhances the effect of his circumlocutory and painfully awkward utterances. But no rhetoric stands in the way of his conveying his real sentiments to the reader. No sort of art or orderliness assists him in putting his material together. But no artificiality tempts him to say what he does not mean. There is no barrier between him and his reader. He is one of the most honest men who ever wrote Latin, perhaps the most honest of all who ever wrote Christian Latin.

The result is that he sometimes attains effects in writing which no contrived art could ever achieve. He can, for instance, suddenly produce a strikingly effective image, and one not even taken from the Bible:

sed illud scio certissime quia utique priusquam humiliarer ego eram velut lapis qui iacet in luto profundo: et venit qui potens est et in sua misericordia sustulit me et quidem scilicet sursum adlevavit et collocavit me in summo pariete.[1]

Clearly this metaphor comes from the depths of Patrick's subconscious, and it makes an appeal which no rhetoric could enhance. Even his well-known *crux interpretum*, the challenge to the 'skilled master-rhetoricians', which immediately follows this passage,[2] extraordinary Latin though it is, is amazingly effective, with its *Quis me stultum excitavit de medio eorum* and its ungrammatical but fine *detestabilis huius mundi*. His account of the most important vision of all is almost like a child's essay in its paratactical simplicity:

And there it was that I saw in the vision of the night a man coming as if from Ireland whose name was Victoricus with countless letters and he gave me one of them and I read the beginning of a letter what contained 'The cry of the Irish', and when I began to think that at that very moment I heard the cry of those who were by the wood of Foclut which is near the Western sea, and this is what they cried out as if with one mouth, 'We beseech you, holy boy, to come and again walk among us', and I was greatly pricked at the heart and I was not able to read further and so I woke up.[3]

One could well imagine how Ambrose or Jerome would have transformed the account of this experience by elegant and dramatic writing. But neither of them could have conveyed the sense of immediacy that Patrick's artless words convey, nor convinced us so surely that he is telling us precisely what he did see and hear, no less and no more. Or we can instance Patrick's noble protestation of his readiness to accept poverty and distress on behalf of Christ because Christ himself became poor for us (*Conf.* 55), or his fine address in the *Epistle to Coroticus* to the souls of those who have been butchered in the massacre (*Ep.* 17 and 18). Patrick did not learn rhetoric, but his subject-matter and the strength of his feelings at times fuse his inadequate Latin into an unstudied rhetoric which is better than the artificial kind.

We now reach what is probably the most interesting and perennially fascinating feature about Patrick, the secret of that

---

[1] *Conf.* 12.   [2] *Conf.* 13.
[3] *Conf.* 23. I have tried to reproduce the ungrammatical *principium* . . . *continentem* by ungrammatical English.

attraction which those who have once looked into his writings inevitably feel.[1] The reader feels that he can understand Patrick's very soul, that he is pouring out his heart directly to the reader of his pages. Far be it from any historian to attempt the task of psycho-analysing Patrick. But it is clear even to the austerest and most dispassionate investigator of his writings that in his captivity at the age of sixteen Patrick suffered what we would now call a severe psychological trauma from which in a sense he never recovered. Even when as an old man he is writing his *Confession*, at least forty and perhaps fifty years after the event, he still cannot stop regarding himself as a helpless adolescent, cruelly torn from home and kindred and forced to do slave labour in hunger and cold,[2] without proper clothing, by unfeeling un-Christian barbarians speaking a foreign language. Even as a venerable bishop who can on occasion thunder forth excommunication and boycott, who is the object of devotion on the part of pious women, who can associate with petty kings and their sons, and who can attract aristocrats to the life of religion, he is still *proselitus et profuga*,[3] *servus*,[4] *profuga indoctus scilicet*,[5] *servulus*,[6] *proselito et peregrino*,[7] *pauperculum pupillum*,[8] *miser et infelix*,[9] he desires to be with *proselitis et captivis*,[10] and lastly, once again *Patricius peccator indoctus scilicet*.[11] He could never quite lose this image of himself as utterly helpless, utterly defenceless, and abandoned. That is why we feel an inextinguishable sympathy with Patrick. He has managed to convey to us so movingly his own feeling about himself, not what he would like us to feel or to

[1] But comparatively few Patristic scholars have done more than glance fleetingly at Patrick. It is an extraordinary fact that, as far as I know, none of the major series of publications of Patristic texts has proposed printing Patrick's works, the *Corpus Scriptorum Ecclesiasticorum Latinorum*, the *Corpus Christianorum*, the *Sources Chrétiennes*, and he does not, of course, appear in the *Loeb* series of texts. The best-established Latin text of Patrick, equipped with an *apparatus criticus*, lies buried in the pages of a recondite Danish periodical, and every single edition of the text and translation into English of his work is at the moment of writing out of print. As far as I know, the only other language into which Patrick's works have been translated is Irish.

[2] *Conf.* 27.   [3] *Ep.* 1.   [4] *Ep.* 10.
[5] *Conf.* 12.   [6] *Conf.* 15.   [7] *Conf.* 26.
[8] *Conf.* 35; this is the most remarkable of all, for *pupillum* here must mean 'orphan'; it is not that Calpornius was killed in the raid which saw Patrick taken captive, but, as the context makes clear, this is an epithet which Patrick chooses to characterize his whole career; during his captivity at the wood of Foclut he was indeed an orphan, deprived not only of parents but also of friends.
[9] *Conf.* 55.   [10] *Conf.* 59.   [11] *Conf.* 62.

think, but what he really felt himself. But we never imagine that he is indulging in futile self-pity. Patrick does not pity himself, because, as he himself tells us, in his moment of helplessness and extreme need he found a helper and a friend in God. He could never forget his terrible experience as an impressionable boy, but neither could he forget that through this experience he had met 'him who is powerful', who drew him out of the deep mud and set him on top of the wall.

APPENDIXES

1. MENTION OF ST. PATRICK IN THE IRISH ANNALS

2. THE 'HIGH-KING' OF IRELAND

APPENDIX 1

MENTION OF ST. PATRICK IN THE
IRISH ANNALS

Six different sets of Annals will be surveyed here, the *Annals of Ulster* (abbreviated to *AU*), the *Chronicum Scottorum* (*CS*), the *Annals of Innisfallen* (*AI*), the *Annals of Tigernach* (*AT*), the *Annals of Clonmacnoise* (*AC*), and the *Annals of the Four Masters* (*A IV M*).

A. The *Annals of Ulster*[1]

These *Annals* run from A.D. 431 to 1131 and from 1155 to 1541. It was Ussher who called them 'the Annals of Ulster', because of the preponderance of entries in them concerning the (old) province of Ulster. *A IV M*, however, more correctly calls them 'the Book of Senad of Mac Manus of Lough Erne'. There are four main manuscripts of these *Annals*, denominated by MacCarthy A, B, C, and D. The last three in one way or another are all dependent on the first, A, though B contains a little material later than the year 1507. B is, however, for the most part an abridged version of A, made in the fifteenth and sixteenth centuries. C is a very bad English version of large portions of the entries in Irish of A, retaining the Latin entries of the original, probably made by Conry in the seventeenth century, and D is a bad Latin version of A's section extending from 1200 to 1300, probably made by Lynch in the seventeenth century. The greater part of A, which is a manuscript of the fifteenth and sixteenth centuries, now kept in the Library of Trinity College, Dublin, was compiled by a cleric called Cathal MacManus, chief of the junior branch of the sept of Maguire, vicar of Inishkeen and dean of the rural deanery of Lough Erne in the diocese of Clogher, a canonist and a competent chronicler, who resided in the stronghold of his clan on an island in the Upper Lough Erne in Co. Fermanagh, then called Shanad and now Bellisle. Some entries bringing the chronicle beyond the date of Cathal MacManus's death (1498) up to 1504 were later added.

---

[1] The *Annals of Ulster* were edited, with an English translation of the entries in Irish, by W. H. Hennessy (Dublin, 1887), in three volumes. The Introduction and Index were issued as a fourth, very large, volume by B. MacCarthy (Dublin, 1901). The information here given about these *Annals* therefore comes from MacCarthy, but the extracts from Hennessy's text.

B. The *Chronicum Scottorum*[1]

These *Annals* run from the earliest times to 1135, and there is a supplement containing the events from 1142 to 1150. The text comes from a manuscript preserved in the Library of Trinity College, Dublin, collated with another in the possession of the Royal Irish Academy. The first manuscript was copied by the Irish scholar and antiquary, Dugald mac Firbis (*c.* 1585–1670), at some point before 1650, and the second is a copy of the first made by mac Firbis himself. It is difficult to determine the date of the original manuscript copied by mac Firbis, but it is likely that it was originally compiled in Clonmacnois. It is clear that the compiler had before him Bede's *De Rerum Natura et Temporibus*, some other ancient work, on English history, and the *Anglo-Saxon Chronicle*.

C. The *Annals of Innisfallen*[2]

These *Annals* run from the earliest times to 1326. They are represented by a manuscript in the Bodleian Library, Oxford; they have borne their present title since at least the early part of the seventeenth century. The chronicle mainly covers the history of Munster, and is, indeed, the main historical source for our knowledge of medieval Munster. About one half of the codex, from the beginning to 1092, was written by a single hand. The rest was compiled by different hands, which up to 1214 were contemporary with the events narrated. The work can be divided into a Pre-Patrician Section and a Post-Patrician Section.

The Pre-Patrician Section is one version, at one stage of its evolution, of a compilation known as the 'Irish World Chronicle', a summary mainly in Latin of the history of the world from the Creation to A.D. 432, including much material from ancient Church historians and some Irish pseudo-history. *AT* contains another version of this (in fact, two versions, for the First Fragment contains a bit of one and the Second Fragment a bit of another); there is another version in a Cotton MS. *AI* contains one of the earliest known versions of this 'Irish World History', for it certainly was transcribed before 1092. The 'Irish World History' was a brief work, later enlarged by glosses, and in some versions then reduced by abridgement. After the 'Irish World History' in *AI* there follows a list of the High-Kings of Ireland with their regnal years, beginning

---

[1] Edited by W. H. Hennessy (Dublin, 1866). The information given here about the book is from Hennessy's Introduction, pp. i–lvii.

[2] Edited with an Introduction (pp. vii–lii) and translation by S. Mac Airt (Dublin, 1951). The information given here is derived from Mac Airt's Introduction.

with Loeghaire mac Neill and ending with Mael Sechnaill mac Domnaill (*ob.* 1022). At the very end of this part the Irish annalistic record proper begins, with the reign of Loeghaire mac Neill (dated as beginning in A.D. 429), and entries covering the years 430–2, largely concerned with Palladius and Patrick. The main sources of the 'Irish World Chronicle' are clearly Jerome's translation of, and continuation of, Eusebius's *Ecclesiastical History*, Bede's *Chronica Maiora et Minora*, Isidore's *Chronicles* and *Etymologies*, Orosius's *Historia adversus Paganos*, the Vulgate, and commentaries on the Vulgate. It is not known for certain whether the compilers had access to all these sources independently or from their being used in Bede's *Chronica*, but as the use of Bede is undisputed, the compilation of the 'Irish World History' cannot be placed before the eighth century. The recension of this work that appears in *AI*, however, must date from after 1056. A long poem in Irish, a versified form of a list of the main world dynasties down to the Byzantine Emperor Leo III (725/6), called from its opening lines *Réidig dam, a Dé do nim*, by Flann Mainistrech, a well-known eleventh-century poet, is given in the Pre-Patrician Section. Flann died in 1056 and wrote this poem in the year of his death. From this and various other evidence Mac Airt concludes that the recension of the 'Irish World Chronicle' which appears in *AI* was probably made between 1056 and 1072.

The Post-Patrician Section can be divided into two parts: (i) the *Annals* from 433 to *c.* 1092, which is the transcript of a single exemplar; and (ii) the remainder, a series of annual of nearly annual entries by contemporary or almost contemporary annalists, and after that annals by subsequent compilers. The earlier of these two parts can in its turn be divided into three:

(1) a section at the beginning containing material common to almost all early Irish annals;
(2) a section coming down to about the middle of the tenth century, consisting mainly of obits; and
(3) a fuller record from the mid-tenth century onward.[1]

Divisions (2) and (3) give some evidence of preference for Munster events and a partiality for the abbeys of Emly and Lismore.

The evidence suggests that shortly after 1130 the codex changed ownership, from East Munster (probably Lismore) to West Munster

---

[1] As we have seen above (p. 98), O'Rahilly conjectured that the common early section in (1) derived from a hypothetical 'Ulster Chronicle', a compilation from existing local and foreign records made probably at Bangor, Co. Down, *c.* 740. Mac Airt believes that this 'Ulster Chronicle' cannot be detected in *AI* later than the early years of the seventh century.

(probably Innisfallen, the island monastery in the Lower Lake of Killarney). About the year 1092 the transcript of the Pre-Patrician Section and of the historical annals 433–1092 was probably made for the use of the monastery of Lismore, and it was probably a transcript of a document which came from the monastery of Emly. The chronicle was continued at Lismore until some point between 1130 and 1159, when it passed to South-West Munster, probably Innisfallen, and there continued up to the date 1214, perhaps by people writing between 1258 and 1285. Later, in the fourteenth century, the blank years were filled in from other sources.

D. The *Annals of Tigernach*[1]

The first two pieces of this collection are in fact two separate fragments, perhaps two separate fragmentary recensions, of an 'Irish World Chronicle', unconnected with the annals that follow, running respectively from the time of the prophets Hosea, Amos, Isaiah, Jonah, and Malachi to the time of the Emperor Antoninus Pius (138–61), and from *c.* 322 B.C. to A.D. 360.[2] The next two fragments are parts of a continuous chronicle by Tigernach hua Braein, a learned Abbot of Clonmacnoise, who died about 1088, covering respectively the years A.D. 489 to 766 and 975 to 1088. The fifth piece is an anonymous continuation in Irish from 1088 to 1178. The Irish sources of *AT* are unknown, but the Latin sources can be reconstructed. They comprise: Jerome's translation of Eusebius's *Ecclesiastical History*; *Chronicon sive de sex huius saeculi aetatibus*, printed in Bede's works; Orosius's *Historia adversus Paganos*; the Vulgate; Isidore's *Etymologies*; a Latin translation of Josephus's *Antiquities of the Jews*; and possibly a lost *Chronicon* of Julius Africanus.

E. The *Annals of Clonmacnoise*[3]

The title of these *Annals* is rather arbitrary, but it was given partly because the doings of families which lived in the vicinity of Clonmacnoise, on both sides of the Shannon, figure prominently in its pages. The original was certainly in Irish. Its author is unknown, and the original text even of the English translation has disappeared. There are, however, several copies of this translation, one in the

---

[1] The documents called by this collective name have all been printed by Whitley Stokes, with the Irish parts translated into English, in *Revue Celtique* ('First Fragment', xvi (1895), pp. 376–419; 'Second Fragment', xvii (1896), pp. 6–33; 'Third Fragment', ibid., pp. 119–263; 'Fourth Fragment', ibid., pp. 337–42; 'Anonymous Continuation', xviii (1897), pp. 9–59, 150–97, 267–303). They are all to be found in a manuscript in the British Museum (Rawlinson B 488).

[2] So O'Rahilly (*Early Irish History and Mythology*, p. 258, n. 1). These are the two documents called 'First Fragment' and 'Second Fragment' by Stokes.

[3] *The Annals of Clonmacnoise*, edited by D. Murphy (Dublin, 1896).

British Museum and one in the Library of Trinity College, Dublin. It is from the latter that the edition of Murphy is taken; this copy was made in 1684. The original English translation, of which this is a copy, was made by Conell or Conla Ma Geogehan, of Lismoyne, Co. Westmeath; he finished it in the castle of Lemanaghan, near Clara in Co. Leix, in 1627. The *Annals* run from the Creation till 1408, so presumably the original, or final, compiler lived at, or some time after, that date. Among the sources the compiler quotes are Bede and Eusebius. After recording the sending of St. Patrick to Ireland, the compiler makes a clean break. First he gives an account of St. Patrick, a very brief and legendary one, clearly derived from some of the later Lives of Patrick, and then begins a new chronicle of the kings of Ireland, dating them by Anno Domini.

F. The *Annals of the Four Masters*[1]

These *Annals* were compiled, in Irish, at the Franciscan monastery of Donegal between 1632 and 1636 by a number of scholars, of whom by far the most prominent was Michael O'Clery. The number of the compilers has always been reckoned as four (though in fact it seems to have exceeded four) since the time of Colgan, and their names are recorded as Michael O'Clery, Conary O'Clery, Cucogry O'Clery, and Ferfeasa O'Mulconry. They accomplished their task at the request and under the patronage of Fergal O'Gara, Lord of Moy O'Gara and Coolavin in the County of Sligo. The *Annals* run from the earliest times to the sixteenth century. It is clear that they represent the most developed state of the legend about Patrick, though they do not give the date of his birth. There is almost no curious story or fancy which they do not embody.

It should finally be noted that though some of these six sets of *Annals* sometimes give datings Anno Domini, it can only have been at a comparatively late date that these reckonings were added, and many of those in the printed texts of today were added by their later editors. Their accuracy, therefore, must often be regarded as doubtful.

In the following lists, quotations in English between inverted commas are translations of original Irish in the case of *AU*, *CS*, and *AT*, but in the case of *AC* and *A IV M* are reproductions of the English of the text as we have it. Reasons of space have compelled me to abridge and paraphrase most of the entries in the case of *AC* and *A IV M*. My own explanations are given in square brackets [ ].

[1] *Annals of the Kingdom of Ireland by the Four Masters*, ed. J. O'Donavan (Dublin 1851), vol. i, and especially the Introduction, pp. vii–liv.

MENTION OF PATRICK IN ANNALS

(i) *Birth and Captivity of Patrick*

AU	CS	AI
	353 *Patricius natus est in hoc anno.*	313 *Patricius episcopus natus est.*
	364 *Patricius in Hiberniam adductus in hoc anno.*	315 *Patricius baptizatus est.*
	369 *Patricius a captivitate solutus est per angelum*	317 *Patricius in captivitate in Hiberniam ducitur et vi annis servivit.*
	376 *Patricius ad Germanum.*	320 *Patricius captivitate (ab) solvitur ab angelo.*

(ii) *Patrick's Arrival as Bishop in Ireland*

431 *Palladius ad Scotos a Celestino urbis Romae episcopo ordinatus episcopus.*

432 *Patricius pervenit ad Hiberniam.*

432 *Patricius, id est archiepiscopus, in Hiberniam venit atque Scotos baptizare incohavit.*

433 *Conversio Scotorum in fidem Christianam.*

AT	*AC*	*A IV M*
[From the 'Second Fragment'.] [*c.* 340] *Patricius nunc natus est* ([i.e. between] *Constantinus a ducibus Constantis fratris sui in bello occisus est* [and] *Constans Arianus effectus catholicos toto orbe persequitur* [and the death of Arius]). [*c.* 355] *Patricius captivus in Hiberniam ductus est* ([i.e. between the return of Hilary of Poictiers from the East and the importing by Constantine (*sic*) of the bones of Andrew the Apostle to Constantinople and the sending of Julian to be imperator in Gaul]).	The captivity of Patrick is recorded in the reign of king Eochy Moymean [the nearest absolute dates given to this are Martin's becoming Bishop of Tours 'in the year 319' (the annalist calls him uncle of St. Patrick) before the captivity and the death of St. Anthony the hermit, aged 100, and the *floruit* of Martin *c.* 360 after the captivity].	
	Record of the sending of Patrick by Pope Celestine, but of his landing in the reign of Sixtus, Celestine's successor, in the year 425 [corrected by translator to 432]. A brief and legendary account of Patrick follows. Then Palladius is mentioned as sent by Celestine before Patrick [under the rubric 'others say that']. Palladius converted only five parishes in Leinster and then departed for Rome, but died on his way to Pictland.	430 Landing of Palladius, sent by Pope Celestine. He landed in Leinster, with twelve men. Nathi, son of Garchu, refused to admit him. He baptized a few people, built three wooden churches, and left four men in these churches, Augustinus, Benedictus, Silvester, and Solinus. He returned to Rome (for 'he did not receive respect' in Ireland) and died of a disease in the country of the Cruithnigh. 431 Patrick ordained by Pope Celestine, who sent him to Ireland. 432 Patrick lands and baptizes the Irish 'as his life relates'. Ath-Truim founded by Patrick.

(iii) *Events in Patrick's Ministry in Ireland*

AU	CS	AI
439 *Secundus, Auxilius, et Serninus mittuntur et episcopi ipsi in Hiberniam in auxilium Patricii.*	438 *Secundinus et Auxilius et Esserninus mittuntur ad Hibernenses,* 'but they obtained not pre-eminence nor authority in the time of Patrick alone'.	439 *Secundinus et Auxiliarius et Esserninus mittuntur in auxilium Patricii, nec tamen tenuerunt apostolatum.*
441 *Leo ordinatus xlii Romanae ecclesiae episcopus et probatus est in fide Catholica Patricius episcopus.*	446 *Quies Secundini filii Restituti lxxv anno aetatis suae cuius mater Culmana Patricii soror.*	441 *Probatio Sancti Patricii in fide Catholica.*
443 '*Patricius episcopus ardore fidei et doctrina Christi florens in nostra provincia.*	457 *Dormitatio Sancti Senis Patricii Episcopi id est Glosdoniensis* [Glastonbury] *ecclesiae.*	443 *Patricius in Christi doctrina floruit.*
444 *Ard Macha fundata est.*	465 *Quies Benigni successoris Patricii.*	448 *Quies Secundini sancti.*
447 *Quies Secundini sancti lxx anno aetatis suae.*		460 *Auxilius dormivit.*
457 *Quies senis Patricii ut alii libri dicunt.*		465 *Essurninus dormivit.*
459 *Auxilius episcopus quievit.*		468 *Quies Benigni episcopi. In Roma moritur.*
461 *Hic alii quietem Patricii dicunt.*		481 *Quies Iarlaithe* 'third abbot of Armagh'.
467 *Quies Benigni episcopi successoris Patricii.*		492 *Quies Meicc Caille episcopi.*
468 *Isserninus episcopus moritur.*		
481 *Quies Iarlathi mic Trena tertii episcopi Ardmacai.*		

AT	AC	A IV M

[From the 'Third Fragment'.]
 	
c. 489 *Quies sancti Ciannaini Daimlaig* 'He gave Patrick his Gospel'.
	Record of Patrick founding Armagh. Legendary encounters with Loeghaire and his family.
	
	430 Mention of Pope Leo 'by whom St. Patrick was approved in the Catholic religion and by the rest of the Popes of Rome that succeeded in his time and then after flourished in the heat of Christian religion in this land'.
	
	433 Secundinus or Seachnall patron of Dunshaughlin and Auxilius were sent by the Pope to help in the conversion of Ireland.
	
	Somewhere between 427 and 450 Death of Secundinus.
	
	468 Death of Benignus the bishop.
	
	469 Iserninus bishop died.
	    Brandon, Bishop of Armagh, died.
	    Earlahy, third Bishop of Armagh, died.
	
	487 [or at some time between 487 and 497] 'Bishop Moyle (Mel) died in Ardacah'.
	    'St. Kineann of Dowliag Dowleeke to whom St. Patrick gave his one book of the Holy Evangelist died.'
	    'The Bishop m'Caille dyed.'
		438 The History and Laws of Ireland collected at Patrick's request by 3 kings, 3 saints, and 3 antiquaries.
		
		447 Death of Secundinus (Seachnall), son of Patrick's sister, Bishop of Ardmacha, aged 75. A poem follows detailing the 24 persons of Patrick's court or *familia*, among them Secundinus, Benignus, 'German, his tutor', and 'Martin, his mother's brother'.
		
		454 St. Usaille (Auxilius) Bishop of Cill Usaille (Killosy) died.
		
		457 Armagh founded by Patrick, having been granted by Daire. 'Old' Patrick yielded his spirit.
		
		467 Death of Benignus, Bishop of Armagh.
		
		481 Death of Jarlath, Bishop of Armagh.
		
		487 Death of Mel, Bishop of Ardagh, disciple of Patrick.
		
		488 Death of Cianan, Bishop of Duleek.

(iv) *Patrick's Death*

AU	CS	AI
491 *Dicunt Scoti hic Patricium defunctum.*	489 *Patricius archiepiscopus et Apostolus Hibernensium anno aetatis suae centessimo xxii, xvi Kal Aprilis quievit, et dicitur,*	496 *Quies Patricii, hi xvi April anno ccccxxxii a Passione Domini.*
492 *Patricius archipostolus* [gloss *archiepiscopus et apostolus*] *Scotorum quievit cmº xxº etatis suae, 16 kal Aprilis, lxº autem quo venit ad Hiberniam anno ad baptizandos Scotos.*	'Since Christ was born, a joyful reckoning, Four hundred and fair ninety, Three exact years after that To the death of Patrick, chief Apostle' [i.e. 493].	

It will be obvious to the reader that all these *Annals* are compilations of many different sources, coming from widely different periods. The contradictions and confusions which are evident even to a superficial glance at them have for long taxed the ingenuity of Patrician scholars. In a brief review such as this only a few main points can be made.

Three facts emerge clearly from a comparison of these six sets of *Annals*:

1. None of the *Annals*, and none of their sources, have any reliable information about the date either of Patrick's birth or of his captivity.

2. All the compilers (except of *AI*) assume that the late date for Patrick's death, about 493, is the accepted and correct one, but they all have some traces of an earlier date, *c.* 461, for his death (except *AT*, whose surviving fragments do not cover this period).

3. The dating of all of them revolves round two facts which the compilers and their sources apparently knew with unanimous certainty:

   a. That Palladius was sent to Ireland by Pope Celestine in

AT	AC	A IV M
[From the 'Third Fragment'.] c. 490 *Patricius Arciepiscopus et Apostolus Hibernensium anno etatis suae centensimo vigessimo xvi die kl Aprilis quievit.* 'From Christ's birth a pleasant step, Four hundreds on fair ninety, Three noble years after that To the death of Patrick chief Apostle' [i.e. 493].	Patrick died in the 123rd year of his age: 'others say that he lived not long, but my author, whose written booke of him is no less than 300 years written, sayeth that his age was no less.' Nobody can be sure whether he was Welsh or Breton or Scottish or English. 'Hee was borne in a village called Taburna neer Emptor town in the south of England.' 487 [or at some time between 487 and 497] 'St Patrick the Apostle and Archbishop dyed in yᵉ 123rd yeare of his age the 16th day of the Calends of Aprill'.	493 Record of the death of Patrick with a long eulogy on his merits and achievements. He received the Body of Christ from Bishop Tassach. He was aged 122. There follows an account of a conflict between the Uí Néill and the Oirghialla on the one hand, who wanted to bring the body to Armagh, and the Ulaid on the other, who wanted to keep it to themselves. A miracle caused them to abandon the dissension and Patrick was buried at Dun-da-lethglas [i.e. Downpatrick].

431 (a fact which could have been learnt from Prosper or some similar source).

b. That Patrick arrived as Bishop in Ireland shortly after the mission of Palladius.

Some scholars have been ready to explain the later date for Patrick's death as arising out of a desire to give Patrick a life of 120 years in imitation of Moses, but the difficulty in this view is that it assumes that the writers who produced this fancy knew Patrick's birth-date, but not his death-date. The evidence, however, is wholly against this assumption. None of the vague guesses about Patrick's birth to be found in these *Annals* place it at about the year 370, which this theory would necessitate. It is much more likely that the attempt to equate Patrick's life with that of Moses arises from the desire to reconcile two widely separated dates which were associated with Patrick in the tradition, 432 and 493. Anyway, it would have been quite possible to envisage Patrick as dying in 461, and still to equate his life with that of Moses, by assuming that he was born c. 340. It may be that the date for Patrick's birth in *AT*, and perhaps even in *CS* and *AI*, can be accounted for by this very assumption. On the other hand, the year 461 as a date for Patrick's death is suspiciously like an assimilation to the death-date of Pope Leo I. One thing is virtually certain, the man who wrote the *Confession* and the *Epistle to Coroticus* could not have died as late as 493.

All that can be said here as a general verdict on these *Annals* is that they do not give the impression that the accuracy of the dates allotted in the fifth century is trustworthy. They certainly do not suggest that we can assume that behind the earliest sources to be detected in them lies any document such as a calendar of the fifth or even of the sixth century.

APPENDIX 2

THE 'HIGH-KING' OF IRELAND

BURY in his *Life of St. Patrick* had accepted almost *au pied de la lettre* many of the statements in the *Annals* about the fifth century, as well as much of the material in the *Book of Armagh*. He was ready to believe that King Loeghaire had drawn up a code of the Laws of Ireland, following here the very late and wholly untrustworthy tradition to be found in *A IV M* (see above, p 219). He reconstructed confidently the career and the dates of Niall of the Nine Hostages, of Nath I, whom he imagined to be Niall's first, and of Loeghaire, whom he thought to be his second, successor. He saw no difficulty in recognizing Loeghaire as 'High-King' of Ireland. Succeeding scholars, such as McNeill and Ryan, have accepted Bury's findings, and have painted a picture of the fifth-century High-King exacting homage from the lesser kings and holding a 'Fair' or national assembly at Tailtiu (modern Teltown, Co. Meath) and/or at Tara, either annually or once in his lifetime, where the affairs of the kingdom were discussed. Morris has recently championed the view that this High-Kingship not only existed in the fourth century, but existed more effectively in the fourth century, when it 'co-ordinated overseas military expeditions', than it did in the fifth and sixth, 'when fighting was virtually confined to domestic wars'.[1]

There are many reasons for doubting the validity of this reconstruction. The first and simplest arises from the writings of Patrick himself. He nowhere mentions a High-King. In fact, the title 'High-King' is a misnomer for any king in Ireland until after the time of Brian Boru in the eleventh century. In his famous insertion in the *Book of Armagh* Brian very early in the eleventh century describes himself as *Briani imperatoris Scotorum*, apparently in imitation of Charlemagne. Earlier kings who aspired to a position like that of High-King had called themselves 'Kings of Ireland'. As Morris points out, Adomnan had described a mid-sixth-century king as *totius Scotiae regnator*, and Muirchú at the end of the seventh century called Loeghaire *imperator barbarorum regnans in Temoria* [i.e. Tara] *quae erat caput Scotorum . . . filius Neill, origo stirpis regiae huius pene insolae.*[1] This could, and probably does, mean no more than that this king was, as far as Muirchú knew, the most powerful king in Ireland

[1] 'Celtic Saints', p. 387, n. 4.

of his day, and the title *imperator barbarorum* was an honorary one. Similarly, as Binchy points out,[1] Adomnan was capable of calling Oswald, King of Northumbria, *totius Britanniae imperator*, not meaning, of course, 'High-King of Britain', but using this as an honorary title for the most powerful king in Britain. Patrick mentions *reges* (*Conf.* 52) and *reguli* (*Conf.* 41), which are almost certainly two different titles for the same class of people, and refers to the *tyrannidem Corotici* (*Ep.* 6), but nowhere does he suggest that he encountered a *rex* who was different from or superior to the *reguli/reges*. Had he met a High-King, there are several places where he might have made a telling reference to him in order to further his argument. Our sole contemporary record for mid-fifth-century Ireland, therefore, yields no evidence for the existence of a High-King.

Next, we may note a point well made by Binchy.[2] If there was a High-King in Ireland during Patrick's missionary activity there, presumably he was Loeghaire, of the Uí Néill dynasty, and presumably his headquarters were at Tara. So Muirchú certainly assumes. Why, then, did Patrick found his chief church and headquarters at Armagh, in Ulster, which was either not under Loeghaire's jurisdiction or had recently been conquered and sacked by him, or by his immediate predecessor? As far as we can reconstruct the historical Patrick, we must allow that he seems to have had little or nothing to do with Tara.

But in fact we must go much further in scepticism concerning the existence of the fifth-century High-King. It must be realized that all our historical sources for fifth-century Ireland, apart from Patrick's writings, have been composed with the intention of rewriting history for ideological purposes, whether we take the writers in the *Book of Armagh*, the compilers of the *Annals*, or the Irish medieval writers who have handed down to us the earliest myths and legends of the Irish race. There is no source which gives us straightforward history for Ireland before the fifth century. The medieval Irish writers who purported to do this were in fact indulging in a large scheme of euhemerization or historicizing myth, because they wanted to represent the gods and goddesses of pagan Ireland as historical and not supernatural characters.[3] Their accounts were quite wrongly taken as sober history by seventeenth-century scholars such as Keating and Mac Firbis, and the influence of these names lingers yet. The entries in the *Annals* for the fourth

---

[1] 'The Passing of the Old Order' (*Proceedings of the International Congress of Celtic Studies*), p. 125.
[2] *PB*, p. 149.
[3] See O'Rahilly, *Early Irish History and Mythology*, cap. xiv, 'History and Fable', pp. 260–85.

century are historically worthless, and we can no more rely on their accounts of a High-King for that period than we can on their apparently 'historical' accounts of the period immediately after the Creation. Far less can we speak with any confidence of the existence in that century of a High-King who could 'co-ordinate overseas military expeditions'. O'Rahilly showed with devastating effect the frailty, indeed the worthlessness, of almost all Bury's assumptions about the dates and the career of Niall of the Nine Hostages,[1] and, indeed, of his reconstruction of the reigns of the fifth-century kings of Connaught.[2] The figures of Niall and of Loeghaire are much mistier and less well-established than Bury ever imagined, and the figure of Nath Í is altogether questionable.

The attempt to associate the fifth-century High-King with a national feast or assembly at Tailtiu or Tara, whether held annually or more rarely, is equally ineffectual. In an article devoted to these two feasts,[3] Binchy has given many weighty reasons for concluding that in the fifth century the 'fair' at Tailtiu was an occasion which concerned no territory more extensive than that of the over-king of the Uí Neíll dynasties, and did not involve any other kings, and that the Feast of Tara, originally a pagan fertility-rite held at some point after the accession of the King of Tara, had become obsolete in the sixth century and was only later invested by historians with a fictitious national significance. It is the last function which one would have expected Patrick, as an opponent of paganism, to visit. But both feasts were fastened upon by later, medieval, Irish writers to forward their ideological aims:

It is, I think, highly significant that the eclipse of Óenach Tailten should have coincided with the period during which the pseudo-historians were busily engaged in creating the myth of the 'high-kingship'. Unhampered by contemporary realities, poets and storytellers might safely 'remould it nearer to the heart's desire'. The failure to hold the Fair during most of the tenth and almost the whole of the eleventh century thus helped to clear the way for the legendary Óenach Tailten which now emerges as one of the constitutional organs of the 'high-kingship', a nation-wide gathering of the 'men of Ireland'.[4]

The mythological reconstruction of the feast of Tara occurred even earlier, in the seventh century:

The historical Feast of Tara was a primitive fertility-rite culminating in the apotheosis of the sacred king. It was last held by Diarmait mac Corbaill in 560, after which it was discarded as a relic of paganism. More than three

---

[1] *Early Irish History and Mythology*, pp. 209–34. [2] Ibid., p. 399.
[3] 'The Fair of Tailtiu and the Feast of Tara.' [4] Ibid., p. 126.

centuries later, however, the pseudo-historians resurrected it in the form of a 'constitutional organ' of the 'high-kingship', and we can actually trace the expansion of the legendary Feast of Tara until by Keating's day it has eclipsed the Fair of Tailtiu in importance and became the equivalent of a 'national assembly' or 'parliament'.[1]

It is true that O'Rahilly believed that the claim to High-Kingship had originated in the second half of the fifth century, after the Uí Neíll dynasty had overthrown the Ulaid and sacked Emain Macha. He did so because he thought that the *Irish Annals'* entries for the fifth century were based on information written in the fifth century in the margins or the blank spaces of Paschal Tables, and that the hypothetical 'Irish World Chronicle', composed in about 740 in Bangor, Co. Down, incorporated these entries.[2] But this theory too rests on insecure foundations. Binchy points out that marginal entries made in a Paschal Table in Ireland in the fifth century would postulate the introduction of a quite new technique of recording into Ireland, involving 'a total revolution in the native Irish methods of reckoning time', the formation in Ireland of monastic communities, and the fostering and developing of this technique in them. He doubts if these conditions could all have been present until well after 500.[3] He is sceptical about O'Rahilly's theory of the existence of an 'Irish World Chronicle' as early as 740 in Bangor, and suspects that the fifth-century entries in the *Irish Annals* were composed on much the same principles and with as little respect for fact as the fourth-century or third-century ones.[4]

J. V. Kelleher, in a recent article, is even more sceptical about the early existence of the institution of High-Kingship.[5] From some early period, whose exact time cannot be ascertained, the kings of the Uí Neíll dynasty did indeed increase their control in various parts of Ireland, so that by the ninth century they dominated all Ulster and the midlands, and at least exercised influence over Connaught and Leinster. But nobody who could be called a High-King appeared until the ninth century. The first High-King who exercised effective control over all other kings was Brian Boru early in the eleventh century. Kelleher does not believe that we can detect in the existing *Annals* an 'Irish World Chronicle' compiled about 740. A much later record has replaced the original annalistic texts for the period up to about 590, and from 590 to 735 has gravely altered them. This later text had four propaganda purposes:

---

[1] 'The Fair of Tailtiu and the Feast of Tara', pp. 137–8.
[2] *Early Irish History and Mythology*, pp. 251–2, 253–9, 408–18.
[3] *PB*, pp. 71–72.   [4] *PB*, pp. 73–74.
[5] 'Early Irish History and Pseudo-History.'

1. The sole domination of Tara by the Uí Neíll is dated from the first century A.D.
2. The fall of Emain Macha, and with it the Uí Neíll conquest of central Ulster, is placed at A.D. 327 instead of about the middle of the fifth century.
3. The latest version of the Uí Neíll regnal lists and pedigrees is woven into the *Annals*.
4. Patrick is associated with the Uí Neíll and with Tara. This last feature reveals that the Uí Neíll dynasty and the ecclesiastical establishment at Armagh have joined hands in a common ideological policy.[1]

This reassessment of the *Annals* means that we must assign the compilation of the earliest parts of the documents as we have them now to a much later period than has been commonly supposed: 'Apart from interpolations it would appear that up to 910 all the annals are but selective versions of one common source, a text very likely composed in that year and both fuller and more national in its purview than any of the recensions derived from it.'[2]

It is therefore not without reason that this work refuses to accept the view that the institution of High-Kingship in Ireland existed in the fifth century, that Loeghaire occupied that position, or that Patrick ever met a High-King.

[1] Ibid., p. 125.   [2] Ibid., p. 126.

BIBLIOGRAPHY

ANCIENT TEXTS

1. St. Patrick's Works

Libri Sancti Patricii, ed. N. J. D. White, Texts for Students (minor ed., London, 1918).

Libri Epistolarum Sancti Patricii Episcopi, ed. L. Bieler, text reproduced by L. Mac Philibín in *Mise Pádraig* (Dublin, 1961).

Commentary on this text by L. Bieler in *Classica et Mediaevalia* xii. 1–2, fasc. 1–2, Part II: Introduction and Commentary (Copenhagen, 1951).

Latin text of the *Confession* and the *Epistle to Coroticus* is also printed in *The Tripartite Life of Patrick and other Documents relating to that Saint*, by Whitley Stokes, vol. ii (London, 1887).

Translations into English:

> N. J. D. White, *St. Patrick, his Writings and Life*, with a Commentary (London, 1920; translations issued separately as *The Writings of Saint Patrick*, London, 1932, repr. 1954).

> L. Bieler, *The Works of St. Patrick*, Ancient Christian Writers (London, 1953), with a Commentary.

2. Annals, etc.

The Tripartite Life of St. Patrick, etc., ed. Whitley Stokes, contains the *Vita Tripartita* in vol. i, and in vol. ii the Lives of Muirchú of Tirechan, the *Liber Angueli*, and other materials.

Liber Ardmachanus: The Book of Armagh, ed. J. Gwynn (Dublin, 1913).

Chronicum Scottorum, ed. W. M. Henessy (London, 1886).

Annals from the Book of Leinster, ed. Whitley Stokes, *The Tripartite Life etc.*, vol. i, pp. 512 ff.

Annals of Ulster, ed. W. M. Henessy (London, 1887–1901).

The Annals of Tigernach, ed. Whitley Stokes (*Revue Celtique*, xvi (1895) pp. 376–419; xvii (1896) pp. 6–33, 119–263, 337–420); also extracts in *The Tripartite Life etc.*, vol. ii, pp. 572, 573.

The Annals of Clonmacnoise, translated into English by C. Mageoghan, ed. D. Murphy (Dublin, 1896).

The Annals of Innisfallen, ed., with English translation, S. Mac Airt (Dublin, 1951).

The Annals of the Kingdom of Ireland by the Four Masters, vol. i, ed. J. O'Donovan (Dublin, 1851); vol. iv, ed. B. MacCarthy (Dublin, 1901).

Chronicles of the Picts and Scots, ed. W. F. Skene (Edinburgh, 1867).

Two Gallic Chronicles, ed. T. Mommsen, *Monumenta Germaniae Historico, Auctores Antiquissimi* ix, *Chronica Minora* i (Berlin, 1892, repr. 1961).

Historia Brittonum, cum additamentis Nennii, ed. T. Mommsen, *Chron. Min. Saec. iv–vii*, vol. iii, *MGH Auct. Ant.*, xiii (Berlin, 1898, repr. 1961), pp. 113–222.

Fontes Historiae Religionis Celticae, ed. J. Zwicker, Pars Altera (Bonn, 1935).
Catalogus Sanctorum Hiberniae, ed. with Commentary, P. Grosjean, *Analecta Bollandiana*, lxxxiii, 1955, pp. 197–213, 289–322.
Lives of the Saints from the Book of Lismore, ed. Whitley Stokes (Oxford, 1890).
Vitae Sanctorum Hiberniae, ed. C. Plummer (Oxford, 1910).
Acta Sanctorum Hiberniae ex codice Salmaticensi, ed. C. de Smedt and J. de Backer (Edinburgh, London, and Bruges, 1888).
Sanctae Brigidae Virginis Vita a Cogitoso Adornata (*PL* 72), 775–90.
Adomnan's Life of Columba, ed. A. O. and M. O. Anderson (London, 1961).

3. Other Texts

Councils and Ecclesiastical Documents relating to Great Britain and Ireland, vol. i, ed. A. W. Haddan and W. Stubbs (Oxford, 1869).
The Anglo-Saxon Chronicle, translated with Introduction by O. N. Garmonsway (London, rev. edn. 1954 of 1953 edn.).
Corpus Inscriptionum Latinarum vii, ed. A. Hübner (Berlin, 1873).
Ephemeris Epigraphica, Corp. Inscr. Lat. Supplementum vii (Rome, 1892).
Ibid. ix (Berlin, 1913).
The Roman Inscriptions of Britain, ed. R. G. Collingwood and R. P. Wright (Oxford, 1965).
Ammianus Marcellinus, *Rerum Gestarum Quae Supersunt*, ed. V. Gardthausen (Leipzig, vol. i, 1873; vol. ii, 1875).
Augustine of Hippo, *Sermones* 273 (*PL* 38. 1251), 325 (*PL* 38. 1447–50), 326 (*PL* 38. 1475), and 356 (*PL* 39, 1578).
Celestinus Papa, *Epistola* iv (*PL* 50. 430, 431).
Constantius, *Vita Germani Episcopi Autissiodorensis*, ed. B. Krusch and W. Levison, *Mon. Germ. Hist. Script. Rer. Meroving.* vii, i (Hanover and Leipzig, 1909).
Epistolae Imperatorum, Pontificum, Aliorum: Collectio Avellana, ed. O. Guenther, *Corpus Scriptorum Ecclesiasticorum Latinorum* xxxv (Prague, Vienna, and Leipzig, 1895):
  Epistola Maximi Tyranni ad Valentinianum Augustum Iuniorem contra Arianos et Manichaeos, 39, pp. 88–90.
  Epistola Maximi Tyranni ad Papam Siricium, 40, pp. 90–91.
Epistola Papae Innocentii ad Victricium episcopum Rotomagensem (*PL* 20. 468–81).
Epistolae Papae Siricii (*PL* 13. 1131–94).
Etheria, *Peregrinatio*, ed. and translated into French by Hélène Petré, *Sources Chrétiennes* (Paris, 1948).
Excerpta Valesiana Anonyma, ed. V. Gardthausen (in vol. ii of *Ammianus Marcellinus*).
Fastidius, *De Vita Christiana* (*PL* 40. 1031–46).
Gildas, *De Excidio Britanniae* etc., ed. H. Williams, with English translation (London, Part I, 1899; Part II, 1901).
John Chrysostom, *Homiliae* viii (*PG* 63, 501).
Orosius, Paulus, *Historia adversus Paganos*, ed. C. Zangemeister (Leipzig, 1889); also *PL* 31.

Prosper of Aquitaine, *Chronicle* (*PL* 50. 535 ff.).
— *Contra Collatorem* (*PL* 51. 271 ff.)
Sidonius Apollinaris, *Epistula et Carmina*, ed. C. Luetjohann, *MGH Auct. Ant.* viii (Berlin, 1877, repr. 1961).
Sozomenus, *Historia Ecclesiastica*, ed. J. Bidez and G. C. Hansen (Berlin, 1960, Series *Griech. christl. Schrift.*).
Sulpicius Severus, *De Vita Martini* (*PL* 20. 159 ff.).
— *Historia Sacra* (*PL* 20. 146 ff.).
— *Epistolae Tres* (*PL* 20. 175–84).
— *Dialogi* (*PL* 20. 185 ff.).
Victricius of Rouen, *De Laude Sanctorum* (*PL.* 20. 443–4)
Zosimus, *Historia Nova*, ed. L. Mendelssohn (Leipzig, 1887, repr. Hildesheim, 1963).

BOOKS

Bieler, L., *The Life and Legend of St. Patrick* (Dublin, 1948).
Blair, P. Hunter, *Roman Britain and Early England* (Edinburgh, 1963).
Blaise, A. (rev. H. Chirat), *Dictionnaire latin-français des Auteurs chrétiens* (Strasbourg, 1954).
Bulloch, J., *The Life of the Celtic Church* (Edinburgh, 1963).
Bury, J. B., *The Life of St. Patrick* (London, 1965).
Carney, J., *The Problem of St. Patrick* (Dublin, 1961).
Chadwick, H. M., *Early Scotland* (Cambridge, 1949).
Chadwick, Norah (ed.) *Studies in Early British History* (Cambridge, 1954).
— *Poetry and Letters in Early Christian Gaul* (London, 1955).
— (ed.), *Studies in the Early British Church* (Cambridge, 1958).
— *The Age of the Saints in the Early Celtic Church* (Oxford, 1961).
— (ed.), *Celt and Saxon* (Cambridge, 1963).
— *Celtic Britain* (London, 1963).
Collingwood, R. B., and Myres, J. N. L., *Roman Britain and the English Settlements* (Oxford, 2nd edn. 1937).
Courcelle, P., *Les Confessions de saint Augustin dans la tradition littéraire* (Paris, 1963).
de Plinval, G., *Pélage, ses écrits, sa vie et sa réforme* (Lausanne, 1943).
Duke, J. A., *The Columban Church* (Edinburgh, 1932, repr. 1957).
Frend, W. H. C., *Martyrdom and Persecution in the Early Church* (Oxford, 1965).
Hanson, R. P. C., *Tradition in the Early Church* (London, 1962).
— *St. Patrick, a British Missionary Bishop* (Nottingham, 1965).
Harden, D. B. (ed.), *Dark-Age Britain* (London, 1956).
Haverfield, F., *The Romanization of Roman Britain* (Oxford, 2nd. edn. 1912).
— *Victoria History of Hampshire*, 'Romano-British Hampshire', vol. i, pp. 265–349.
Henry, Françoise, *Irish Art in the Early Christian Period to A.D. 800* (London, rev. edn. 1966 of edns. of 1940 and 1947).
Hughes, Kathleen, *The Church in Early Irish Society* (London, 1966).
Jackson, K., *Language and History in Early Britain* (Edinburgh, 1953).

Jarrett, M., and Dobson, B. (eds.), *Britain and Rome* (Kendal 1966).
Jones, A. H. M., *The Later Roman Empire*, 3 vols. (Oxford, 1964).
Kenney, J. F., *Sources for the Early History of Ireland* (New York, 1929).
MacNeill, E., *St. Patrick*, ed. J. Ryan (Dublin, 1964).
MacQueen, J., *St. Nynia* (Edinburgh, 1961).
Map of Roman Britain (Ordnance Survey, Chessington, 3rd edn. 1956).
Meates, G. W., *Lullingstone Roman Villa* (London, 1955).
Mélanges offerts à Mademoiselle Christine Mohrmann (Utrecht, 1963).
Meyer, K., *Learning in Ireland in the Fifth Century* (Dublin, 1913).
Mohrmann, Christine, *The Latin of St. Patrick* (Dublin, 1961).
Olden, T., *The Church of Ireland* (London, 1892).
O'Rahilly, T. F., *The Two Patricks* (Dublin, 1942).
— *Early Irish History and Mythology* (Dublin, 1946).
Oulton, J. E. L., *The Credal Statements of St. Patrick* (Dublin, 1940).
Phillips, W. A. (ed.), *History of the Church of Ireland*, vol. i (Oxford, 1933).
Radford, C. Ralegh, and Donaldson, G., *Whithorn and Kirkmadrine: Official Guide* (Edinburgh, 1953).
Richmond, I. A., *Roman Britain* (London, repr. 1960 of 1955 ed.).
Ryan, J., *Irish Monasticism* (Dublin, 1931).
— (ed.), *St. Patrick* (Dublin, 1958).
Salway, P., *The Frontier People of Roman Britain* (Cambridge, 1965).
Simpson, W. D., *St. Ninian and the Origins of the Christian Church in Scotland* (Edinburgh, 1940).
Souter, A., *Pelagius's Expositions of the Thirteen Epistles of St. Paul*, vol. i; *Texts and Studies* (Cambridge, 1922).
Thompson, E. A., *The Visigoths in the Time of Ulfilas* (Oxford, 1966).
Todd, J. H., *St. Patrick, Apostle of Ireland* (Dublin, 1864).
Van der Meer, F., and Mohrmann, Christine, *Atlas of the Early Christian World* (E.T., London, 1958).
Wainwright, F. T. (ed.), *The Problem of the Picts* (Edinburgh, 1955).
Wall, J., *Christian Evidences in the Roman Period*, Part I (Gateshead, 1965).
— 'Christian Evidences (Archaeological and Documentary) in Roman and Sub-Roman Britain' (dissertation submitted to the University of Bristol, October, 1966).
William, H., *Christianity in Early Britain* (Oxford, 1912).

ARTICLES

Bieler, L., 'Der Bibeltext des heiligen Patrick' (*Biblica*, xxviii (1947), 1, pp. 31–58, 239–63.)
— 'The "Creeds" of St. Victorinus and St. Patrick' (*Theological Studies*, ix (1949), pp. 121–4).
Binchy, D. A., 'The Fair of Tailtiu and the Feast of Tara' (*Ériu*, xvii, pp. 113–38).
— 'Patrick and his Biographers' (*Studia Hibernica*, ii (1962), pp. 7–173).
— 'Varia III' (*Ériu*, xx (1966), pp. 232–7).
— 'The Passing of the Old Order' (*Proceedings of the International Congress of Celtic Studies*, 1962, pp. 119–32).

Bullough, D. A., 'Columba, Adomnan and the Achievement of Iona' (*Scottish Historical Review*, xliii, no. 136 (October 1964), pp. 112–30; and xliv, no. 137 (April, 1965), pp. 17–33).

Bury, J. B., 'The Origins of Pelagius' (*Hermathena*, xiii (1905), pp. 26–35).

Esposito, M., 'Notes on the Latin Writings of St. Patrick' (*Journal of Theological Studies*, o.s. xix (July, 1918), pp. 342–6).

— 'The Patrician Problem and a Possible Solution' (*Irish Historical Studies*, x, no. 38 (September, 1956), pp. 129–56).

Evans, R. F., 'Pelagius, Fastidius and the Pseudo-Augustinian *De Vita Christiana*' (*Journal of Theological Studies*, n.s. xiii (April, 1962), pp. 72–98).

Frend, W. H. C., 'Religion in Roman Britain in the Fourth Century A.D.' (*Journal of the British Archaeological Association*, 3rd ser. xviii (1955), pp. 1–18).

Frere, S. S., 'Excavations at Verulamium 1959' (*The Antiquaries Journal*, xl (1959), pp. 1–21).

— 'Excavations at Verulamium 1960' (ibid. xli (1961), pp. 72–148).

Grosjean, P., 'Analyse du livre d'Armagh' (*Analecta Bollandiana*, lxii (1944) pp. 32–41).

— 'Notes sur les documents anciens concernant S. Patrice' (ibid. 42–73).

— 'Notes d'hagiographie celtique' (ibid. lxiii (1945), pp. 65–130).

— 'Recherches sur les débuts de la controverse pascale chez les Celtes' (ibid. lxiv (1946), pp. 200–43).

— 'S. Patrice d'Irelande et quelques homonymes dans les anciens martyrologes' (*Journal of Ecclesiastical History*, i (1950), pp. 151–71).

— 'Dominicati Rhetorici' (*Archivum Latinitatis Medii Aevi*, xxv. i. (1955), pp. 41–46).

— 'Notes d'hagiographie celtique' (*Analecta Bollandiana*, lxxv (1957), pp. 158–226).

— 'Les Pictes apostats dans l'épitre de S. Patrice' (ibid. lxxvi (1958), pp. 354–78).

Kelleher, J. V., 'Early Irish History and Pseudo-History' (*Studia Hibernica*, iii, pp. 113–27).

Levison, W., 'An Eighth-Century Poem on St. Ninian' (*Antiquity*, xiv (1940), pp. 280–91).

Morris, J., 'Pelagian Literature' (*Journal of Theological Studies*, n.s. xvi (April 1965), pp. 26–60).

— 'The Dates of the Celtic Saints' (ibid. xvii (October 1966), pp. 342–91).

Myres, J. N. L., 'Pelagius and the End of the Roman Rule in Britain' (*Journal of Roman Studies*, l (1960), pp. 21–36).

Nerney, D. S., 'A Study of St. Patrick's Sources III' (*Irish Ecclesiastical Record*, 5th ser. lxxii (August 1949), pp. 97–110).

Richmond, J. A., 'Contribution about a wooden writing tablet from Walbrook, London' (*The Antiquaries Journal*, xxxiii (1953), pp. 206–8).

Stevens, C. E., 'The British Sections of the "Notitia Dignitatum"' (*Archaeological Journal*, xcvii (1940), pp. 125–54).

— 'Marcus, Gratian, Constantine' (*Athenaeum*, n.s. xxxv (1957), pp. 316–47).

Thompson, E. A., 'A Note on St. Patrick in Gaul' (*Hermathena*, lxxix (1952), pp. 22–29).

— 'Zosimus on the End of Roman Britain' (*Antiquity*, xxx (September 1956), pp. 163–7).

Toynbee, Jocelyn, 'Christianity in Roman Britain' (*Journal of the British Archaeological Association*, 3rd ser., xvi (1953), pp. 1–24).

Turner, E. G., 'A Roman Writing-Tablet from Somerset' (*Journal of Roman Studies*, xlvi (1956), pp. 115–18).

— (with Skutsch, O.), 'A Roman Writing-Tablet from London' (ibid. l (1960), pp. 108–11).

(Also short reports from others, ibid. xxl (1930), p. 247; xxviii (1928), p. 206; xxx (1940), p. 187; xxxviii (1948), p. 103, no. 18).

Wright, R. P., 'Roman Britain in 1963: II Inscriptions' (ibid. liv (1964), p. 182).

INDEX OF NAMES

Aaron (martyr), 30, 147.

Abernethy, 145–6.

Abraxas, 30.

Adelfius (bishop), 31, 32.

Adeodatus, 136.

Adomnan, 23, 67, 88, 95, 226, 227.

Aedh (Bishop of Sletty), 77, 83–84, 85, 89, 94, 189.

Aetius, 4, 14, 15, 21, 26, 50, 172, 190.

Agricola (Pelagian), 47, 48.

Ailred (of Rievaulx), 57, 58, 61.

Alans, 7, 56.

Alaric, 4, 8, 39, 184.

Alban (martyr), 30, 70, 47. *See also* St. Albans.

Alexander Severus (emperor), 167.

Allectus, 3, 44.

Alypius, 36.

Amator (Bishop of Auxerre), 78, 82, 88, 90, 94, 185.

Ambrose, St., 206, 207.

Ambrosius Aurelianus, 15, 18, 19, 20.

Anatolius of Alexandria, 67.

Anderson, A. O., and M. O., 87.

Andrew, St., 219.

Anthony of Egypt, St., 219.

Antonine Wall, 1, 15.

Antoninus Pius (emperor), 216.

Arcadius (emperor), 176.

Argobast, 44.

Arianism, 34, 45, 196.

Ariminum, Council of, 32, 33.

Arles, Council of, 31, 66.

Armagh, 66, 74, 75, 77, 79, 80, 82, 85, 88, 92, 191, 196, 197, 220, 221, 227.

Armagh, Book of. See Index of Ancient Texts.

Arminius (deacon), 31.

Armorica, 8, 11, 20, 21, 50, 52, 65, 70, 123, 153.

Arraglen, 60.

Arthur, 18, 19, 20, 170.

Atalphus, 4.

Athanasius, 32.

Atkinson, R., 76.

Attacotti, 1, 37.

Attalus, 44.

Audurus, 148.

Augustalis, 67, 68.

Augustine (of Canterbury), 66, 68, 151, 170.

Augustine (of Hippo), 36, 40, 41, 42–43, 111, 128–9, 140, 147–8, 163, 183, 200, 205, 206.

Augustinus (companion of Palladius), 219.

Auvergne, 65.

Auxerre, 47, 48, 54, 61, 81, 83, 86, 88, 89, 90, 109, 129, 141, 165, 184, 197, 199.

Auxilius, 73, 78, 79, 82, 90, 98, 187, 190–1, 195, 196, 220, 221.

Avitiacum, 65.

Avitus (Bishop of Vienne), 62.

Bangor (Ireland), 98, 215, 229.

Bangor (Wales), 17, 52.

Bannavem Taburniae, 113–16, 117, 118, 224.

Barrovadus, 59–60.

Bath, 167.

Bede, 53, 57–59, 61–62, 104, 151, 190, 193, 214, 215, 216, 217.

Belgae, 20.

Benedictus (companion of Palladius), 219.

Benignus, 79, 97, 98, 191, 220, 221.

Bernard, J. H., 76.

Bertha (queen), 151.

Bieler, L., 24, 41, 51, 54, 72–73, 74, 75, 76, 83, 98, 106, 108, 110, 111, 113, 119, 120, 122, 125, 126, 128, 129, 131, 132, 135, 136, 154, 156, 158, 161, 162, 172–3, 180–2, 196.

Binchester, 14.

Binchy, D. A., 22, 23, 26, 27, 51, 53, 55, 56, 57, 63, 66, 70, 74, 75, 77, 80, 83, 85, 91, 92, 94, 95, 96, 104, 110, 111, 123, 128, 135, 138, 139, 153, 154, 165, 166, 191–2, 193, 194, 195, 196, 197, 198, 227, 228.

Bodleian Library, 75, 214.

Bordeaux, 55.

Brading, 30.

Brampton, 149–50.

Brandon, Mt., 60.

Brechin, 146.
Brian Boru (king), 226, 229.
Bridget, St., 78, 89, 145–6.
British Museum, 216, 217.
Britu, 64.
Bromwich, Rachel, 18, 19, 20, 22.
Brougham, 1, 14, 62, 150.
Bulloch, J., 41, 57, 60, 61, 67, 83, 114, 115, 122, 138, 142, 144, 151, 154, 165, 173, 181, 184, 197.
Burgh Castle, 5.
Bury, J. B., 5, 24, 25, 26, 36, 37, 53, 55, 67, 74, 75, 76, 82–83, 98, 104, 113, 114, 122, 123, 125, 128, 135, 136, 138, 141, 144, 153, 154, 171, 177, 179–80, 193, 195, 196, 197, 199, 226, 228.

Caelestius, 36, 37, 39, 46, 152.
Caerleon, 30, 31, 32, 147.
Caerwent, 12, 31, 113.
Caistor, 14.
Calpornius, 112, 114, 115, 116, 117, 118, 176–9, 208.
Canterbury, 190.
Carausius, 3, 5, 44.
Carlisle, 14, 150, 168–9.
Carney, J., 25, 26, 70, 73, 77, 83, 86, 108–9, 110, 111, 121, 123, 124, 135, 136, 153, 161, 171–2, 187, 191–2, 194.
Carrawburgh, 31.
Caspari, C. P., 40, 44, 46, 47.
Cassian, 141, 174.
Cassiodorus, 61.
Celestine (pope), 47, 48, 51, 52, 53, 62, 78, 80, 81, 82, 94, 96, 97, 99, 100, 141, 190, 195, 218, 219, 223–4.
Censurinus, 47.
Ceretic, 22, 23, 24.
Chadwick, H. M., 10, 12, 15, 17, 18, 20, 22, 24, 25, 99, 103–4.
Chadwick, Mrs. N. K., 3, 4, 5, 10, 12, 17, 18, 19, 20, 22, 24, 31, 33, 34, 37, 40, 41, 48, 49, 50, 51, 52, 54, 56, 63–64, 66, 94, 95, 98–99, 103–4, 114, 118, 130, 142, 143, 144, 147, 149, 151, 154, 161, 168, 193, 197.
Chadwick, O., 138, 146, 147, 149.
Charlemagne, 226.
Charles the Bald (king), 51.
Chedworth, 30.
Christian (Bishop of Whithorn), 57.
Cianan (Bishop of Duleek), 221.
Cicero, 112, 205.

Cirencester, 30.
Clogher, 43.
Clonmacnoise, 99, 214, 216.
Cogitosus, 78, 89, 94.
Colchester, 2, 31, 32, 167, 183.
Colgan, 76.
Collingwood, R. G., and Myres, J. N. L., 5, 8, 10, 13, 14, 31, 41, 48, 57, 82, 117, 171, 179.
Collingwood, R. G., and Wright, R. P., 167, 168, 179.
Columba, 23, 57, 66, 80, 81, 88.
Columbanus, 53, 69.
Concessa, 78.
Constans (emperor), 219.
Constans (son of Constantine III), 44, 151–2.
Constantine I (emperor), 176.
Constantine II (emperor), 219.
Constantine III (usurper), 7, 8, 9, 10, 43, 44, 151–2.
Constantinople, 3.
Constantius (emperor), 5, 219.
Constantius (patrician), 10.
Coolavin, 217.
Corbridge, 1, 30, 168.
Cornovii, 12.
Coroticus, 11, 22, 23, 24, 25, 72, 101, 107–8, 114, 115, 137, 169–70, 175, 193, 203.
Cothiarthiacus, 79.
Coulanges, F. de, 87, 88.
Courcelle, P., 128–9.
Coventina, 31.
Croagh Patrick, 198.
Culmana, 220.
Cummian (Abbot of Durrow), 66, 98, 104.
Cunedag, 21, 22, 23.
Cyprian, 128, 181, 206.

Daire, 91–92.
Daithi or Nath I, 26, 81, 171–2, 192, 219, 226, 228.
Dalriada, 12, 22.
Darlugdach (Abbess of Kildare), 145–6.
Daventry, 113.
David I (king), 57.
Decius (emperor), 30.
Demetia, 12, 117.
Demetrias, 38, 144.
Dichu, 91.
Didymus, 151.

Diocletian (emperor), 2, 3, 30, 172.
Dionysius of Alexandria, 67.
Dionysius Exiguus, 68, 69, 80.
Diospolis, 39, 42.
Donaldson, G., 60, 61, 149–50.
Donegal, 217.
Downpatrick, 78, 82, 198, 224.
Ducange, 110.
Duke, J. A., 29, 57, 60, 83, 108, 122, 146, 148.
Dumbarton, 12, 23, 24, 81, 114.
Dumnonii, 20.
Dunshaughlin, 221.

Eborius (Bishop of York), 31.
Eccles, 35.
Eccleston, 35.
Elafius, 50.
Elmet, 12, 23.
Elvodug (Bishop of Bangor), 52.
Emain Macha, 197–8, 229, 230.
Emly, 215–16.
Eochy Moymean (king), 219.
Epillicus, 166.
Esposito, M., 38, 54, 77, 83, 92, 106, 110, 123, 130, 136, 161, 172, 184, 189, 191.
Ethelberth (king), 151.
Eugenius, 44.
Euric, 65.
Evans, R. F., 40, 41, 43.
Exeter, 12.
Exuperantius, 48.

Fastidius, 35, 40–41, 44, 70, 181, 199.
Faustus (Bishop of Riez), 63–65, 111, 153, 162, 164, 181, 199.
Ferdomnach, 75, 81, 84, 85, 97.
Fifehead Neville, 31.
Firmus, 4.
Flann Mainstreach, 215.
Flavius Antigonus Papias, 169.
Florentius, 60.
Foclut, wood of, 91, 120, 131.
Frampton, 30.
Franks, 1, 129, 130, 175.
Frend, W. H. C., 30, 31, 34, 147.

Gaianas, 4, 44.
Gallus, 125, 143.
Gamp, Sarah, 132.
Gavidius (bishop), 32, 33.
Gelasius (pope), 73.
Gereint ap Erbin, 19.

Germanus (Bishop of Auxerre), 18, 21, 30, 47–52, 54, 55, 62, 70, 77, 78, 80–81, 88, 90, 94, 101, 102, 136, 137, 141, 142, 175, 218, 221.
Gervasius, 148.
Gildas, 11, 13, 14, 15, 16, 18, 19, 20, 27, 45, 94, 117, 147, 182, 184, 199.
Gildo, 4.
Gilla Coemgin, 17.
Glastonbury, 97, 116, 153–4, 159, 189, 220.
Gloucester, 2.
Goths, 55, 184, 196.
Grampians, 62.
Gratian (emperor), 3, 5, 172.
Gratian (usurper), 7, 151.
Gregory the Great (pope), 102.
Gregory (Bishop of Tours), 104.
Grosjean, P., 24, 25, 35, 38, 49, 58, 59, 67, 68, 72–73, 76, 83, 84–85, 85, 86, 95, 104, 106, 107, 110, 115, 116, 129, 130, 131, 136, 138, 142, 143, 144, 145, 151, 153, 154, 157, 175, 189, 197.
Guitolinus, 18.
Guorthemir, 18, 52.
Gwynn, J., 75, 79, 82, 83, 86, 92, 135.
Gwynnedd, 17, 21.

Haddan, A. W., and Stubbs, W., 29, 32, 33, 36, 38, 45, 95.
Hadrian's Wall, 1, 5, 15, 49.
Hanson, R. P. C., 83, 96, 169, 171, 173.
Harden, D. B., 13.
Haslehurst, R. S. T., 41.
Hauseiter J., 172.
Haverfield, F., 6, 31, 113, 117, 159, 166–7, 169.
Heiric, 51.
Henghist, 18, 23, 52.
Hennessy, W. H., 213, 214.
Henry, Françoise, 27, 60, 149.
Hilary of Arles, 53.
Hilary of Poictiers, 28, 32, 180, 206, 219.
Hinton St. Mary, 30.
Hippo Regius, 148.
Honoratus, St., 63, 140, 153.
Honoriaci, 151–2.
Honorius (emperor), 6, 7, 9, 11, 39, 47, 151, 176.
Hübner, A., 166.
Hughes, Kathleen, 30, 66, 67, 70, 74, 98, 139, 177.

Huns, 55.
Hunter Blair, P., 5, 6, 8, 12, 15, 18, 19, 31, 49, 52, 69, 117.

Inishkeen, 213.
Innisfallen, 99, 215–16.
Innocent I (pope), 39, 177–8.
Inver Dea, 78, 81, 91.
Iona, 80.
Irenaeus, 164.
Iserninus, 73, 78, 79, 81, 82, 90, 98, 187, 190–1, 195, 196, 220, 221.

Jackson, K., 15, 17, 21, 24, 31, 35, 38, 41, 48, 57, 82, 94, 99, 110, 115, 116, 118, 128, 153, 158, 159–60, 162, 163–4, 166, 167, 170.
Jarlath (Bishop of Armagh), 220, 221.
Jerome, 18, 36–38, 39, 40, 42, 163, 172–3, 179–84, 207, 215, 216.
Jerusalem, 144.
Jocelin of Furness, 76.
John I (pope), 68.
John of Tinmouth, 76.
Jones, A. H. M., 2, 8, 10, 48, 116, 177, 179.
Josephus, 216.
Jovinian, 140.
Julian (Bishop of Eclanum), 47.
Julian (emperor), 1, 219.
Julius (martyr), 30, 147.
Julius Africanus, 216.

Kattenbusch, 172.
Keating, 227, 229.
Kelleher, J. V., 104, 229.
Kenney, J. F., 38, 56, 76, 77, 82, 95, 98, 100, 109, 122, 131, 143, 150.
Kilsaggart, 149.
Kirkmadrine, 60, 70.

Labriolle, de, 113.
Lactantius, 206.
Latinus, 59–60.
Leicester, 168.
Lemanaghan, 217.
Leo I (pope), 53, 68–69, 70, 100, 101, 101–2, 102, 103, 195, 220, 221, 224.
Leo III (emperor), 215.
Leporius, 147–8.
Lérins, 41, 63, 83, 140, 153, 165, 181, 196, 197, 199.
Leucius (king), 29.

Levison, W., 57, 58, 59, 149.
Leyden Glossary, 55–56.
Ligugé, 140, 150.
Lincoln, 2, 32.
Lismore, 215–16.
Lismoyne, 217.
Livy, 205.
Llanfelteg, 117.
Loeghaire (king), 25, 26, 27, 77, 78, 79–80, 81, 82, 83, 91, 94, 196, 215, 221, 226, 227, 228, 230.
London, 2, 31, 166.
Longborth, 19.
Lothair (abbot), 51.
Lough Erne, 213.
Louth, 86.
Lucillus (Bishop of Castellum Sinitense), 148.
Luetjohann, C., 63, 65.
Lullingstone, 30, 70.
Lupus (Bishop of Troyes), 30, 48, 51, 142.
Lydney, 6, 168.
Lyons, 47.

MacAirt, S., 214–15.
Macalister, 148.
MacCarthy, B., 67, 69, 213.
MacCorbaill, Dirmait, 228.
MacFirbis, Dugald, 214, 227.
McGeogehan, Conla, 216.
MacManus, Cathal, 213.
McNeill, E., 26, 51, 74, 76, 77, 83, 83–84, 85, 100, 122, 123, 131, 136, 154, 172, 195, 197, 198, 226.
MacQueen, J., 12, 59, 60, 61, 62, 94, 108, 146, 151.
Maelgwynn, 21, 22.
Mael Sechnaill MacDomnaill, 215.
Magnentius, 44.
Magnus Maximus, 2, 3, 4, 5, 6, 15, 19, 34, 39, 44, 51, 64, 178–9.
Magonus, 79, 82.
Malton, 5.
Manau Gogoddin, 12, 21.
Mansuetus, 21, 65–66.
Marcus (bishop), 51.
Marcus (usurper), 7.
Marseilles, 141.
Martin, St., 33, 52, 57, 58, 59, 60, 66, 70, 75, 81, 116, 140, 143, 145–8, 150–1, 152, 157–8, 184, 203, 219, 221.
Maryport, 167.

Massilienses, 174.
Mavortius, 60.
Mearns, the, 62.
Meissner, J. L. Gough, 2, 49, 55, 75, 76, 82, 86, 96, 114, 122, 128, 155, 159, 195, 197.
Mel (bishop), 221.
Melania, 144.
Merthyr Iun, 147.
Messina, straits of, 45.
Meyer, Kuno, 55–56, 109.
Milan, 3, 61, 140, 148.
Milliuc, 77, 78, 79, 82, 91.
Minucius Felix, 206.
Mocteus, 86–87.
Mohrmann, Christine, 55, 83, 106, 108–9, 110–11, 118–19, 120, 122, 128, 128–9, 129–30, 138, 141–2, 154, 158, 160–6, 172–3, 182.
Mommsen, T., 17, 21.
Mons Badonis, 16, 19, 20.
Monte Cassino, 40.
Morris, J. R., 9, 10, 12, 15, 18, 19, 20, 21, 22, 27, 34, 35, 37, 40, 41, 43, 44, 45, 46, 49, 51, 54, 58, 87–92, 96, 99–103, 108–9, 114, 132, 135, 138, 143–4, 144, 150, 152, 153, 164, 165, 165–6, 170, 175, 193, 226.
Moses, 195, 224.
Moy O'Gara, 217.
Muirchu, 22, 26, 27, 75, 76, 77, 77–78, 79, 82, 83, 84, 85, 87–92, 94, 96, 103, 108, 113, 116, 123, 125, 126, 138, 192, 198, 226–7, 227.
Murphy, D., 216.
Myres, J. N. L., 9, 18, 19, 41, 117, 143.

Nath I. See Dathi.
Nechtan Morbet, 145–6.
Nemthor, 81, 113, 114, 224.
Nennius. See Index of Ancient Texts.
Nerney, D. S., 173–4.
Nestorianism, 201.
Netherby, 150.
Niall of the Nine Hostages, 5, 22, 25, 26, 171–2, 197, 228.
Nicaea, Council of, 32, 67, 68.
Nicholson, E. B., 113.
Ninian, St., 56–63, 108, 145–51, 168, 186.
Nodens, 6, 168.
Novara, 75.
Novatian, 206.

Nynekirks, 62, 150.

O'Brien, M., 121.
Ochta, 18.
O'Clery, Conary, 217.
O'Clery, Cucogry, 217.
O'Clery, Michael, 217.
Odoacer, 6.
O'Donovan, J., 217.
O'Gara, Fergal, 217.
Olden, T., 91, 105, 122, 184, 189, 191.
Olympiodorus, 8, 10.
O'Meara, J. J., 128–9.
O'Mulconry, Ferfeasa, 217.
O'Rahilly, T. F., 23, 24, 25, 26, 53, 54, 70, 76, 77, 80, 83, 85, 86, 91, 98, 100, 104, 116, 118–19, 120, 135, 153, 171, 187, 190–2, 193, 194, 197, 198, 215, 216, 227, 228, 229.
Origen, 29, 174.
Ostia, 46.
Oswald (king), 227.
Oswy (king), 149.
Oulton, J. E. L., 172–3.

Palladius, 47, 48, 51, 52–54, 55, 56, 59, 78, 80, 81, 82, 90, 96, 97, 98, 99, 137, 142, 153, 175, 189–90, 191, 192–4, 196, 218, 219, 223–4.
Papebroch, 150.
Paschal Cycles or Tables, 66–69, 70, 80, 98, 99, 104, 192, 229.
Paschasinus (Bishop of Lilybaeum), 68.
Patiens (Bishop of Lyons), 47.
Patricius Senex vel Secundus, 97, 103, 189–92, 220, 221.
Paul, St., 164, 180, 202, 205.
Paulinus of Nola, 143, 177.
Peiper, R., 63.
Pelagianism, 19, 45, 46, 47, 48–49, 50, 51, 52, 64–65, 70, 173–5, 186, 201.
Pelagius, 35–46, 111, 136, 144–5, 162, 164, 183, 199.
Peronne, 73.
Perth, 62.
Peter, St., 148, 149.
Pevensey, 5, 6.
Picthelm (Bishop of Whithorn), 58–59, 149, 150.
Picts and Scots [P means Picts only], 1, 3, 4, 5, 13, 14, 15, 19, 22, 24, 25, 27, 46, 49, 47P, 61–62P, 81P, 82P, 107–8, 186P, 192P.

Plinval, G. de, 37, 38, 39, 40, 41, 42, 43, 44, 128, 144, 183.
Plummer, C., 88.
Portchester, 5, 20.
Potitus, 112, 118, 176, 178.
Priscillianists, 39.
Probus, 76, 113.
Prosper of Aquitaine, 18, 36, 46–47, 48, 50, 51, 52–53, 54, 103, 193.
Protasius, 148.
Puteoli, 45.

Quartodecimans, 67.
Quintilian, 112.

Radagaesus, 6, 9.
Radford, C. Ralegh, 60, 61, 83, 122, 149–50.
Ravenglas, 25, 115–16.
Ravenna, 7, 101, 102.
Ravenscar, 5, 167.
Restitutus (Bishop of London), 31.
Rheged, 12, 114, 115, 186.
Rhun, son of Urbgen, 51, 99.
Richborough, 10.
Richmond, I., 30, 31, 149–50, 166.
Ricimer, 4.
Riderch Hen, 23, 175.
Riochatus, 35, 63–65, 153.
Robin Hood Bay, 5.
Rome, 2, 8, 39, 53, 54, 57, 58, 59, 67, 68, 69, 78, 80, 82, 83, 88, 90, 96, 100, 102, 103, 109, 135, 140, 144, 145, 146, 149, 150, 158, 177, 184, 196, 218, 221.
Ronan, son of Comgall, 60.
Royal Irish Academy, 214.
Rufinus (Church father), 36, 206.
Rufinus (Praetorian prefect), 44.
Rufus, son of Callisumus, 214.
Ryan, J., 26, 51, 54, 57, 63, 72–73, 83, 86, 95, 98, 121, 128–9, 131, 136, 138, 182, 195, 197, 226.

St. Albans (Verulamium), 2, 14, 30, 31, 144, 147.
Sallust, 205.
Salway, P., 1, 11, 13, 14, 115–16, 117, 149–50, 167, 168, 169, 186.
Sarauw, 153.
Sardica, Council of, 32.
Saul (Co. Down), 78, 82, 91, 198.
Saxons (Anglo-Saxons), 1, 8, 12–13, 14,

15, 16 18, 19, 20, 23, 49, 70, 130, 149–50, 160, 185, 192, 199.
Scilly Isles, 39.
Secundinus, 76, 77, 79, 83, 189, 191, 195, 196, 220, 221.
Segene (of Iona), 66, 98, 164.
Senicianus, 31, 168.
Severianus (Pelagian), 47, 48.
Severus (Bishop of Trèves), 49, 50.
Silchester, 14, 31, 166–7.
Silvester (companion of Palladius), 219.
Silvianus, 168.
Simpson, W. D., 5, 14, 22, 24, 34, 41, 57, 60, 114, 143, 144, 146, 148, 149–50, 150.
Siricius (pope), 3, 34, 101, 177, 179.
Sixtus II (pope), 219.
Skene, W. F., 76, 145–6.
Slemish, Mt., 77, 78, 79, 81, 91, 198.
Sochet, 78, 79.
Soissons, 51.
Solinus (companion of Palladius), 219.
Souter, A., 37, 38, 183.
Stephen, St., 148.
Stevens, C. E., 5, 6, 8, 9, 10, 11, 13, 151, 167.
Stilicho, 4, 6, 22, 44, 151, 172, 179.
Stirling, 62.
Stokes, Whitley, 22, 66, 73, 76, 77, 78, 80, 81, 82, 84, 88, 90, 91, 113, 184, 190, 191, 192, 198, 216.
Strathclyde, 12, 23, 24, 34, 62, 108, 114, 115, 186.
Suevi, 7, 8.
Sulpicius Severus. See Index of Ancient Texts.
Sutherland, C. H. V., 13, 14.
Symmachus (pope), 59.
Synesius, 49.

Tara, 26, 27, 66, 78, 91, 226, 227, 228, 229, 230.
Tarragon (Bishop of), 177.
Tassach (bishop), 224.
Taylor, Joan and Harold, 154.
Telltown, 226, 228, 229.
Ternoch, son of Ciaran, 149.
Theodoret, 29.
Theodoric, 4.
Theodosian Code, 26, 115–16.
Theodosius the elder, 1, 3, 5.
Theodosius (emperor), 2, 6, 7, 80, 96, 176, 178.

Theophilus (Bishop of Alexandria), 136.
Thompson, E. A., 8, 10, 13, 21, 50, 54, 123, 196.
Tibatto, 11.
Tigernach, 216.
Tirawley, 91, 129.
Tillemont, 138.
Tirechan, 26, 27, 75–76, 77, 79–81, 83, 84, 86, 87, 88, 91, 92, 96, 97, 98, 99, 103, 138, 189–90, 191, 192, 195, 197, 198, 203.
Todd, J. H., 17, 51, 55, 76, 91, 95, 100, 108, 135, 138, 172–3, 187, 190, 203.
Torbach (Abbot of Armagh), 75.
Tours, 21, 57, 58, 59, 65–66, 81, 140, 146, 150, 152, 219
Toynbee, Jocelyn, 30, 31, 169.
Trim, 219.
Trinity College, Dublin, 213, 214, 217.
Troyes, 48.
Tutwall, 61, 175.

Uí Neill dynasty, 66, 80, 197, 224, 227, 228, 230.
Ulidian dynasty, 197, 224, 229.
Ultan (bishop), 79, 84, 86, 92, 94.

Valens (emperor), 44, 176.
Valentia, 2.
Valentinian I (emperor), 2, 61, 176.
Valentinian II (emperor), 3.
Valentinian III (emperor), 176.
Valentinianus or Valentinus (usurper), 2–3, 9.
Valentinus (Bishop of Chartres), 143.
Vandals, 7, 8, 55.
Verinianus, 151.
Verulamium. See St. Albans.
Victor (angel), 79, 80, 81, 82, 91, 97.
Victoricus, 120, 131.
Victorinus of Pettau, 172–3, 201.

Victorius (bishop), 79.
Victorius of Aquitaine, 68, 69, 80, 192.
Victricius of Rouen, 54, 143–4, 145, 150, 177–8.
Vienne, 143.
Visigoths, 187.
Viventius, 60.
Vortigern, 18, 19, 20, 23, 52, 64.
Votadini, 12, 21.
Voteporigis, 117.
Vulgate, 75, 179–84, 216.

Wainwright, F. T., 146.
Walbrook, 166.
Wall, J., 31, 34, 62, 148, 150, 169.
Wallop, 18.
Ware, Sir James, 126.
Weymouth, 10.
Whitby, Synod of, 66, 149.
White, J. Newport, 35–36, 51, 73, 75, 76, 82, 108, 112, 123, 126, 132, 135, 156, 172–3, 175, 180, 181, 197, 201.
Whithorn, 57, 58, 59, 60, 62, 70, 108, 144, 145, 146–7, 248–9, 150, 151, 168.
William of Malmesbury, 76.
Williams, H., 13, 15, 21, 29, 31, 32, 34, 37, 38, 45, 48, 50, 54, 63, 65, 66, 69, 83, 114, 141, 144–5, 146, 147, 152, 184, 199.
Wimborne, 19.
Winchester, 6, 20, 190.
Wright, R. P., 167, 168.
Wroxeter, 12, 14.

York, 1, 2, 31.

Zeitz, 69.
Zimmer, H., 17, 38, 45, 55, 153.
Zosimus (historian). See Index of Ancient Texts.
Zosimus (pope), 39.
Zwicker, J., 29, 117.

INDEX OF ANCIENT TEXTS

I. THE WORKS OF PATRICK

Confession

1	33, 112, 118, 119, 125, 176
2	118
3	202
4	172, 201, 203
6	109
8	202
9	35, 111, 118, 119, 126, 158, 163
10	106, 126, 127, 158
11	125, 126–7, 127, 185, 202
12	125, 127, 206–7, 207, 208, 209
13	35, 109, 127, 128, 163, 207
14	130, 172, 173
15	106, 208
16	120
17	120, 205
18	61, 121, 200
19	120, 121, 200
20	123, 125, 203, 205
21	91, 123, 124, 125, 205
22	123, 125
23–25	131
23	91, 113, 120, 124, 128, 150, 205, 207
24	203, 205
25	203, 205
26	131, 132, 133, 157, 208
27	118, 128, 131, 135, 156, 208
28	132
29	132, 133, 205
30	132, 156
31	31, 132
32	132, 133–4, 169, 205
33	203
34	185, 202
35	208
36	118
37	112, 124, 134, 138, 155, 163
38	56, 137, 139, 185, 202
40	137, 200, 202, 203
41	11, 137, 141, 155, 195, 197, 200, 227
42	56, 137, 141, 155, 157
43	113, 129, 138, 157, 174, 187, 203
44	156, 174
46	56, 101–2, 126, 134–5, 169, 174, 186, 202, 203, 205
47	109, 202–3
48	109, 138
49	106, 126, 137, 139
50	106, 137, 139, 204
51	56, 106, 109, 137, 138, 185, 192
52	11, 107, 124, 137, 138, 139, 197, 227
53	107, 109, 139
54	139, 204
55	138, 139, 157, 203, 204, 207, 208
56	101–2, 126, 204
57	56, 138, 203
58	138, 185
59	208
60	200
62	106, 126, 138, 208

Epistle to Coroticus

1	108, 126, 137, 193
2	107, 108, 114, 137, 185
3	101, 136, 137, 192, 197
5	185
6	10, 24, 102, 136, 185, 200, 208, 227
7	24, 107, 137, 203
9	185
10	112, 119, 162, 174, 176, 185, 208
11	108, 114, 185, 202
12	24, 107, 108, 126, 137, 141, 154, 195, 197
14	24, 107, 129, 175
15	108, 112–13
16	24
17	73, 137, 207
18	207
19	24, 108, 137
20	202
21	107, 130, 127

II. ANCIENT IRISH TEXTS

The Book of Armagh
(pages of the folio in Gwynn's edition,
with pages of Stokes's edition in
parentheses)

Generally: 72–75, 84–85, 150, 180,
181, 189–90, 226, 227

Introd. xiii–xv	75
xii	79
xv	92
lii	86
lix	92
2 a 2 (273)	78, 192
2 a 7–7 a 2 (271–93)	88
2 a 7 (272)	78
2 b 1 (275–6)	91
3 b 1 (273–4)	91
6 b 2–7 a 2 (290–2)	92
6 b 2 (29)	198
7 a 2 (295–6)	78, 198
8 b 2 (300)	96
9 a 1 (301)	73
9 a 2 (303)	79, 96
9 b 1 (304)	79
11 a 1–11 a 2 (311–12)	80
11 a 1 (311)	92
12 a 7 (314)	84
14 b 2 (326)	91
15 b 2 (332)	198
16 a 1 (332)	190, 192
18 b 1 (342)	81
18 b 2 (348)	81
20 a 1–20 a 2 (269–71)	88
20 a 1 (272)	78, 90
20 a 3 (273)	90
20 a 7 (269)	89
20 b 1 (271)	22–23

Vita Tripartita, 76, 77, 81–82, 84–85, 87,
92, 97, 103, 114, 123, 125, 192, 198

Letter to the Bishops of Mag Ai, 74, 196

Annals of Ulster, 67, 68, 69, 97, 98, 99,
100, 213, 218–25

Chronicum Scottorum, 97, 103, 189, 214,
218–25

Annals of Innisfallen, 68, 100, 190, 214–
16, 218–25

Annals of Tigernach, 216, 218–25

Annals of Clonmacnoise, 100, 216–17, 218–
25

Annals of the Four Masters, 189, 217, 218–
25, 226

Annals from the Book of Leinster, 97, 103

Book of Lecan, 189

Hymn of Fiacc (Génair Patric), 76, 77, 114,
189

Hymn of Secundinus, 75–77, 83, 191

Acta Sanctorum Hiberniae, 76, 89

Catalogus Sanctorum Hiberniae, 95

Vitae Sanctorum Hiberniae, 88

*Lives of the Saints from the Book of Lis-
more*, 88, 89

Cogitosus, Life of St. Bridget, 78, 89

Bangor Antiphonary, 77

Martyrology of Oengus, 77, 86, 189, 191

Stowe Missal, 191

III. OTHER ANCIENT CHRONICLES

Chronicles of the Picts and Scots, 76,
145–6

Book of Llandaff, 147

Two Gallic Chronicles (ed. Mommsen)

p. 646	3
p. 654	8
p. 660	13

Anglo-Saxon Chronicle, 143, 190, 214

Annales Cambriae, 17, 68, 99

Nennius, *Historia Brittonum*
Generally: 16, 17, 17–18, 76, 77, 94,
95, 99, 184

cap. 22	164
26	150
32 ff.	52
36–38	19
37	23
43–46	19
50–55	82
50	192
62	22

IV. OTHER ANCIENT TEXTS

ADOMNAN, *Vita Columbae*
Generally   23
2nd Praef., 3a   86–87
AMMIANUS MARCELLINUS, *History*
27. 7. 5   61
27. 8. 1   1
28. 3. 7   2
AUGUSTINE
Confessions
Generally   140
iii. 11. 20. 4   128–9
De Gestis Pelagii, 6   42
De Civitate Dei, xxii. 8   148
Epistles, 186   36
Sermons
273. 7   147
325   148
326   148
336   148
356. 10   147–8
BEDE
Chronica Maiora et Minora   215
Chronicon   216
De Rerum Natura et Temporibus   214
Historia Ecclesiastica
i. 13   53, 190
26   151
iii. 4   57, 61–62
v. 24   53
THE BIBLE
Job xx. 15, 16, 26   182
Psalm xviii. 4   119
Ecclesiasticus vii. 16   127, 202
Matthew xxviii. 19, 20   181
John viii. 43   119
Romans xii. 3   172
Revelation xi. 1 ff   172
CELESTINUS PAPA
Epistulae
Praef. 1 and 2   141
4   53, 54
CHRYSOSTOM, JOHN
Homiliae, viii   29
CONSTANTIUS
Vita Sancti Germani
Generally   204
Praef.   125
1   48
14   48
15   48–49, 117
16   30

17   35, 49
25   49
26   49
27   35, 50
EPISTULAE IMPERATORUM, PONTIFICUM,
ALIORUM
39. 4   3
40. 1   3
ETHERIA
Peregrinatio
Generally   120, 158, 159, 165
1. 7. 2   112
EUSEBIUS CAESARIENSIS
Historia Ecclesiastica, 7. 20   67
EXCERPTA VALESIANA ANONYMA   158
FASTIDIUS
De Vita Christiana
Generally   40–44
Praef.   43, 125
3   43
11   41–43
15   44
GENNADIUS
De Viris Illustribus
56   41
85   53
GILDAS
De Excidio Britanniae
Generally   182, 183–4, 199
10   30, 147
11   30
15   15
17   15
18   15
20   13, 15
21   13
22   15
23   15
25   15, 20
26   16
27   11
31   117
38   44–45
62   125
93   125
HIPPOLYTUS
Elenchos, 10. 34   29
Historia Lausiaca
i   144
ii   145

INNOCENS I PAPA
Epistulae, ii   143, 177–8
ISIDORE OF SEVILLE
Chronicles and Etymologies, 99, 215, 216
JEROME
Comm. on Jeremiah
   PL 24. 68032   36
     757/8   36
Comm. on Ezekiel
   Praef. to Bk. I   37
   Praef to Bk. VI   37
Epistulae
   50. 2   39, 144
   69. 3, 6   37
   133. 9 (to Ctesiphon)   2, 37
   (for Epp. 7 and 13, see under
   'Pelagian Works')
Adversus Iovinianum, 11. 17   38
Dialogus, 3. 14   42
Ecclesiastical History   98, 215, 216
Letter to Pope Damasus   182
JORDANES
History of the Gothic War
   (pp. 118, 119)   21
MARIUS MERCATOR
Liber Subnotationum in Verba Iuliani
   Praef. 2. 1   36, 144
NOTITIA DIGNITATUM   2, 4, 5, 10
ORIGEN
Hom. on Ezekiel, 4   29
Hom. on Luke, 6   29
OROSIUS, PAULUS
Historia Adversus Paganos
   Generally   215, 216
   vii. 3, 4   3
     25   3
     36   4
     38   4
     40–42   8
     50   151–2
Liber Apologeticus, 12   30
PELAGIAN WORKS
   Edited or referred to by Caspari. See
     pp. 40, 45–46, 141, 144, 152
PROCOPIUS
Bellum Vandalicum, i. 38   9

PROSPER OF AQUITAINE
Contra Collatorem, 21. 2   11, 47, 53
De Ingratis, 1   36
Chronicle
   Generally   98, 103
   sub ann. 413   36, 46–47
     429   47, 52
     431   53, 54, 55
SIDONIUS APOLLINARIS
Epistulae et Carmina
   Carmen Eucharisticum
     (p. 241, ll. 84–87)   63
   Epistles i. 7   21
     ix. 6   64–65, 110
SIRICIUS PAPA
Epistulae
   i. 8–11. vi   177
   13. ix   101
SOZOMENUS
Dialogi
   Generally   75
   i. 26   125
   ii. 2   143
     11   178
Historia Ecclesiastica, ix. 11. 4   152
SULPICIUS SEVERUS
Historia Sacra, xli. 152   32
Vita Martini
   Generally   75, 150, 157, 204
   Introd.   125
   ii. 161   116
TERTULLIAN
Adversus Iudaeos, 7.4   29
De Oratione, 13   42
VICTRICIUS OF ROUEN
De Laude Sanctorum, i   143
ZOSIMUS
Historia Nova
   i. 64   38
   iii. 5   1
   iv. 29   2–3
     35   3, 4, 38
   v.   8
   v. 38   11
   vi. 5   8, 152
     10   9